COMPUTERS IN CONGRESS

MANAGING INFORMATION
A Series of Books in Organization Studies and Decision-Making

Edited by **AARON WILDAVSKY,** *University of California, Berkeley*

What impact does the computer have on organizations (both public and private), and the individual decision makers within them?

How can "data" be converted into "information for decision"?

Who produces (and who consumes) such data? with what effects? under which conditions?

What are the sources of error—and the means of overcoming them—in contemporary management information systems (MIS)?

What is the state of the art in MIS theory?

How can we increase our understanding of information and its management, as well as the surrounding organizational environment?

These are critical questions in an era of information overload, coupled with the need for decision-making by managers and policy makers dealing with finite resources. The **Managing Information** series meets the need for timely and careful analysis of these vital questions. Studies from a variety of disciplines and methodological perspectives will be included. The series will analyze information management from both public and private sectors; empirical as well as theoretical materials will be presented.

STEPHEN E. FRANTZICH

Volume 4
MANAGING INFORMATION:
A Series of Books in Organization
Studies and Decision-Making

Series Editor: **AARON WILDAVSKY**

COMPUTERS IN CONGRESS

THE POLITICS OF INFORMATION

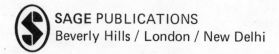

SAGE PUBLICATIONS
Beverly Hills / London / New Delhi

To my parents, who nurtured, encouraged, and cared.

For information address:

SAGE Publications, Inc.
275 South Beverly Drive
Beverly Hills, California 90212

SAGE Publications India Pvt. Ltd.
C-236 Defence Colony
New Delhi 110 024, India

SAGE Publications Ltd
28 Banner Street
London EC1Y 8QE, England

Printed in the United States of America

Library of Congress Cataloging in Publication Data

Frantzich, Stephen E.
  Computers in Congress.

  (Managing information ; v. 4)
  Bibliography: p.
  Includes index.
  1. United States. Congress—Data processing.
2. United States. Congress—Information
services. I. Title
JK1083.F7   328.73'0761   82-3285
ISBN 0-8039-1840-2   AACR2

FIRST PRINTING

CONTENTS

PREFACE

IN A BOOK on information, it seems only right to give the reader a bit of information on its genesis, and some hint as to the people on whom I was dependent for information. The beginnings of this research go back to the period when I was directing internship programs in Washington, D.C., for Hamilton College. In trying to create an academic seminar that would synthesize the experiences of interns in a variety of settings, it became clear that the one commonality in all divisions of government, from the congressional office to the agency, was information processing. It also became obvious in the early 1970s that modern information technology was invading government and few observers were tracking its progress or evaluating its implications. Seminar discussions with students led to more serious research involving interviewing and data collection.

Initial attempts to publish my findings on the process of technological innovation in Congress highlighted a problem. The study of innovation in information technology in a political setting fell between the cracks of established academic disciplines and their accompanying journals. Political science journal editors directed me to sociological or anthropological journals, which traditionally publish works concerned with the process of societal innovation. The editors of these journals argued that, while I "spoke their theoretical language," the focus on a political institution was out of their traditional realm. Eventually the log jam broke and the study of information technology emerged as an interest of professionals in many fields. With increasing evidence that modern information technology had the potential for changing the nature of politics, it became clear that we could not close our eyes to this important phenomenon just because it did not fit into traditional academic boundaries.

It was with excitement that I became aware of the Managing Information series, edited by Aaron Wildavsky. This series verifies the importance of studying the impact of information technology and seems unconstrained by traditional disciplinary boundaries.

This book provides a look at the introduction of information technology to the Congress as a social phenomenon. I have attempted to avoid both the technical jargon and technical issues of computerization, and instead focus on processes of innovation, patterns of usage, and political consequences. On the bottom line, this is a book about how technological change in such a vital area as information opens the door to changes in power among individuals and institutions. While the particular focus is on the U.S. Congress, both the trends and implications go well beyond those institutional walls.

One cannot write a book such as this without incurring a number of debts. Over 50 members of Congress and their staffs took part in interviews, and although their requests for anonymity are honored, their insights and perceptions—as shown in quotes throughout the book—are crucial to an understanding of the topic, and I would have been at a loss without them. My wife, Jane, served as a primary research assistant, taking on numerous editorial and analysis duties. Sandra Erb taught two "greenhorns" how to use the word processor efficiently, and consistently found ways to push the machine to its utmost capabilities. Rod Tomlinson shared his computer expertise and made the data analysis task more manageable. Donna Hurley cut many weeks off the initial research by creatively employing a wide variety of computerized bibliographic searches. Mrs. W. S. Frantzich took on the thankless task of editing the manuscript for grammatical errors. The entire manuscript was read by Aaron Wildavsky, Robert Chartrand, and Jim Williams, while other colleagues digested segments. Their comments significantly strengthened its content and format. Part of the research period was funded by a grant from the Naval Academy Research Council. My colleagues and students deserve credit for providing encouragement and giving me enough leeway in my other responsibilities to make research and writing possible. Finally, although I threatened my children that this might be the first book in which the author commented that the book was finished *despite* his children, entreatments to "be quiet" and "let Daddy work" were generally heeded.

As is always the case, I alone bear full responsibility for errors of omission and commission.

—S. E. F.
Annapolis, Maryland

1 WHAT CONGRESS NEEDS TO KNOW

No man can be a competent legislator who does not add to an upright intention and a sound judgment, a certain degree of knowledge of the subjects on which he is to legislate—*Federalist no. 53* [Hopkins, 1972: 452].

There is, in fact, no subject to which a member of Congress may not have occasion to refer—*Thomas Jefferson* [Chartrand, 1978: 11].

An assembly must be informed before it can act. . . . Information is to be had only by debate and examination of evidence—*John Adams* [1851].

The judgments of the 535 members of Congress, like anyone else's, can hardly be better than the information on which those judgments are made—*Joseph Califano* [1971: A18].

On the most basic level, the U.S. Congress serves an information-processing function. It translates information on societal needs and desires into public policy by evaluating information on potential options. The ability of individual members of Congress and Congress as a whole to effectively process the best available information determines the kind of public policy enacted, the relative power of policy participants, and, eventually, the viability of Congress and its members.

In recent years, the importance, magnitude, and nature of information processing in Congress have been significantly altered by changes in the environment and in the motivations and behavior patterns of the participants. Such changes set the stage for Congress to look at modern information technology as a possible solution to its new information needs.

THE CHANGING CONGRESSIONAL ENVIRONMENT

Increasing Decision-Making Demands

With the growth of big government and the increasing complexity of policy decisions, members of Congress began to echo congressional scholar Ernest Griffith's poignant question, "How can a group of nonspecialists elected as representatives function in a specialized and technological age?" (U.S. Congress, House, Select Committee on Committees, 1974: 17). As American society became more complex in its composition, needs, and desires, this trend was reflected in the agenda set for Congress. While earlier sessions of Congress were dominated by one or two key issues, modern sessions must now grapple with numerous issues on which there is disagreement over the facts as well as the underlying values. As John F. Kennedy reflected:

> During the 19th Century, America had many distinguished Senators, Presidents, Congressmen . . . but most of these men dealt in their entire political life . . . with only four or five major problems. . . . Now the problems swarm across the desks of political leaders [U.S. Congress, House, Select Committee on Committees, 1974: 101].

The growth in the number of issues and conflicts which must be dealt with was accompanied by the increased complexity of each issue and by a growing body of knowledge that had to be mastered before a satisfactory decision could be made. The generalist member of Congress, who knew just enough about everything to make educated guesses, is gone.

Members of Congress themselves quickly became aware of their inability to acquire and process the requisite information. In one study, 78 percent of the House members surveyed indicated that a lack of adequate and useful information hindered them in doing their job. Former Senator James Buckley (R-NY) emphasized this point from personal experience:

> As for trying to do all the "necessary reading" . . . all that is required to develop in-depth personal understanding and knowledge. . . . It can never be done. The amount of reading necessary to keep a Senator minimally informed on matters of maximum importance is

always double that which he can possibly accomplish in the time allotted [Weiss, 1977: 101].

The problem is not confined to the U.S. Congress, nor even to the American context. One commentator on the British Parliament echoed the same refrain:

A generation ago it was enough for an MP to be 'well read' . . . but today the revolution in the social sciences which stresses the importance of quantifying and analyzing information so as to reach conclusions that are other than impressionistic is coming [Worthley, 1976: 57].

The problem is not totally ameliorated by specialization. One congressman with significant expertise in the area of his subcommittee expressed his frustrations during a hearing in the following way:

I don't know if I have been eating magic mushrooms or wandering around Alice's Wonderland, but the more I learn about this field the bigger it gets. I'm always losing ground. I think I'm going to cry [Congressman Al Swift, quoted in Hornblower, 1981: 1].

Increasing Constituent Demands

In the not-so-distant past, constituents "spoke" on election day and were not heard from again until the next election. While the nostrum "Write your congressman" always stood as a safety valve to ameliorate government mistreatment and verify democracy, relatively few constituents communicated with their elected representatives. In the contemporary congressional office, assessing constituent opinions and managing constituent correspondence has become a major commitment. With constituents watching them more closely, members of Congress need to take public opinion within their districts into account and produce more sophisticated responses to constituent correspondence. The amount of constituent mail entering congressional offices has grown astronomically, to the point where it is not unusual for a Senate office to handle over 1000 letters per week. Not only do constituents expect responses to their specific demands, but they also expect to be informed of their representative's stand on issues and performance in office. As Table 1.1 reveals, constituents have high expectations of their legislators, and their expectations concerning communications almost match those in the legislative area.

TABLE 1.1   Constituent Prescriptions for Congressional Effort*

Activity	Percentage Ranking Activity "Very Important"
Making sure district gets its fair share of government money and projects	77
Debating and voting on legislation on the floor of the house	76
Studying and doing basic research on proposed legislation	71
Getting back to the district to stay in touch with constituents	68
Taking time to explain to citizens what their government is doing to solve important problems and why	67
Helping people in district who have personal problems with the government	62
Working in committees to develop legislation	62
Sending newsletters about the activities of Congress to people in district	49

SOURCE: U.S. Congress, House, Commission on Administrative Review (1977b).
*Responses to: "I'd like you to tell me how important you feel your congressman ought to treat each of these activities."

The demands of constituent communications are reflected in the ways in which congressional offices are organized. One Senate survey indicated that, prior to the use of computers, over 50 percent of the average senator's clerk-hire funds were being expended to deal with constituent communications. In the House the figure approached 75 percent.

The Changing Information Environment

Congress does not exist in a vacuum. It is subject to the environmental strains that affect all segments of society. Since the 1960s there has been a quantitative as well as a qualitative jump in our awareness of the importance of information and in the availability of information itself.

To use Bell's (1973) term, we have moved into the "postindustrial" age. The agricultural age ended in the 1900s, when the majority of the work force migrated from the fields to the factories (see Figure 1.1). The industrial age in America ended in the 1950s, when "the production and dissemination of information replaced manufacturing as the principal activity of the U.S. economy" (Thomas, 1978: 803). Not only is the work force dominated by information creators and transmitters, but this segment of the economy is growing at 10 percent per year, a rate twice that of the total U.S. economic growth (Thomas, 1978: 803).

The postindustrial society differs from its predecessors not only in terms of the work force, but also in its underlying dynamics:

> A Pre-Industrial Society is essentially based on raw materials, as a game against nature in which there are diminishing returns. An Industrial Society is organized primarily around energy and the use of energy for the productivity of goods. A Post-Industrial Society is organized around information and the flow of knowledge; it is also a society uniquely dependent upon the compilation of theoretical knowledge. Now, every society has always been dependent upon knowledge in order to grow. But it is only in the last decades that we have become uniquely dependent on the codification of theoretical knowledge in order to know where we are [Bell, quoted in McHale, 1976: 22].

Not only must the Congress deal with the development of an "information society" as a substantive issue, but it must also deal with the outputs. The "information explosion," or "white plague," means that members of Congress are not faced with a lack of information, but with a problem of selectivity (U.S. Congress, Senate, Committee on Rules and Administration, 1977a: 8). In Weaver's (1972: 3) words: "The problem is not that Congress gets too little information, but that too little of the great mass it gets is relevant and readily, rapidly available."

Commentators on the arrival of the information society speculate on numerous likely consequences. Perhaps the most important consequence for Congress lies in redefining personal competence and affecting personal power.

Information can be categorized under two headings: "Resident" information is that body of data and knowledge which the individual "carries around" and has readily available. It is usually the product of a long-term process of assimilating facts and putting them in some structure to reduce their randomness. Experts who base their status on resident information are being challenged by the information explosion. The fast pace of information production and the human limitations in keeping abreast of new information and absorbing it into one's body of resident information set the stage for eventual incapacity to "keep up with the field."

"Access" information serves as another route to status and power. The person endowed with access information carries around relatively little substantive information, but exhibits proficiency in, and knowledge of,

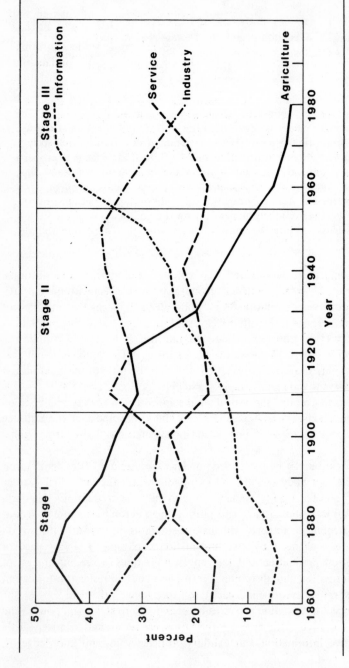

Figure 1.1 Four Sector Aggregation of the U.S. Work Force by Percentage, 1860-1980 (using median estimates of information workers)
SOURCE: Porat (1976: 189).

how to tap into the resident information of others and information and knowledge codified in printed and other storage formats. Gaining access information is not inherently less difficult than gaining resident information; it is more flexible in times of change in information formats and probably requires less use of the individual's personal "storage" capability.

The kinds and availability of information in the legislative setting would be of little interest if it were not for the fact that they affect power relationships. While it has become a cliché that "information is power," there is a great deal of truth in the expression. In the information society, "what one *knows* rather than what one *has* is becoming the new property base for political, social, and economic power" (Futurist, 1978: 55). With the information explosion, resident information becomes obsolete in a much shorter period of time than does access information. Power will shift to those who know how to get the necessary information and will not wait for the old experts to update their resident information. In the pithy words of Marshall McLuhan, "This is the age of the hunter," and the prey is better information.

Increasing codification and formalization of knowledge reduces the significance of personal experience that leads to resident information. "One can no longer count on a venerable old age with increasing responsibility, respect and remuneration" (Thompson, 1969: 97). In a system such as Congress, in which the seniority system rewards longevity with respect and power and justifies the action by referring to expertise and experience, the implications portend a significant change. Current members advantaged by the seniority system might find some comfort in the prediction that similar power shifts will affect all in that society. According to McHale's crystal ball:

The use of knowledge as the principal commodity in Post-Industrial Society will tend to break down the rigidity of hierarchical forms of management organization and replace these with more democratic participatory processes [McHale, quoted in Futurist, 1978: 56].

The composition of Congress has been changing, and with it the capabilities and information demands of its members. A veteran staff member observed that "Congress is getting more sophisticated. New members have backgrounds in economics, finance and the sciences. Staff are more likely to be experts than the cronies they replaced."

The existence of information as a power resource introduces a qualitatively different situation. Resources in the previous periods were exhaustible and concrete, and took on the character of a "zero-sum" game in which one participant's gain was the other's loss. Information and knowledge as resources in themselves are not lessened or reduced by increased use or sharing (McHale, 1976: 19), although limiting access to relevant information may itself be a power source. In the current age, power "comes to the individual with access to such information. The politically smart manager controls others by manipulating this information" (Hellriegel, 1979: 552).

CHANGED CONGRESSIONAL MOTIVATIONS AND BEHAVIOR

Along with the environmental changes impinging on Congress came a more direct change: the influx of a new breed of legislator. Careerism grew as members began to see legislative service as a long-term goal rather than as a brief interlude from some other career. The growth of careerism meant that members of Congress increasingly looked for ways in which to make their work more manageable and pleasant. For many members inprovements in information processing held out hope for reaching both job satisfaction and reelection goals.

Newer members also adopted decision-making patterns that required expanded information capabilities. While the traditional member felt comfortable following the party and chamber leadership with little questioning, newer members increasingly wanted independent guidance and information.

INFORMATION NEEDS

Before describing the kind of information Congress needs, it is important to make a distinction between "information" and "data." "Data" refers to the raw facts and figures from which information is created. While the distinctions are not absolute, "information" consists of facts and data that have been organized and put into a conceptual framework that makes it useful for answering questions of interest to policy makers. For example, in isolation the raw data on infant mortality rates would have little utility for decision-making. But when data are compiled to show that we are doing poorly relative to other countries—that rates have increased over time or that the rates differ significantly for subdivisions of society— the data become information that may trigger further action. Placing data in the conceptual context of relative desirability, change over time, or differential condition enhances them.

Developing an exhaustive catalog of Congress's information needs is no easy task. To begin with, the term "Congress" implies many players, from individual members, to committees, to legislative service staffs and agencies. Each participant has different types of needs and may require the same basic information presented in a unique format. The following listing will focus on, but will not be limited to, the key types of information needed by individual members of Congress in the performance of their official duties. Particular emphasis will be given to information needs with significant policy and political impacts.

While focusing on individual members of Congress makes the task a bit easier, a true composite picture is difficult to develop, for each has varying information requirements beyond the common minimum needed to participate in corporate decisions. Individual information needs vary according to particular constituents, interests, committee assignments, and personal expertise (Dechert, 1966). A second problem arises from the multifaceted job of U.S. legislators. Their duties include: (1) representing and communicating with constituents; (2) monitoring societal problems, originating legislation, evaluating alternatives, and making authoritative decisions; and (3) overseeing the work of the bureaucracy. In carrying out their constitutional duties, members of Congress are aided by staffs; this forces them to become administrators, with all the attendant information needs for hiring, planning, and monitoring work efficiency. If a legislator moves into a leadership position or has a particular interest in a specific piece of legislation, he or she must become a strategist. While members might be aided in carrying out some of these functions, the ultimate responsibility is on their shoulders.

A number of authors have attempted to develop an exhaustive list of information needs and bring some order to the confusion. I have drawn on their work and insights in developing the following scheme (see Maisel, 1979: 4; U.S. Congress, House, House Information System, 1979b: 3; O'Donnell, 1980: 10).

Decision-Making Information

The primary function of the U.S. Congress, both constitutionally and in terms of impact, lies in translating citizen desires into legislation. Although individual members may place more emphasis on personal goals, such as reelection or serving the intermediary role between citizens and the bureaucracy, they are ultimately responsible for dealing with legislation and casting votes. Ideally, members of Congress need a legislative decision-making information system that defines current and impending problems, canvasses and evaluates possible solutions, provides legislative activists with strategy information, provides relevant political information for individual decisions, creates an efficient authoritative and recorded decisional mechanism, and provides a means by which enacted programs can be monitored and evaluated.

Problem-definition information

Members of Congress need information about emerging societal problems to determine whether these problems have valid claims to their time and effort. Ideally, this foresight stage should be lengthened, so that Congress does not remain solely a reactive institution dealing with the crises of the moment, but can begin monitoring long-term trends and changes in economic and social indicators to spot emerging problem areas (Dechert, 1966: 42-43). In defining problem areas, information can help overcome human limitations by "providing reasonable assurance that preconceived biases (conscious or unconscious), ignorance and myth do not rule out important possibilities" (Kornbluh, 1977: 25).

While the availability of information will not assure that it traverses the perceptual screens of decision makers, the lack of available information on a current or emerging problem will assure that it is not considered. Information useful for determining problems might include quantification of external demands, dramatic downturns or disturbing long-term trends in social or economic indicators, or information from other social settings that would lead to changed expectations concerning the potential for positive governmental impact.

Canvassing alternatives

The desirability of a match between a problem and a potential solution is likely to increase as the number of reasonable and relevant alternatives is expanded. Alternatives not uncovered in an information search cannot be evaluated. Alternatives uncovered too late in the decision-making process are often not given full consideration because of the "sunk costs" involved in analyzing the alternatives introduced earlier. The more legislators can have "all the cards on the table" from the beginning, the better the chances of choosing the optimal solution.

Projecting consequences

For members of Congress creatively participating in the legislative process, a great need exists for methods of quickly and efficiently projecting the consequences of various alternatives. This may mean no more than developing an awareness of the consequences of similar programs in other jurisdictions or realms that are often missed with ethnocentric information searches. More sophisticated projection capabilities would allow riskless experimentation through the use of models.

Understanding the potential consequences not only holds importance in the creative stage of developing alternatives, it also serves a very important purpose for all members of Congress when it comes to the authoritative decision stage. Without sophisticated information, members may become captives of intuitive limits or untested myth and/or ideology. As the complexity of society and the issues faced by Congress increase, information beyond current capacity is needed to assess the interrelated impacts of various decisions.

As a representative of a state or congressional district, members of Congress must consider both the overall impact of their policy choices and the more narrow, but politically crucial, parochial impacts. In projecting the impact of policy alternatives, they need to know specifically how the alternatives will affect their constituents. While legislating for the "national interest" (if such a thing can ever really be defined) is viewed as a higher calling, it is neither politically possible nor perhaps even desirable in all cases. As one member of the House put it:

> I am the only person in Washington representing my district. If I do not take a particular interest in their unique needs no one will. The so-called public interest lies in all of us taking care of our own people by coming to a decision we can all live with and under which no one segment inordinately prospers.

This process of representation includes absorbing both shreds of evidence on constituent desires, such as poll results and mails counts, and specific data on how governmental decisions will affect specific districts. In the not-so-distant past, decision information was limited largely to projections of aggregate or national impact, while modern legislators want such data broken down to show the specific costs and benefits for their districts. This requires new methods of presenting taxation, program expenditure, and performance data on a district-by-district basis.

Budget information

Acting on Congress's responsibilities in the budget realm forces members of Congress to delve into a mass of data organized around 16 functional categories divided into over 1200 account numbers, with numerous programs under each account. The maze of information sources using misleading terminology, differing accounting methods, and noncomparable classifications traditionally has put Congress at a great disadvantage. Congress needs information on budget requests, authorizations, and appropriations organized according to committee jurisdictions, subject areas, and constituency characteristics (U.S. Congress, Joint Committee on Congressional Operations, 1974: 513-514). In the words of Congressional Budget Office Director Alice Rivlin (1978: 25):

> Ideally when the President and the Congress make decisions on the budget they should have reliable information for each type of federal activity on how much is being spent, who is being affected, what is being accomplished, and what are the alternative ways to achieve the same ends more effectively.

Political Information

Many analysts of congressional information needs give short shrift to the fact that Congress is a political institution and no amount of information is going to eradicate that fact. An underlying assumption of those who wish to improve Congress's information capabilities is that the mere interjection of information will guide them to *the* right answer. As one proponent put it:

> "Men of good will" can be counted on to do the "right" thing if they are only provided with the information, knowledge and means of determing what the right choice is [Grumm, 1979: 2].

Members of Congress fought their way into office through a political process, and they are unlikely to change weapons just because they have reached their immediate goal. There are very few absolute facts in a political battle. Facts are like bullets in a battle: They can be used by either side. What counts more than the facts per se is access to the relevant information, the ability to package it in a form relevant to those you wish to impress, and the skill to link facts with the values underlying political choices. Information is rarely neutral. Political advantage can be derived from misinterpreting information, distorting it, selectively disseminating it, or ignoring it (Krevitt Eres, 1980: 3-4). Members of Congress must keep an eye on the facts (if discoverable) and on those on whom they depend (constituents, colleagues, and so on), whose interpretation of the facts may be more important than reality.

Objectivity does not stand as a virtue and a goal to the Congress member as it might for other users of information. In one congressman's words:

> You have a general position. Once you assume that posture you use the . . . testimony as ammunition. The idea that a guy starts out with a clear slate and weighs the evidence is absurd [Kingdon, 1981: 236].

Or, as has been said about the Senate:

> A Senator is not a research coordinator. The ranges of choice in decision-making for Senators are usually narrowly constrained by political circumstances. Senators do not operate in an open decision-making world, where all relevant objective information is gathered, sifted, and the most promising options selected. On the contrary, Senators typically seek information that justifies previous positions, or at most resolves limited finite questions within a small range [U.S. Congress, Senate, Commission on the Operation of the Senate, 1977d: 122].

The adversarial role, in which the information search involves seeking out facts to bolster a case, lies comfortably on most members of Congress, given their previous political experience and the fact that many of them are lawyers (Kingdon, 1981: 232). If we even partially accept Mayhew's (1974) picture of Congress members as "single-minded seekers of reelection," it is clear that they are "unlikely to invite objective analyses that may not support their preconceptions of what is needed in the district or state to get them reelected" (Jones, 1976: 251-264).

Rather than harboring the hope that increased information will somehow transform politicians into philosopher kings for all decisions, proponents of improved information for the Congress are better off accepting the status quo and reveling in those cases (perhaps rare) in which politicians are free to eschew political considerations for more traditionally objective ones. Furthermore, an improved information system could provide members of Congress with the information they need to anticipate fully the political implications of their actions (such as public opinion polls), while democratizing the distribution of such information so that all members are on equal footing in looking out for the well-being of their constituents.

Monitoring and Strategy Information

With the tremendous amount of legislation wending its way through the legislative process and touching the various decision-making units in different ways, anyone with an interest in a specific piece of legislation needs a quick and efficient method of determining where it is in the process. Compared to other legislatures, Congress deals with massive amounts of legislation. During the 96th Congress, over 25,000 bills were introduced in the U.S. Congress, compared to 679 in the Canadian Parliament during the same period (Clayton, 1979: 9). In planning strategy, members must know when authoritative decisions are likely, who will be making them, and the likelihood of success for their perspectives, in each decision setting. As the final decision comes closer, strategists need to know voting intentions and possible clues for swinging particular members over to their side.

Decision-Authorizing Mechanisms
and Creating a Legislative Record

Congress not only absorbs information from the outside, but must also create a record of its rationale and authoritative decisions. Congressional participants and outsiders alike need information on past decisions and an efficient method of recording current decisions.

Oversight Information

Congress is charged with both passing legislation and overseeing its implementation. Congress needs information to monitor bureaucratic activity to determine consistency with legislative intent and general standards of efficiency and honesty. The individual member of Congress often wants to monitor bureaucratic effort and effectiveness within his or her state and district as compared with other constituencies.

While the above listing of information needs comes largely from observers of Congress, it reflects quite closely what the members themselves perceive. Two recent surveys of House and Senate members indicate that they concur with the observers and see similar needs for each chamber (see Tables 1.2 and 1.3). As one might expect, with two-year terms and closer

TABLE 1.2   Information Needs as Perceived by Members of the Senate

Needs	Percentage of Senators Ranking "Very" or "Fairly Important"
Improving the scheduling of floor and committee activities to avoid conflicting demands on a senator's time	93
Improving access to and usability of information available to the Senate in its oversight of the executive branch	89
Improved research and analytical support available to committees and the Senate as a whole in the development of legislation	81
Better systems for learning about the status of legislation	73

SOURCE: U.S. Congress, Senate, Commission on the Operation of the Senate (1976c: 8).

ties with their constituencies, House members were more interested in determining the parochial impact of legislation, while the Senators gave top priority to receiving more and better oversight information. Understandably, given the relatively negative connotation of "political" considerations, even in an anonymous survey members did not feel free to call for specific help in this area.

Information Needed by Individual Offices

Constituent communications and representation information needs

The individual member of Congress not only must face up to public policy decisions, but is also responsible for representing his or her constituents and developing lines of communication. In their representational role, members of Congress are aided by staffs whose functions and organization have been likened to that of a small business (Loomis, 1979). Given the heavy job demands, members of Congress need information, both to manage their own time and that of their staffs efficiently and to deal with the two-way flow of information in and out of their offices.

TABLE 1.3   Information Needs as Perceived by Members of the House of
Representatives

	Percentage of Representatives with "Greatest" Legislative Information Problems in This Area
What the likely impact of the legislation will be on your district	40
Information about existing needs or problems to be addressed by the legislation and what past efforts to solve those problems have produced	39
Information about other proposals currently being considered which relate to the problem being addressed by the legislation	35
When and how legislation like this is to be considered on the floor	34
What the likely impact of the legislation will be nationally	30

SOURCE: U.S. Congress, House, Commission on Administrative Review
(1977b: 965).

Handling the mail

For most congressional offices, constituent mail becomes the most
burdensome and time-consuming activity. In a system that prides itself on
giving citizens the right to "petition government for the redress of griev-
ances," the mail must go out. Most members of Congress are aware of at
least one former colleague who lost an election in a "safe" district because
he or she had "lost touch" with his or her constituents. Thus the motivation for "getting the mail out" stems from both philosophical and practical grounds.

In recent years, incoming mail has inundated congressional offices.
While there is great variation in mail volume from office to office,
depending on such factors as educational level of constituents, proximity
to Washington, and the current hot issues, the number of letters per week
in a Senate office can approach 1000, while members of the House report
receiving over 600 per week (U.S. Congress, House, Commission on
Administrative Review, 1977b: 890).

The mail can be divided into two categories. "Legislative mail" is that
which deals with current public policy questions being debated in Con-

gress, while "casework" involves individual requests for information or benefits, or requests to have the representative mediate constituent concerns with the bureaucracy. The bulk of mail is legislation oriented. Casework increases with seniority. Junior members classify 19 percent of their mail as casework, while senior members have a comparable figure of 33 percent (O'Donnell, 1980: 29).

Legislative mail is characterized by repetition. Most months, "over 80 percent of the mail deals with the same two or three issues" (confidential interview). Constituents want to express their opinions, find out where their representatives stand on certain issues, and determine where certain legislation stands in the legislative process. On the big issues, these questions could be answered by any staff member, but on more esoteric subjects, the representative's record must be searched and sources within the legislative system tapped. Legislative mail is not a one-way street. The mail provides a useful way in which members of Congress can "feel the pulses" of the most politically active and concerned members of their constituencies.

Casework mail represents both more variety in subjects and the need for unique personalized responses. Casework may involve something as simple as a one-shot request—for tour information, a flag flown over the Capitol, help with term paper sources from the Congressional Reference Service, or a VIP tour of the White House—to more complicated requests, such as for intervention in the bureaucracy to shake loose a Social Security check or introduction of a private bill to override the immigration quotas. For the simple matters, such as official information or benefit requests, the congressional staff simply needs to know whom to ask and what procedures to follow. In dealing with claims against the bureaucracy, the congressional office needs to determine the legitimacy of the claim, find out the process for filing claims, discover where the claim is in the process, locate ways to expedite the claim, and monitor the system to make sure that promises of action are actually carried out (O'Donnell, 1980: 30).

The caseload of member offices has been increasing in recent years "as constituents are becoming more aware of the influence of the Federal Government and are demanding more responsive action from their elected representatives" (O'Donnell, 1980: 25). In 1979, the Social Security Administration dealt with over 300,000 congressional inquiries, while the Bureau of Immigration and Naturalization dealt with 78,000, and the Veterans Administration handled 45,000. The 4 military liaison offices on the Hill deal with over 30,000 congressional inquiries per year (O'Donnell, 1980: 25). With the growth of district offices, the problem of information is exacerbated. With extensive "walk-in traffic" the luxury of time to search for information is reduced, and in face-to-face meetings, constituents expect immediate answers (O'Donnell, 1980: 27).

Casework mail is important not only for the petitioning constituent and the receiving member of Congress, but also as a measure of the performance of the political system. Casework can serve as an input to the oversight function of Congress by pointing out where the system is falling down. Legislators receiving numerous complaints about particular programs can use this information as ammunition in the next set of authorizing or appropriating debates, particularly if they are able to show an imbalance or inordinate growth of problems.

When House members represent districts with over one-half million individuals and senators' districts number in the millions, any individual contact with a potential voter is important. Not only does the legislator want to leave a good impression by dealing with the specific problem at hand, but he or she also wants to develop and secure the nascent relationship that has evolved so that it can be pursued in the future. This might involve little more than developing a general mailing list for "educational" newsletters, or setting up an information filing system whereby individuals with similar interests can be tapped for targeted mailings on subjects near and dear to their hearts.

Federal projects information

With the federal government playing an active role in funding research, experiments, and local projects, the congressional office has become a clearinghouse for grants and aid information. House offices report receiving an average of 25 inquiries per week on federal programs, and the volume in the Senate is invariably higher (O'Donnell, 1980: 33). Congressional offices become involved in identifying programs most likely to provide assistance, reviewing applications for strengths and weaknesses, seeking out individual contacts within agencies to expedite the process, tracking the progress of decisions, and evaluating grant decisions for fairness, equality, and correspondence to legislative intent (O'Donnell, 1980: 35) In performing such functions the congressional office needs massive amounts of information. Members of Congress who represent small towns and rural areas perform a particularly important function, informing their constituents of programs otherwise known only to cities with large research staffs or paid consultants (Gregory, 1980: 41). As such funding decreases and grants become more competitive, access to quick and relevant information may well determine success or failure. In such an environment information sharing is unlikely, and each congressional office is likely to "go it alone" to reserve the right to take credit for its successes.

Public relations and outreach information needs

Members of Congress are public servants who have the responsibility to inform and educate the public. They have unique access to information and, while not denying the political advantages of good public relations, there is an advantage in sharing their information with the public. In developing a good public relations program, the congressional office must monitor congressional activity for newsworthy items, with a special eye to those items of particular interest to its district or state. They must know how to get in touch with the relevant members of the general and specialized press, and know their constraints (publishing dates, lead time, format limitations, and so on) and capabilities. They must also be cognizant of the past public pronouncements emanating from their offices, to maintain consistency (O'Donnell, 1980: 52).

Assessing constituent opinions

While few congressional participants or observers expect members of Congress to follow constituent opinion blindly, this opinion should be a factor in the decision-making process. Legislators need to know not only how people feel in general, but how particular subgroups feel. These subgroups may encompass those most deeply affected by a particular policy or those of special importance to a member's reelection. In some cases measurement of changes in opinion over time, especially those following important events, would be desirable.

Administrative Information

Congress is a large entity, with a staff of over 20,000 who need to be paid, communicated with, and monitored. By law Congress must produce numerous documents and keep authoritative records of expenditures and official legislative actions. Individual members of Congress must administer an office, with all its attendant administrative tasks of hiring, work scheduling, filing, monitoring, and the like. As a collective decision-making body, Congress needs to find ways to coordinate the activities of 535 "prima donnas" and their supporting entourages. This involves scheduling numerous and potentially conflicting meetings in the most efficient way possible. Those doing the scheduling must know who is being scheduled and the importance and extent of their other commitments. Individual members of Congress need to know both their organizational commitments and the form and extent of other requests for their presence. In a political environment, it is important that an elected official give constituents as equal and explainable attention as possible. This requires a balancing act of careful scheduling and strategic attentiveness, both of which depend on information from the "field" and within the office. Knowing who can be snubbed with little risk when a scheduling conflict arises may well determine political success or failure.

While not as exciting, and perhaps not having as much political or policy impact, the information necessary to make the Congress as a whole and individual congressional offices run smoothly will reduce the amount of attention that must be focused on these organizational requirements and increase the time for other concerns.

The most important kinds of data Congress needs to translate into useful information can be placed into three categories. First, Congress needs to select, assimilate, and organize *secondary data* that will shed light on public policy problems. The problem for Congress lies in creating a selective sieve to separate the important from the inconsequential, and a method of searching it for alternative purposes. The output of this process will tend to resemble selective bibliographies.

Second, Congress needs to collect and manipulate *primary data* on its own activities and policy concerns. Such data include everything from legislative status files, which can be mined for strategic information, to raw data on governmental activity, budgets, and performance, which can be monitored to determine emerging problems or assess policy consequences, or be enhanced through simulation models to predict future states.

Finally, in their role as communicators individual members of Congress need *word processing* capabilities to create and disseminate efficiently the messages they wish to spread.

The menu of congressional information needs could go on and on. When one's political future is on the line or when the nature of public policy is in the balance, there is no such thing as enough information. The question is not, "How do we get all the information to Congress?" but rather, "How, given the uniqueness of Congress and the limitations of information management, can we get enough relevant information so that Congress can survive as a viable institution?"

UNIQUENESS OF CONGRESS
AS AN INFORMATION CONSUMER

Before one can discuss improving Congress's information-handling capacity, it is important to point out that Congress is not just another information-processing organization. It has unique characteristics that must be considered and it performs a very crucial function in the political system that is far too important to tamper with unless a particularly good cause can be found.

Structurally, Congress is unique. It is part of a governmental system in which power is shared among a number of institutions. In hierarchical organizations, such as business firms, one common goal is the acquisition of profit. Under such conditions cooperation is common and sharing of information is more likely to be seen as a benefit for all. In the competitive environment of Congress, where decentralized committees artificially fragment policy problems, where one chamber competes with the other and both compete with the other branches of government, the motivation for efficient information gathering and sharing is diminished (Norton, 1980: 4-7).

The congressional information problem is exacerbated by its workload. Over 25,000 bills are introduced in each session of Congress, and each member is subject to close to 2000 recorded decisions as well as numerous unrecorded ones. Congress does not completely control its own agenda and therefore must have a reactive information system rather than one which can be planned out well in advance (U.S. Congress, House, Commission on Administrative Review, 1977b: 676-677).

The time pressure in congressional decision-making is staggering. Events can move with dazzling speed in the legislative arena, and the energies of most staff are devoted in a significant way to the avoidance of surprise (Zweig, 1979: 147). Decisions cannot wait until all the information is in; if one waits for the experts to come to a conclusion, it may be too late. In Congressman Charlie Rose's words, "Sometimes we forget what the problem was by the time we get the answer to the question" (Government Executive, 1977b: 48). Congress is task oriented and has a short time perspective (Schneier, 1970); the typical member of Congress "wants his answers *now*" (Jones, 1976: 259-260).

Because Congress is a political arena dealing with tough issues, congressional information requirements

> cannot be analyzed solely in terms of the factual inputs needed to
> define an issue, generate the alternatives, select the "best" solution
> to meet some simple objective such as cost or profit, and then
> control implementation in terms of economy and efficiency
> [Dechert, 1966: 169].

The domain of Congress revolves around norms of bargaining. Politics is essentially a "strategic game in which information is intelligence in the military sense. The legislative process is a highly stylized 'combat' played out by partisan troops who serve under different flags" (Worthley, 1976: 46-47). Information is not a "collective good" that all participants want shared around, but rather a source of power." Information is not only scanned, but it is also traded among congressional staff as goods may be traded in any marketplace (Zweig, 1979: 147). In using information, members of Congress are on the horns of a dilemma. If they maintain objectivity and share their information with all, they lose impact within the chamber. If they compromise objectivity, they may well lose their credibility (Jones, 1976: 259-260).

Given the nature of congressional issues that hinge on value choices laced with a good dose of intuitive guesswork, members of Congress are used to tempering information with personal advice. Loyalty and trust are very important. Valid information may be discounted if the source is not trusted, or if it runs counter to the personal advice of a trusted advisor (U.S. Congress, House, Commission on Administrative Review, 1977b: 676-677).

In many cases, members of Congress are less interested in information that enlightens them on general problems and more concerned with how a particular proposal affects their individual districts:

> The "facts" rarely speak for themselves. Members need to know how
> a particular proposal will affect their districts. . . . All members of
> Congress claim that they seek the "best" public policy, but they
> would also admit that there is no objective answer to what is "best"
> [Maisel, 1979: 7].

Unlike organizations in which information is a direct cost that must be subtracted from any profit, or the academic realm, where one is attempting to find the most efficient path to total truth, Congress has less concern for efficiency or completeness for completeness's sake in information gathering. Redundancy is not necessarily bad. "Economy of information is unimportant. What is important is how useful the research results are for policy purposes, a criterion which often dictates redundancy rather than economy" (Coleman, 1977: 29).

On the bottom line, one must remember that members of Congress are primarily motivated by the desire for reelection. As one member put it, "I can't do all the good things I want for my people and the nation unless I win the next election." The reelection goal underlies much of the concern for improving Congress's information resources.

One can be misled by viewing Congress solely as a single institution. It is made up of over 500 individuals, each of whom has a different view of information needs. Some of these differences reflect different approaches to the job, while others stem from differing objective conditions. "One congressman may represent a few blocks of mid-town Manhattan or the entire state of North Dakota" (Jost, 1979: 47). No matter the differences in individual members' views of congressional information needs, the 1960s dawned as an era in which traditional searching, retrieval, and analysis procedures were inadequate for the job.

CHARACTERISTICS OF
DESIRABLE CONGRESSIONAL INFORMATION

Congress must function as a massive scanning machine, sucking in data and arguments from many sources and refining them into legislative material [Schick, 1976: 228].

The quality of information entering the legislative system helps determine the quality of ultimate policy decisions. While poor information may not predetermine faulty decisions, it does nothing to help avoid them. The term "information" is being used in the broad sense and includes facts, data, opinions, analysis, and interpretations. Information serves as the raw material for knowledge. "Knowledge" is information that has been evaluated, refined, and organized. While the knowledge of others may enter an individual's consciousness as a new bit of information, it cannot be viewed as personal knowledge until it is absorbed and integrated into his or her individual repository. Neither information nor knowledge is enough on which to make decisions. Decisions are goal oriented and the goals are determined by one's values. Values are definitions of what is desirable for an individual or a society; they cannot be verified completely by empirical means. I might value a limited government and you might champion an activist one. All of the information and knowledge in the world would still lead us to talk past each other unless we could find some common ground of a higher value on which we could both agree. Thus from the outset there are limits on the utility of any available information. Information can lead to knowledge, but cannot guarantee it. Information may be available on potential value choices and the implications of choosing one over the other, but it does not predetermine an individual's choice. Information can tell us how to build a bomb and what it might accomplish, but it takes wisdom based on knowledge and value commitments to determine whether that bomb should be dropped.

In focusing on the characteristics of desirable congressional information, we will pay attention to information rather than to knowledge or values. The potential for wisdom and value choices is dependent as much upon the recipient as on the quality of information. Ideally, members of Congress need information that is complete, accurate, timely, relevant, independent, action oriented, and, at times, confidential. While at least the first four of these criteria are desired by all information users, members of Congress put unique emphasis on some.

For the sake of emphasis, congressional information needs and desires will be counterposed against those of objective researchers in the academic world. A number of authors have made the distinction between the "world of action," wherein Congress falls, and the world of the academic researcher (Coleman, 1977).

Completeness/Timeliness

The goal of complete information beckons all analysts, but for members of Congress completeness must often be sacrificed in order to avoid information overload and meet the demands of timeliness. A complete information-gathering process would leave no stone unturned in the search for potentially useful information and would develop a series of data collection points in order to assess changes over time. Unlike the academic researcher, whose deadlines for finding the "truth" are ultimately constrained only by personal longevity (I could rewrite this book in ten years, change my conclusions, and excuse my oversights in a line or two with few repercussions), the legislator in the world of action must often make crucial decisions before all the facts are in. In this situation, "partial information available at the time action must be taken is better than complete information after that time (U.S. Congress, Senate, Commission on the Operation of the Senate, 1977b: 29). In the words of former Congressman Charles Mosher:

> I'm skeptical of so-called "factual information. . . . Political decision-makers seldom can wait for the scientific process to produce confirmed factual information. The scientist, by the very nature of the way he thinks and works, wants to research, research and research again . . . but the political decision-maker can practically never wait for that type of information [Chartrand and Morentz, 1979: 73].

If completeness can be approached without sacrificing timeliness, it will be sought as a desirable goal.

Despite the heavy time pressures, Congress is not starved for information. The danger of information *overload* exists concurrently with the potential for information *underload* With too much information, it is possible to "lose the forest for the trees" (Rosenthal, 1981: 88). As one observer warned in the budget realm, it is possible for Congress to get "caught up in the web of economic numbers and lose sight of the substance of the issue" (U.S. Congress, House, House Information Systems, 1979b: 4). The plaintive cry of a current congressman points out the general problem:

> The real information difficulty I have as a member of Congress is the frustrating knowledge that I have that everybody would like to educate me more than I am able to absorb [U.S. Congress, House, Select Committee on Committees, 1973a: 318].

Members of Congress are not going to seek out additional information and increase the load on their staffs and themselves simply to have more information. The push for increased information will be based on a desire either to change the balance of information on a particular side of an issue or to compensate for biases in the current collection pattern. One member revealed the utility of increased information to improve the reliability of information available from current sources:

> The problem of information as I see it is primarily one of keeping the gatekeepers honest, . . . a problem . . . of keeping the system pluralistic, or of making sure there is competition (U.S. Congress, House, Select Committee on Committees, 1973a: 333).

Accuracy

Accuracy is the hallmark of good information. The information used by members of Congress can have dramatic impact on momentous decisions affecting their own political futures and, more importantly, national policy. Unlike academic researchers, anonymous staff members in Congress, or the bureaucracy, members of Congress are held responsible for their actions. When challenged by a constituent, an opponent, or some other interested party, it just does not wash to say, "I was misinformed." Members of Congress "keep book" on the accuracy of information provided them by various sources. Once a source has fallen from grace and lost the reputation for accurate and reliable information, it is a long route back to acceptance. In the words of one congressman referring to a lobbyist:

> I took his facts and incorporated them into my speech. I was stopped mid-sentence on the floor and challenged. My so-called facts were outdated and incomplete. I felt like a fool. I never want to see another representative from ———."

Relevance

The utility of information for solving the problem at hand is the legislator's criterion for relevance. As the personal and legislative goals of members of Congress vary, so will the information they perceive as important. In general, judgments of relevance made by members will differ in two ways from those made by academic researchers. Whereas the academic researcher holds as an ultimate goal the explanation of causes of phenomena, the legislator's need for strategic information is often satisfied when information allows him or her to predict with some certainty the effects of various decisions. The member of Congress is less concerned with why something works than with the fact that taking a particular course of action at a particular time will help him or her to reach a certain goal. In order to plan strategy, members of Congress need to know the problems faced (constituent demands, societal conditions, votes to be made, and so on), the options available, and the expected political and actual consequences of each option. They need to have at least a general conception of all these components, while the academic researcher working in the same substantive area might focus on a single component and study its internal workings.

A second factor that differentiates the congressional information user from the academician in judgments of relevancy is the congressional user's interest in political information, along with a willingness to eschew objectivity. The job security of members of Congress depends on their ability to monitor information on their own political strength, both within the chamber and in their constituencies. While academic researchers seek generalizations that apply across cases, members of Congress want to have very specific information about their own unique situations. The academician's objective evaluation of a particular policy may well be based on some criterion such as "the greatest good for the greatest number," while the member of Congress wants information on how the policy will affect his or her constituency or how it will relate to his or her value choices. While objectivity is the hallmark of academic research, the member of Congress often wants explicitly evaluative information useful for making a case for his or her preferred policy option.

Independence

Information is a source of power. Whoever controls the creation and dissemination of information can control its content and impact. To the degree that Congress is dependent on others for its information, Congress loses its role as a free participant in the decision-making process. Members of Congress want to control the creation and dissemination of information in such a way that it can be used to their best personal and institutional advantage. Although "territorialism" exists in all realms of human endeavor, the values of academic researchers lie in the direction of cooperation, open publication, and open access (U.S. Congress, Senate, Commission on the Operation of the Senate, 1977b: 40). Although open access to information and cooperation may seem to be a desirable goal in the abstract, it is unrealistic to expect members of Congress to renounce their political aims for the sake of fairness, better decisions, or efficiency in information gathering (Schick, 1976: 217). When creating independent information sources or limiting information access enhances a member's power, it is probable that he or she will choose that course of action.

Action Orientation

"Legislators want information that leads to action; and not to education. They want to solve problems rather than discover them" (Rosenthal, 1981: 222). In the words of Edward Schneier:

> The best possible intelligence you can get is a reliable directive to vote yes or no. . . . The worst possible kind of information you can have is 5000 pages stuck on your desk with no evaluation [U.S. Congress, House, Select Committee on Committees, 1973a: 326].

Confidentiality

Information is a power resource that facilitates persuasion, allows for planning, and contributes to legislative and electoral strategies. Members of Congress are not interested in information per se, but in its ability to help them reach their legislative and/or political goals. The very fact that some information is collected and available to a member may serve as an embarrassment politically. Some strategic information loses its utility if too widely shared. While academic researchers are committed to open sharing of information, political activists want the availability and use of their information to be a closely guarded secret (Coleman, 1977: 40).

TYPICAL INFORMATION SEARCH PATTERNS

In searching out information, members of Congress are hampered by limited time and resources. They tend to follow a "problematic" search pattern, that is, they limit their searches to those decisions they have problems making, and avoid search for search's sake (Kingdon, 1981: 228). If a decision is predetermined, completely one-sided, or one for which members of Congress will not have to take responsibility, no further information search is initiated. Members attempt to be parsimonious in their information searches, only gathering as much information as they absolutely need. "The marginal utility of information is a decreasing function of the amount of information at hand" (Grumm, 1979: 5).

In some situations, members of Congress find that an information search is not only impractical, but also a waste of time. One member complained: "Once I studied something for hours, went over to the floor, and it went through on a voice vote" (Kingdon, 1981: 229). Information may be less important for making decisions than for serving as insurance so that members can justify their decisions (Mayhew, 1972).

Academic researchers tend to use a "clinical" style of information gathering. Emphasis is on the internal logic of the problem rather than on the external ramifications. Great amounts of information are collected, compared, and contrasted in the search for relationships and causal factors. Legislators tend to eschew this method for an "advocacy" approach. Emphasis is on the external logic and, particularly, on the external political ramifications. Information is used to justify decisions made on other grounds. Members of Congress pick and choose the information that supports their biases (Caplan et al. 1963: 63).

It is not so much a case of "My mind's made up, don't confuse me with the facts," as a realization that there are "facts" and there are "facts." Members of Congress are dealing in an area where ambiguity clouds self-evident answers. Facts, and the interpretations of them, often disagree. "Soft," impressionistic information must be merged with "hard" facts. Political orientations and goals screen information and distort perceptions of it. The so-called facts must be overwhelming and unambiguous to compete successfully with biases and perceptions.

Under conditions of low preexisting information and/or biases, legislators, out of necessity, avoid searches for alternatives that attempt to be comprehensive. There is simply not enough time or resources for such searches. One of two suboptimal strategies is chosen. Using a "sequential" process, the legislator develops a level of satisfactory aspiration for improving the status quo. Alternatives are analyzed until one of them surpasses the minimal aspiration level acceptable. In a "batch" processing mode, the legislator's strategy is driven even more by the physical constraints of time and resources. A predetermination is made concerning the number of alternatives that can reasonable be reviewed. The best alternative from the "short list" of those considered is chosen on the basis of a combination of factual information and existing biases. While no empirical proof exists, at least one close observer feels that the "batch" approach captures more of the essence of reality (Grumm, 1979: 6).

Congressional information searches are clearly selective, both in scope and substance. The use of particular congressional information resources stems more from their ability to provide for the unique information needs of members of Congress than from their information quality as judged by more traditional researchers.

Congressional Information Resources

Members of Congress do not lack for potentially useful information sources. Groups and individuals from the outside beg to be heard, while internal sources find it to their political advantage to be information sources, either to shape the course of public policy or to prove their importance and thereby assure their job security. Until recently we knew little about the relative importance of various information sources. Two recent surveys of House members, using somewhat different approaches, came up with similar findings (see Table 1.4). Kingdon (1981: 18), focusing on the process by which individual members made specific voting decisions, highlights the importance of congressional colleagues, constituents, lobbyists, and the executive branch, while downgrading the importance of congressional staff members and the party leadership. A survey by the House Commission on Administrative Review (1977b: 966-980) specifically asked questions about sources of information for general topics, voting on the floor, and representing constituents. For floor voting, their findings coincide with Kingdon's on the importance of colleagues and constituents and the relative unimportance of party leadership, but they found that congressional staff members were seen as more crucial, and lobbyists and the administration less important, than was shown in Kingdon's study. Part of the variation may be due to the fact that the emphasis of the whole commission study was on ways to upgrade the administrative support given to members of the Congress. In the commission's survey, the congressional support agencies (Congressional Research Service, General Accounting Office, Congressional Budget Office, and so on) came out much better, especially as purveyors of general information.

If we know relatively little about general information flow in Congress, we know even less about individual variation among members. One study found that subject-area specialists embark on a much wider search for

TABLE 1.4 Perceived Relative Importance of Information Sources by Members of the House of Representatives

Sources	Information Used for Policy Decisions				General Information[b]	Casework Information[b]
	Kingdon[a]		Commission on Administrative Review[b]			
	Percentage*	Ranking	Percentage**	Ranking	Percentage	Percentage
Colleagues	40	1	38	3	9	7
District sources (mail)	37	2	21	5	16	22
Lobbyists	31	3	15	6	16	8
Administration	25	4	6	10	16	46
Party leaders	10	5	12	8	4	0
Personal study and reading	9	6	22	4	19	13
Staff***	5	7	57	1	9	51
Party groups (DSG, Republican Research Organization)	—	—	50	2	11	10
Committee staff	—	—	14	7	29	21
Congressional support agencies	—	—	11	9	30	17
Media	—	—	—	—	36	8
Academic research	—	—	—	—	8	—

SOURCES: a. Kingdon (1981: 18-19).

b. U.S. Congress, House, Commission on Administrative Review (1977b: 966-968).

*Percentage who spontaneously mentioned each source when asked: "How do you go about making up your mind?"

**Percentage mentioning each source when asked: "In every session of Congress, you're faced with voting on literally hundreds of bills on the floor which haven't been through one of the committees on which you sit. Thinking about the different places you could go to get what you need to know on bills like these — your personal staff, committee staff, the leadership groups, like the DSG or Republican Research Committee, various sources in your district, groups here in Washington, and the CRS, for example — where do you turn to get what you need to know to vote on the floor on these bills . . . — who do you really rely on for information like this?" (Similar questions were asked to acquire data on general and casework information sources.)

information on their particular topics and depend more on noncongressional sources, while nonspecialists rely on colleagues and constituents in making similar decisions (Zweir, 1979: 1). On the committee level, we know that "policy" committees—using Fenno's (1973:1) classification scheme—use more reports from the congressional support agencies than do "influence," "reelection," or "undesirable" committees (Sciccitano, 1981: 103-110), but we do not know whether these generalizations also apply to usage patterns by individual members.

Even if we discover the point of information transfer, it may not tell us much about the information source. In many cases there is a "two-step flow" of information into the Congress (Porter, 1974: 704). "Policy specialists outside Congress 'wholesale' communications to parallel specialists within the legislature. These men in turn 'retail' to others in the House" (Kovenock, 1967: 26).

INFORMATION SOURCES

The desire to know where members of Congress get their information is more than idle curiosity. The source of information can determine both its content and its perceived validity. "Congressmen often made judgments on the basis of the source of the argument, information, or position, rather than according to content" (Kingdon, 1981: 239).

Colleagues

It should be no surprise that fellow members of Congress stand out as important information sources. The division of labor principle underlying the committee system develops a set of in-house specialists who are readily available and cognizant of both the substance of the issues under consideration and of the unique pressures under which members of Congress make their decisions. Members develop consulting patterns that lead them to fellow members with substantive information who come from districts with similar needs and aspirations. Information transfer is facilitated by numerous informal and semiformal caucuses, cliques, and clubs organized around partisan, ideological, substantive, and/or regional bases. Frequently, a member walks out on the floor during a vote and asks, "What is this all about?" And in the words of a congressman:

Without calling on some information service, we swap information on the floor between people we have confidence in and believe in

[U.S. Congress, House, Select Committee on Committees, 1973a: 319].

Information from colleagues is strong on relevance and confidentiality, but the selective attention process by which information sources are chosen reduces the completeness of the information provided. Much of the information exchange involves "preaching to the choir," that is, like-minded individuals reinforcing each other's biases, rather than a process of changing minds through the influx of information.

For the individual member of Congress, accepting information from a colleague reduces independence, but there can be compensating advantages. Asking someone for information may boost that person's ego and make him or her think, "Why, what a wise person you are for asking me for the information." If the information petitioner comes across as an able person with a seeking mind, rather than as an incompetent, the seeking of information may build a relationship between the petitioner and the source that can work to the advantage of both. The petitioner may "owe" the source one, but the social bookkeeping may give the petitioner some credit also. He or she may be able to go back to the source and implicitly say, "Since I was so wise and paid you the great honor of seeking your counsel, now it is your turn to accept my bit of information."

Constituents

American democratic theory almost predetermines that members of Congress will give at least lip service to paying attention to constituent communications. The mass of mail entering a congressional office represents one piece in the large puzzle that is constituent opinion. The mail cannot simply be weighed or counted, since it reflects only the opinions of those who took the time and effort to communicate. Despite the quantity of mail, it seldom reflects the concerns of more than 10 percent of any constituency. Those who write are obviously more concerned, but are also likely to be better educated, more informed, and better off financially than those who do not (Verba and Nie, 1972: 52).

While mail may contain a great deal of particularly politically relevant information, members of Congress must make some judgments about it. One judgment concerns whether it comes from a "relevant constituency." Each member of Congress legally represents a geographic constituency, but is usually more concerned about some subsection of that geographic area. In most cases the "electoral constituency" weighs more heavily. Letters from likely voters, and especially past or potential future members of that electoral constituency, must be given preference. Members of Congress must also judge the quality of each communication. In most cases, a communication that reveals a great deal of effort, such as a long personal letter, has more impact than a postcard supplied by an interest group. Thus constituent mail is potentially strong on relevance, but is weak on completeness, even if one makes the effort to analyze it, as opposed to just "handling it," which is the term used by many offices.

Staff

The personal, committee, and support staffs of members of Congress have grown dramatically both in terms of quality and numbers in recent years. The personal staff surpasses all other possible sources in terms of confidentiality and independence, but it is unlikely to approach completeness in information gathering. Even with a staff of 15 to 20 in the House or over 30 in the Senate, the purview of Congress is so wide that even with specialization a great deal "falls through the cracks." With 535 independent research units on the Hill (not counting committees and support agencies) duplication is inevitable. As one staff member said:

It is not so bad when I am wading through voluminous information in the congressional reading room to find that I am plowing the same ground as staff members from a half dozen other offices, but it is really disheartening to find that I am doing a carbon copy of the work someone in our own office did just last week.

Congressional offices are hectic places, not well designed for efficient research. Overall planning gives way to "fighting brush fires." Not only do staff members duplicate the work of others, but information gathering is supplanted by other demands. When the big newsletter has to be addressed by hand, everyone is pulled off his or her job to help.

The nature of personal staff recruitment has seldom focused on information-gathering skills as a major priority. Loyalty and ideological compatibility take precedence over other factors. This contributes to confidentiality of information, but means that staff members often have the same "blinders" and biases about information sources and conclusions as their bosses.

The committee staffs are able to fulfill the criteria of information completeness and accuracy a bit more, but are weaker in presenting relevant, independent, and confidential information. Committee staffs are dominated and chosen by the chairperson and ranking minority members and may well have loyalties and even responsibilities to those offices.

The congressional support agencies (Congressional Research Service [CRS], General Accounting Office, and more recently the Congressional Budget Office and the Office of Technology Assessment) are weakest in their ability to approach completeness and accuracy in information, but suffer particularly from their inability to cut through the mass of information to determing what is relevant. Out of necessity for their survival, the support agencies are indoctrinated with the norm of objectivity (Maisel, 1979: 53). The official position of the CRS is that it

> serves as a staff arm of policy-mediated and partisan power structure [which] operates on an entirely different premise. It has no official views regarding which is a better solution to a legislative problem. It attempts to identify choices and to forecast the apparent implications of the alternatives, but it is the individual members and therefore the Congress, who make the decision [Baaklini and Heaphey, 1977: 111].

There is a great deal of truth in the joke that if you ask the CRS to do a report on child abuse, they will return in 3 days with a listing of the 10 good points and the 10 bad points about child abuse, complete with 100 footnotes and the summarized testimony of an equal number of experts on each side. It takes some effort to cut through all the objectivity to find the relevant material. Members of Congress do not want objective analyses, they require evaluations that take their own values into account.

Personal Research

One study showed that individual members of Congress did 30 percent of their general research and 60 percent of the preparation for committee hearings, floor debate, and voting (Saloma, 1969: 187). Members are hampered by many of the same problems as their staffs: The immensity of the task limits their completeness and their biases limit their accuracy. Time pressure is a particular problem. As one House member bemoaned:

> When I came here I vowed that I would set aside two hours per day for reading and research. In two years I have not been able to do that once. A constituent calls, the voting bells ring or a hearing is

called. I feel like a puppet on a string. It is like being in law school and only being able to study in five or ten minute blocks.

Even if the member or his or her staff wants to do research, the traditional bibliographic sources and congressional documents are not always accurate, current, or responsive (Norton, 1980: 11). It is no surprise that members and their staffs try to find ways to get others to predigest and present information.

Committee hearings are designed to provide members with information from outside sources and to provide a forum for sharing perspectives with fellow members. Hearings seldom live up to all the criteria of good information. Completeness falls by the wayside when chairpersons "stack" the witnesses in order to bolster their position; and when members attend selectively those meetings that feature witnesses of their own persuasion or who give them a chance to "grill" an expert, thus reaping the desired press coverage. Outside experts are often the closest thing to complete information sources on a topic, but time pressures of most hearings necessitate a witness giving a brief summary to a handful of committee members, while the bulk of the testimony gets placed in the hearings document, which is seldom read by the decision makers and may at best serve as a source for future "experts" so that they can gear up for the next hearing. Hearing witnesses also seldom have a good feel for what is relevant to members of Congress. They spend a great deal of time talking past each other, without ever having adequate mutual insight to evaluate each other's needs, biases, and potential contributions.

Interest Groups and the Executive Branch

Interest groups and the executive branch can be grouped together since they both approach Congress as lobbyists and their information is subject to similar strengths and weaknesses. Both approach Congress with the particular perspective they want to portray. Useful information can be gained from both sources if members of Congress realize that it is seldom complete, possibly not relevant to congressional concerns, and subject to selective accuracy.

This incompleteness and selective accuracy stems from the desire to present the best possible case for one's legislative goals. Both executive branch and private group lobbyists realize that they live on the basis of their reputations. They cannot afford to lie to a member of Congress. The weakness of their information lies in sins of omission, rather than in sins of commission. They pass on selectively the information and findings that bolster their case. This should not be alien to members of Congress, since it is the same partisan advocacy game they play so well.

Members of Congress expect partisan advocacy on the part of interest groups, but are sometimes less prepared for it from the bureaucracy. Even in areas in which the bureaucracy is required to present Congress with objective data, they are often withheld or presented in useless form. "The legislative branch is informed only to the extent the executive branch wants to inform it" (Hopkins, 1972: 454). Part of the problem is that Congress does not know what to ask for. "It is hard to get answers without first knowing the questions, and Congress has only the most inadequate ways of knowing them" (U.S. Congress, Senate, Commission on the Operation of the Senate, 1976a: xii). Even former Vice President Mondale echoed the problem:

I have been in many debates, for example on the Education Committee, that dealt with complicated formulas and distributions. And I have found that whenever I am on the side of the Administration, I am surfeited with computer print-outs and data that comes within seconds, whenever I need to prove how right I am. But if I am opposed to the Administration, computer print-outs always come late, prove the opposite point or are on some other topic [Jones, 1976: 256].

Even people in the White House realize the imbalance, as exemplified by this exchange between John Dean and Richard Nixon:

Dean—I spent some time on the Hill myself and one of the things I always noticed was the inability of Congress to deal effectively with the executive branch because they have never provided themselves with adequate staffs and adequate information. Nixon—[expletive deleted] don't try to help them out (U.S. Congress, Senate, Committee on Rules and Administration, 1977b: 16].

Awareness of the problem is widespread. Representative Thomas Evans (D-CO) estimates that "80-90% of Congress' information comes from the executive branch" and former Senator Edmund Muskie (D-ME) bemoaned the fact that the administration seeks to "spoonfeed" the information they decide Congress should have (Cohen, 1973: 379). The problem is broader than inequalities in information and directly affects the balance of power in our separation of powers system. In Representative Morris Udall's words:

> Knowledge is power.... And the decline in congressional power can be at least partially attributed to the inability of the legislative branch to develop information sources independent of the executive branch [Hopkins, 1972: 454].

The problem looms particularly acute in the area of the federal budget. Without good budget data, the would-be decision makers are often relegated to grasping at political straws, such as excessive administrative costs or the high price of government wastebaskets, when they should be involved in the job of truly managing the nation's resources (Congressional Record, 1968: 1322).

The lack of independent information sources is the major limitation to use of executive branch and interest group information. Without the ability to check their data and conclusions, Congress is at a tremendous disadvantage. Members of Congress have become particularly wary of using data they cannot validate independently. Al Ullman, who, as a ranking member of the leadership, should have had extraordinary access to information, complained that

> we have an antiquated information system.... We spend hours to get information we should be able to get by pushing a button.... We can't do anything more than pass on the Administration information to the House with some recommendation of our own [Cohen, 1973: 382].

It is probably safe to say that no one is completely satisfied with the types, quality, or amount of information currently available to members of Congress. Outside observers add to these concerns a dismay about the ways in which information is traded, manipulated, and processed once it crosses the congressional threshold. No universally acceptable information is likely to be found since the criteria for evaluating information adequacy vary among individuals. Improving Congress's information will require attacking the problem on many fronts, paying particular attention to the characteristics of the various options and the unique perceived and actual needs of the members themselves.

The following chapters will focus on computerized information systems as a partial answer to Congress's information needs. Chapter 2 evaluates the strengths and weaknesses of computerized data bases for solving the information needs of a political institution such as Congress. Chapters 3 through 6 focus on the adoption of computers, progressing from a discussion of innovation theory (Chapter 3), to discussion of the acquisition of computers by Congress as an institution (Chapter 4), to a description of the data bases available to Congress (Chapter 5), and finally to an analysis of individual members of Congress and their adoption and usage of modern information technology (Chapter 6). Chapter 7 takes up the question of access to information by various groups, both in and out of Congress. Our discussion concludes with an analysis of the impact of modern information technology on the Congress, with special emphasis on the political implications (Chapter 8).

2 COMPUTERS IN CONGRESS: THE POTENTIAL AND THE PITFALLS

Complex technological societies and the role governments play in these societies require new political and administrative machineries and the application of modern technologies [Baaklini and Heaphey, 1977: 23].

Financial support for extensive and accurate informational systems is crucial to the effective and efficient operation of most legislatures and is one of the best bargains legislators can find [Grumm, 1979: 22].

Since their invention in the 1940s, to esoteric usage in the 1950s, to becoming part of standard operating procedures in the 1960s and 1970s, and now in the age of the home computer in the 1980s, computers have revolutionized our lives. Although initially employed as complex calculators to reduce dramatically the time required for mathematical manipulations, modern applications span the whole range of human endeavor. Computer applications include everything from generating our paychecks to guiding our missiles. Few individuals are so isolated that some form of computer application does not touch their lives daily.

In a fluid and open social and political system such as the United States, new technologies cross institutional boundaries with ease. Institutions with similar needs borrow openly and the purveyors of such technology seek to spread their products. Initially, widespread use of the computer developed in the business community, where its ability to take over routine clerical jobs increased efficiency, accuracy, and, most importantly, profits. The executive branch of government called on the computer to manage its massive data files and used it as a "super clerk" to handle such tasks as distributing Social Security checks and organizing information files. While the rush to computerize spread through business and the bureaucracy, the legislative branch sat back either unaware of the developments or uninterested in the possibility of employing computers. While some of the hesitation was well founded in the inherent limits of applying computers to the legislative process or based on realistic fears of the dangers involved, pressures were building to make eventual computer utilization almost inevitable.

PRESSURE FOR COMPUTERIZATION

Probably the first to notice the need for new operating procedures in the postwar era were the members of Congress and their staffs. By every work measure available, from number of hours in session, to number of bills introduced, to the amount of mail received, the traditional picture of the part-time legislator and a small staff leisurely handling a limited workload began to fall by the wayside (see table 2.1).

At first, as the workload increased, members simply spent more time at their desks and expanded their staffs, but the workload expanded faster. Not only was there more to do, but the decisions to be made became more technical and complex. The ability of a member of Congress to be well read, and thereby well informed, fell victim to the complexity of the issues and the information explosion that was making yesterday's knowledge obsolete. Congress was simply being overwhelmed by its immense information needs and the profusion of sources that were "overpowering Congress' old fashioned diffuse information handling capabilities" (Hopkins, 1972: 453). As Worthley (1977b: 155) put it:

> With the growth of information need, there has been a simultaneous explosion in information availability. But mere availability of data does not assure its delivery or useability.... There can be so much data that it is overwhelming.... As a consequence, legislators often receive too little information, that is, not enough of the right kind of information at the right time, in the right form.... All of this has produced a focus on development of computer-based information systems for handling the situation.

TABLE 2.1 Indicators of Legislative Activity and Workload

	Congress						
	84th (1955)	86th (1959)	88th (1963)	90th (1967)	92nd (1971)	94th (1975)	96th (1979)
Legislative Activity[a]							
Number of bills introduced							
House	13,169	14,112	14,022	22,060	18,561	16,982	9,103
Senate	4,518	4,149	3,457	4,400	4,408	4,114	3,480
Number of days in session							
House	230	265	334	328	298	311	326
Senate	224	280	375	358	348	320	333
Number of roll call votes							
House	147	180	232	478	456	810	779
Senate	224	422	541	595	955	1,311	1,055
Number of public bills enacted (total Congress)	1,028	800	666	640	607	588	613
Pages of bills enacted	1,848	1,774	1,975	2,304	2,330	4,117	NA
Number of committee meetings							
House	3,210	3,059	3,596	4,386	5,114	NA	NA
Senate	2,607	2,271	2,493	2,892	3,559	NA	NA
Constituent Communications[b]							
Millions of pieces of mail sent by Congress	103.8	194.5	205.2	371.1	547.3	723.8	800 (est)

SOURCES: a. Stevens and Richardson (1981); all data are from this source, except as noted.
b. Bibby et al. (1980).

The increased workload and the information explosion themselves may not have been the sole impetus for searching out computer applications to the legislative process. The relative disadvantage of legislatures in information handling, compared to the executive branches of government, created in its members a jealousy of the advantages of the competing branch. Members of Congress began to realize that they were losing power to the executive branch, partly due to its speedy access to massive data banks. Numerous proponents of change spoke with envy about the number of computers under the control of the executive branch. Control of access to information serves as a major power resource in a political system. Members of Congress found their incoming information filtered at least twice by "gatekeepers." The executive branch agencies selectively passed information to committees, which in turn selectively released it to members. This process inevitably led to distortions, blockages, and misconceptions. The eventual consumer, the individual member of Congress, was beholden to other individuals, whose goals may have been different and who may have passed on only the information that promoted their interests (U.S. Congress, House, Select Committee on Committees, 1974: 32). Computerization for Congress was promoted as allowing Congress to

respond more efficiently to constituent requests, to approach the legislative process armed with a better array of data, and to oversee and monitor even the most remote agencies of the executive branch [Southwick, 1977: 1045].

PROMISE OF COMPUTERS

While the capabilities and limitations of computers are constantly in flux, congressional consideration of computer applications came at a time when research in other settings both in and out of government had begun to map the terrain. Most simply, computers "make available more information, more rapidly, and in many forms" (Gross, 1969: 67). The primary strengths of the computer lie in its abilities to store massive amounts of information and to deliver that information rapidly in a wide variety of forms tailored to particular needs. Computers do not do work that could not be done by hand, but do make possible tasks that either consume inordinate amounts of human resources or are avoided due to the drudgery of hand collection and manipulation.

In Chartrand's (1976b: 42-43) conception, the computerized information system has the following advantages:

(1) speed
(2) flexibility in the storage of data
(3) cost savings
(4) "massage" of preselected data at various levels of aggregation
(5) use of interactive searching procedures allowing for homing in on problems and information

Given the multiple tasks of the modern legislator, the proposed applications of computers were numerous and varied when they first came to Congress. The most obvious translation from business applications lay in having the computer take over administrative or "housekeeping" functions. By transferring manual record keeping of personnel records, payroll, and tracking of legislation, a payoff would develop not only through increased speed and accuracy, but also in terms of freeing staff for other activities. Our limited attention to purely administrative applications in this book should not be interpreted as demeaning their importance. However, the "most directly beneficial contributions of computers have and still do result from housekeeping applications" (Kraemer and King, 1975: 2-15).

Clerical Functions

Modern word-processing machinery improves the efficiency of clerical personnel by reducing redundancy and increasing the cumulative nature of efforts. Textual material can be edited while the work is in progress. Amendments to legislation can be inserted directly, and personalized letters can be created by combining a set of prewritten paragraphs. Computer-based filing systems allow speedy selective recovery of files based on sophisticated cross-filing indexes. Staff members are thereby relieved of repetitive tasks and the quality of information retrieval is not hampered by the frailties of human memory or the limitations of a filing system that can only deposit the document in a single file folder.

Research Functions

Important as the administrative and clerical applications are, they are somewhat removed from the legislative activities of members of Congress.

Clerical improvements may make the staff more efficient and life on the Hill more pleasant, but they do not necessarily improve the quality of decision-making. The abilities of the computer to serve as a research librarian and repository for original data banks made the prospect of computerization more exciting and potentially more important. As a librarian, the computer promised to give members of Congress access to the best and most current knowledge produced worldwide, instantaneously. Congress would not have to depend solely on the skill and diligence of its own bibliographers in the Library of Congress, but could also tap into the burgeoning list of specialized bibliographies being created by academic institutions and commercial enterprises. Access to such information would help Congress in identifying problems, canvassing alternative solutions, and assessing the probable consequences of particular choices. With creative search and dissemination techniques, such bibliographies could be used to update members and their staffs on new developments in fields of their choice.

Through the development and acquisition of substantive data banks, the Congress could do its own original research, both for the purpose of making legislative decisions and to facilitate monitoring the bureaucracy. These data banks could include everything from the monitoring of chamber activity to helping a member know what has been or is about to be done. Ongoing measures of "social indicators," such as literacy rates or infant mortality data, could be monitored over time for changes that would indicate a need for legislative action (De Sola Pool, 1971: 24).

The proper data banks would give the legislator the best possible information for discovering emerging problems, searching out solutions, and planning strategy for enactment. Some of the potential information existed prior to the advent of computerization, but was often in a form that made it difficult to use. Other information simply was not collected because of the time and effort involved.

Decision-Facilitating Information

While members of Congress would not, and should not, delegate their decision-making responsibilities to anything other than their own judgment, simulation models facilitate predicting the consequences of particular policy choices. A simulation model attempts to predict consequences by linking together a number of assumptions and at times combining this simplified model of reality with some actual hard data. While a simulation model may not predict the future in all cases, repeated use, comparison with reality, and revision can lead to better predictions than intuition alone. To the degree that users of a simulation model agree with the basic assumptions and are satisfied with the quality of its predictions, it can serve as an efficient method of simplifying decisions. The computer makes simulations possible by facilitating complex analysis and data manipulation.

Except for simulation models, the main contribution of the computer lay in its speed in manipulating large bodies of data and presenting them in ways that fit the needs of individual users. Experience from the introduction of modern information technology in local government implies that the development of computerized data banks increases not only the quantity of information, but the quality as well. Governmental units begin to share data, catch each other's errors, and sharpen each other's data collection and analysis techniques (Kraemer and King, 1975: 2-14). The ultimate promise of the computer stems from its potential for providing Congress not *more* information, but *better* information, in terms of organization, coordination, accessibility, delivery, and visibility (U.S. Congress, House, Commission on Information and Facilities, 1976c: 10).

Despite the manifold potential of the computer for increasing the quality and efficiency of legislatures, we must not lose sight of the fact that

> the computer is not a necessary component of an information system. It is merely a tool chosen to implement the information system because it fulfills requirements either to improve the accuracy or timeliness of information, to reduce the costs of obtaining and distributing information, or to make possible new information services [U.S. Congress, House, Commission on Organization and Procedure, 1973: 287].

These temperate words carry even more weight when one realizes that their author, Frank Ryan, served as the head of the computer system in the House.

COMPUTER LIMITATIONS AND DANGERS

The supposed advantages of new technology are accompanied by limitations and dangers that must be considered before adopting the innovation fully. Research from other realms indicates that computerization would bring mixed blessing to Congress.

Mechanical Problems

By delegating one's information collection and analysis to the computer, one becomes dependent on the efficiency and particular quirks of the machine. When speed in information access becomes the expectation, "down time"—when the computer is not available—or slow response time creates frustration and disgust. Individuals accustomed to computerized access can become immobilized at the thought of reverting to the old way of doing things when the computer cannot be counted on. In many cases, information in the computer is locked into the system and unavailable in other forms. Early in the adoption of computerized systems, when it is most important to impress potential users with the utility of such a change, hardware (machine) and software (programming) problems are most likely. It is often difficult to anticipate usage levels that could swamp the system or programming quirks that may produce misinformation rather than information.

While the computer itself seldom makes mistakes, faulty programming, often transparent to even the most sophisticated user, gives meaning to the quip found on the wall of most computer centers:

> To err is human; but it takes a computer to really screw things up.

The computer magnifies human mistakes and faulty logic. Computers are very literal. They do what we tell them to do, not what we mean to tell them to do. By depending on computers, the eventual user of information loses some "feel" for the data and how they are manipulated, and becomes dependent on the skills of the programmer and the limitations of the particular machine being used.

Human Problems

While mechanical problems may plague computer utilization, the weakest link may be the perceptions and attitudes of the humans who must use the computers. Reaction to the introduction of computers is seldom neutral. For some the cry "The Computers Are Coming" strikes a note of fear and repulsion. The computer threatens those comfortable with the traditional methods of collecting and analyzing information and those who foresee a loss of power when others either supersede them as information brokers or have equal access to information that was previously their domain. The introduction of computerized information systems often involves restructuring job descriptions and inevitably entails retraining. Individuals who view themselves as "not being any good with machines" or "terrible with numbers" panic at the thought of becoming anachronistic.

Many individuals fear that computers will diminish the quality of their jobs. While computerization reduces some routine activities, other activities, such as data entry, loom larger in an office. Some individuals fear that the introduction of an information system will expose their past deficiencies and that their future performance will be better monitored. While computers are no substitute for human thought and judgment, misperceptions of their capabilities require careful correction in order for computers to be accepted.

While the major problems with computers stem from the fears and dislocation they produce among the potential users, some individuals are overly receptive They accept computers uncritically, and see them as the source of their emancipation and the basis for their future power and status. For these individuals, the computer becomes an end in itself, rather than a tool that may or may not be appropriate to a particular task. As Congressman Charlie Rose (D-NC) observed:

> Some people tend to worship computers. They use them as security blankets. They can be partners in the work process if everybody knows how they work and what they can and cannot do.

Resource Problems

Little comes cheaply in the modern world, and computers are no exception. While touted as a method of saving money in the long run, computerization involves dramatic personnel and financial start-up costs, which are followed in quick order by updating costs (Downs, 1967: 206). On the human side, personnel must be found who not only understand the technical aspects of computer utilization but who have a feel for the needs of the eventual information consumers. The information battlefield is littered with beautifully designed information retrieval systems reflecting the skill of talented computer technicians who fell short on only one criterion: They did not provide the kind of information needed by the users.

Creating the initial data bases is expensive and often involves duplicating work done under the previous manual system. Although the long-run benefits may be obvious, the initial costs may seem prohibitive for marginal improvement in speed or data flexibility. There are times when one must come to the conclusion that the costs of perfect information exceed the benefits.

Even if the human and financial resources are available, computerization may be inappropriate if the most crucial aspect of an information system, valid and reliable information, is lacking. No discussion of computerized information systems would be complete without reference to "G.I.G.O." (garbage in, garbage out). The quality of an information search outcome is only as valuable as the material available. No information system will compensate for the lack of information or the availability of questionable data. "There frequently are no studies lying around you can grab and use" (Weinberg, 1979: 36). One is often lured into a false sense of optimism by hearing that some other organization has in its possession needed data, only to have the hopes dashed when it is discovered that the data are unavailable for sharing or that they have been collected and categorized in an awkward or unusable fashion (Worthley, 1976: 170). The choices that go into collecting particular bits of information in specific ways reflect the needs and interests of the collecting organization; this information may be of little use to outside users.

The users of information systems often set themselves up for frustration by not knowing the limits of the data bases at hand. Nichols (1976: 4-5) reports the common experience of a state legislator, who, after going to a training session on a bibliographic data base, believed that all the information in the world was waiting at his fingertips. It was not until a search produced a massive bibliography, which would have taken extensive time and work to pursue, that he realized that through this data base he could gain access to information, but not the information itself.

Distortion of the Decision-Making Process

The most serious consideration of the limits of modern information technology must be focused on the potential dangers it presents for affecting the decision-making process and eventually reducing the quality of the ultimate decisions.

Unwarranted enhancement of information

The status of the computer printout invites the turning of "sow's ear data into silk purse knowledge." The public has become conditioned to believe that if it came from a computer it is absolute, when in reality the result is no more reliable than the judgment of the individual who designed the system and the reliability of the data provided it (Nichols, 1976: 4). The temptation to disguise weak data input behind a complex facade in order to reinforce a decision already arrived at looms large (U.S. Congress, House, Select Committee on Committees, 1974: 69). In the battle to have one's preferences prevail, participants often shop around, not only for information that best supports their cause, but information that can be presented in a form that imbues it with legitimacy.

Information users often lack either the skills or the motivation to develop an understanding of the limitations and assumptions under which data was collected and disseminated. As one congressional staff member pointed out:

> There are some dangers of disseminating information recklessly, especially in the budget area. Information users need to know the ground rules by which the data was collected and analyzed. They need to know where the data came from, how valid it is, and the assumptions used in analysis. The computer enhances information. Many people feel that if something comes from a computer it must be "It." Unlike the academic realm where the risks of bad information are less, we must remember that congressmen are going to make important decisions which affect thousands of people based on your information.

A special problem arises with simulation models, which have as their underlying rationale the enhancement and manipulation of current data to predict future states. Despite their value if used correctly, such models can provide solutions that are either unacceptable or undesirable. Simulation models are based on assumptions that may or may not be shared by the users. To the degree that underlying assumptions are not shared or cannot be proved, conflict over policy choices will not be reduced by the availability of such models. Simulation models also find limited utility when the solutions they imply involve policy choices that politicians can or will not make, or when the model fails to take into account such things as political factors.

Overemphasis on empirical data

Although the computer can store and analyze many forms of data, its forte lies in the manipulation of empirical data that can be coded into a discrete set of categories and expressed in numerical summaries. Since the computer excels in dealing with quantity of data, and does little to evaluate quality, a "Gresham's Law" of data develops, in which the more easily collectable empirical data push out those data that are less quantifiable or measurable. Information system planners place undue emphasis on those aspects of reality with which the computer can most easily deal (Michael, 1966: 29). Supposedly "soft" and inexact impressionistic, intuitive, and descriptive data are arbitrarily excluded from consideration (Chartrand, 1976b: 43).

With the marked preference for empirical data, there is a tendency to use what is available, rather than what is desirable. During the late 1970s, one highway department was using the 1960 birthrate figures to plan highways, because that was all that was available on computer tape. Major miscalculations resulted from using such outdated information, which could have been avoided by relying on officials with an impressionistic feel for the situation (Danziger, 1977: 32).

Like the mountain that must be climbed because it is there, the capacity to collect data can set into motion tremendous pressure to collect potentially unneeded or undesirable data. It has become axiomatic that more information is better than less. The introduction of the computer, with its ability to manipulate huge amounts of data, is supposed to turn data mountains into molehills, but the lack of physical constraint to data collection may also turn data mountains into mountain ranges (Danziger, 1977: 32). Without careful screening for need and quality, the supposed advantages of expanded information can turn into a detriment. Sheer volume of information can result in "endarkenment as well as enlightenment" (Webber, 1981: 10). Producers and users of information systems should heed Norman Cousins's charge that too often there is a "tendency to mistake data for wisdom" (Chartrand, 1978: 15). Not only is an overcollection of a limited type of data potentially dangerous for the decision-making process and an inefficient use of resources, it poses the danger of invading the privacy and civil liberties of those on whom data are collected. When the collection of data becomes an end in itself, no one is well served.

Distortions produced by quantifying

Data fed through a computerized information system are simultaneously enhanced in status and reduced in essence. The reduction results from having to simplify and place information in a fixed coding format. In this process, the user loses some "feel" for the more subtle aspects of the information. Once a decision has been made on a particular data entry and retrieval format it is not easy to reverse; the choice of initial collection scheme may mean that some information is lost forever.

Once data are collected in a particular way, "sunk costs" and user familiarity make change unlikely. Changes in data collection systems resemble incremental budgeting processes in which previous data collection decisions are seldom challenged and only the most obvious shortcomings are corrected, with as minor tinkering as possible. Unless the foresight is extraordinary, it is not uncommon for organizations to be stuck with less-than-optimal data systems (Chartrand, 1976b: 43).

Choices in collecting and coding data can have dramatic political and economic implications. Recently the Economic Development Administration needed to collect employment data on towns and cities in order to make decisions on target planning grants for public works projects. Until a number of members of Congress complained that deserving small towns in their districts were bypassed, no one questioned the decision to code all towns under 2500 population as having zero work force and zero unemployment, since the data was so hard to get (Gregory, 1978: 98). The problem probably would not have been exposed if computer-wise Representative Charlie Rose (D-NC) had not been affected. In his words:

> This horror story of faulty decision over life and death economic resources was totally inexcusable. It came about because people who drove the decision process were more concerned about getting the money out than in helping people. They botched it with faulty data, and luckily we exposed it.

Recognizing the Limited Role of Facts in Decision-Making

> The lines between information collection, summarization, analysis and application are blurred and the activities are a continuum. At one end perhaps the activity is fairly neutral and non-political, whether clerical or professional. At some point as one moves to application there are judgments introduced which properly must be conditioned by ideology and political objective [Bolling, 1975: 493].

Proponents of modern information systems for legislatures may assume that the collection, storage, retrieval, and analysis of information will lead to undeniable answers, but most often these answers are to the wrong questions. When it comes to making legislative decisions,

> policy analysis intermingles hard facts carefully analyzed and inter-preted with an unpredictable amalgam of values, experience and judgment. ... This sort of research will only rarely give a "correct" answer or even a weighted preferential one [U.S. Congress, House, Select Committee on Committees, 1974: 222].

The availability of information does not guarantee that it will be used in an effective or objective manner.

> Merely because there is a flow of information is *no* guarantee that the decision-maker is going to act on the basis of that, especially if it tends to contradict his own predispositions, or his own self-percep-tion of how he would like the world to be [U.S. Congress, Senate, Committee on Rules and Administration, 1980: 126].

We each selectively attune ourselves to information sources likely to reinforce our biases and reinterpret collected information in such a way as to limit the conflict with our predispositions.

A legislative information system should be able to tell us what others see as problems and what has been done in the past and its impact, as well as suggest alternatives for the future and their likely consequences; but no information system can tell a politician the relative importance of one problem area over another or determine universally acceptable criteria for evaluating actual or predicted policy outcomes. Legislators remain impor-tant in choosing the values to pursue and in making judgments about the quality of incomplete, conflicting, and possibly biased information. Intel-lect distinguishes between the possible and the impossible; reason dis-tinguishes between the sensible and the senseless. Even the possible can be senseless (Max Born, in Bulletin of the American Society for Information Science, 1978: 5). To this distinction I must add that politics distinguishes between the acceptable and unacceptable.

Computerized information systems can add to the intellect of legis-latures by identifying problems and clarifying alternative solutions (Cooper, 1975: 355), but have much more limited applicability in the bulk of the legislature's work, which focuses on reason and politics. It is in this realm that value choices and more impressionistic perceptions pervade.

In order for an issue to become important enough that overburdened legislators will seek out more information, there must be conflict. Conflict implies a lack of technical certainty. Expert opinions conflict and conflicting predictions abound. The role of the legislature is to evaluate the political strengths of various viewpoints:

> We should not, and fortunately we probably cannot, overwhelm the political judgment of the Congress with masses of factual data and technical analysis [Dreyfus, 1977: 107].

In the bureaucratic setting, Caplan (in Weiss, 1977: 193) found that "the ultimate test of data acceptability is political, particularly in the area of domestic social policy.... Rarely are data in their own right of such a compelling force as to override their political significance." If this is true in the bureaucracy, we would expect it to apply with even more force to the legislative branch, where politics not only affects the decision-making process within the chamber, but defines the very route to individual job security.

Politics is a process characterized by the mediation of competing and contrasting interests. To the degree that computerized information will be important, it will be used to support one-sided arguments that initially stem from value choices rooted in self-interest or unverifiable perceptions and assumptions. Legislators as a matter of necessity will look out for the interests of their parochial constituencies and shop around for data that justify their actions and measures their success. Ideological and policy biases will precede the selective gathering of information that bolsters one's values and makes them salable to a wider group of fellow decision makers.

Only rarely will the kinds of facts a computerized information system can deliver be so unambiguous and overwhelming that the underlying value choices come into question. Generally the legislator will thwart conflicting information from the computer by pointing out that one cannot reduce all the significant variables to numbers, questioning the uncertainties in predicting consequences, mentioning the potential distortions based on the difficulties of controlling those who run the machines, or even frankly admitting the imprecise science of assigning values to different alternatives (Janda, 1968: 430).

The fact that ultimately legislative decisions depend more on values than on facts does not diminish the potential importance of modern information technology in the legislative setting. As long as legislators use information of all kinds as a strategic resource to sway the uncommitted and thwart their opponents, knowing the availability and use of computer-based information in this scheme will be important.

Fear of Upsetting Traditional
Decision-Making Procedures

Legislatures and legislative procedures were designed to facilitate compromise and the building of consensus. Speed and efficiency in decision-making were definitely not the goals of the Constitution writers who instituted bicameral legislatures and separation of powers. Instantaneous access to information changes the chemistry of the decision-making process and the roles of the participants. The time for consensus building is lost and a spirit of data "one-upsmanship" may develop. Quick absorption of massive amounts of data may not be compatible with democratic decision-making (Vagianos, 1976: 148).

Information Misuse

Once information has been collected and deposited in a computer bank, it can be used in ways never intended by and perhaps inimical to the interests of the creators. On the individual level, the computer data banks pose a threat to privacy. Information innocently given in routine transactions as a requirement for receiving a job, product, or government benefit can easily be collected, compared, combined with other data, and used to embarrass or coerce the individual. Information with known limitations can be extracted from data files and either knowingly or unknowingly used to present an unwarranted image of reality.

The computer, lacking judgment or compassion, is unable to distinguish between facts and information that may be half-true or totally erroneous [Thomas, 1978: 813].

Once this misinformation enters the public consciousness, it can become the conventional wisdom, which is more difficult to correct than to implant initially.

Information created for legitimate official purposes often emerges as a resource used by individuals pursuing their own private and personal goals. This is particularly true in the political realm, where data gathered for official tasks is used with impunity for electoral purposes, giving incumbents an unwarranted advantage over nonincumbent challengers.

The advantages of computerization both within and without the legislative branch have been speculated upon, observed, and analyzed. Despite the actual and potential limitations, the trend is clear. The clock will not be turned back and the pressure for innovation toward more extensive and creative computerized information systems will continue. Attempts will be made to avoid or correct the most likely potential flaws, while the advantages will be touted loudly. In the words of Samuel Johnson:

> Few enterprises of great labor or hazard would be undertaken if we had not the power of magnifying the advantages we expect from them.

3 ORGANIZATIONAL INNOVATION AND TECHNOLOGICAL CHANGE

THE STUDY OF technological change has drawn the attention of sociologists, anthropologists, economists, and political scientists as well as researchers from business, agriculture, and the medical profession. Their concern has been focused on the organizational and individual factors that affect the creation of innovation (invention) and the adoption of innovations by eventual users. Our concern will be solely with the adoption stage. Innovation will be defined as follows:

> The successful utilization of programs or products which are new to an organization and which are introduced as a result of decisions made within that organization [Rowe and Boise, 1974: 285].

Innovation is not simply change, but implies some intentional planning. Innovation does not necessarily imply improvement. Innovations are introduced as improvements, but inappropriate applications or faulty adoption procedures doom many to failure. An innovation does not have to be totally new, only new to the setting in which it is being applied (Knight, 1967: 478).

The study of innovation usually involves the organizational decisions making a new approach available and individual decisions to take advantage of the proposed approach. Individual adoption patterns often receive their impetus from factors widely divergent from those that drove the organization to act. "Analysis of technological innovation therefore must consider its use by professionals to achieve their goals, which may be compatible with, contrary to or independent of the goals of the larger organization" (Albrecht, 1979: 280). This chapter will focus on the theory and practice of organizational innovation, while Chapter 5 will delve into the causes of innovativeness among individuals.

While studies of technological innovations by organizations abound in many disciplines, we are still a long way from any general theory. Each discipline tends to focus on different types of organizations, facing decisions on different types of technological innovations. Each discipline also implies different research methods using different classes of independent variables. While some cross-fertilization of knowledge occurs, it is more likely to be the result of lucky happenstance rather than of a well-planned comprehensive search for knowledge. In many ways students of innovation look like the proverbial blind men touching different parts of the elephant and trying to describe reality from their own limited perspectives. After canvassing research attempts in many realms, Mohr (1969: 113) concluded that the existing empirical research

> consists of scattered projects representing different disciplines, motivated by different consideration, and employing a strikingly heterogeneous selection of independent variables.

In a rare moment of self-criticism, Warner (1974: 438) took economists to task in words that should speak to practitioners of all disciplines:

> Diffusion is a complex social phenomenon which clearly involves both economic and noneconomic factors. . . . No single discipline's variables explain the entirety. . . . Economists have shied away from consideration of noneconomic variables (as noneconomists have generally ignored the economic factors).

Psychologists focus on the individual innovators and personality characteristics supportive of change. From an organizational perspective, psychologists assert that innovative organizations will be inhabited by a large number of individuals with a high tolerance for risk taking and a low threshold of fear. Psychologists also add to our knowledge of organizational change by analyzing various techniques for changing the behavior and beliefs of those who will be asked to accommodate change (Knight, 1967: 479).

Sociologists have focused on the communications patterns and personal traits of organizational members that facilitate and thwart organizational change (Warner, 1974: 439). Sociologists also are concerned with the development of resistance to change and the impact of innovation on social structure (Knight, 1967: 480).

Economists, as might be expected, focus on the profitability of innovations as the key variable and limit most of their analysis to the business firm. Innovation is simply explained as a linear function of profitability and inversely related to costs (Knight, 1967: 479-480). In looking at the rate of diffusion, economists have tended to look at the spread of a single innovation through a large number of firms. Above and beyond considering solely financial factors, some attention has been paid to organizational factors such as the differences between small and large firms (Knight, 1967: 479).

Organizational theorists concern themselves with the factors that precipitate the search for changed procedures and the stages through which the typical proposed innovation goes before it is fully adopted. Organizational theorists with a more applied bent concern themselves with the ways in which organizations can facilitate the acceptance of innovation by the eventual users.

Political scientists have paid relatively little attention to technological innovation in general, although some specific writing has been done on the impact of computers in bureaucratic and legislative settings (see particularly the works of Chartrand, Worthley, and Baaklini; see also Downs, 1967). Only sporadic attention has been paid to the power shifts, brought about by technological innovation, that lie at the heart of the political scientist's concern (Baaklini and Heaphey, 1977: 3). Students of public administration have been more attuned to the phenomenon of introducing new technology into governmental organizations, but have focused their major attention on the contributions of such technology to organizational efficiency and the formal stages of adoption.

Not only have political scientists largely failed to use their unique insights to analyze innovation in general, they also have not assessed the pattern of technological innovations among political institutions. After observing the substantial literature in other fields on innovation, Dexter (1969: 205) concluded that "little of it bears explicitly on the adoption, adaptation and diffusion of *political* innovations."

While this book will draw widely from the approaches and applicable theories from a wide variety of disciplines, special attention will be focused on the political precursors, strategies, and consequences of technological innovation in the clearly political setting of the U.S. Congress. I will ultimately attempt to determine whether theories of innovation apply to such a unique political institution and its members, or whether such theories are institution-specific.

Organizational innovations can be studied in two different ways. A case study approach involves a microanalysis of the patterns of internal organizational change (Bigoness and Perreault, 1981: 73-74). As with all case studies, the strength of such an approach lies in the detailed understanding developed about the process being studied. The major weakness lies in the fact that idiosyncratic factors tend to dominate the explanation and generalizations beyond the particular case may be inappropriate.

The comparative approach collects identical data on a large number of organizations or individuals faced with the opportunity to innovate, and assesses the differences between the innovators and the laggards (Bigoness and Perreault, 1981: 73-74). With a careful choice of units of analysis, such an approach facilitates generalization, but the difficulties of data collection often lead to the collection of more superficial, albeit more readily available, information on each case.

This book will use a combination of methods. In studying organizational change, the House and the Senate will serve as a pair of case studies that can be compared with other organizations and with each other. In analyzing the diffusion of technology within Congress, data on individual members will serve as the basis for a comparative study assessing the causes and consequences of different levels of innovativeness and resistance.

THEORIES OF ORGANIZATIONAL CHANGE

Activating Factors:
The Motivation for Change

Survival is a fundamental imperative for all organizations (Davidson and Oleszak, 1976: 39). Little motivation exists for change when the organizational future is bright and portends the easy satisfaction of organizational and individual goals. Adaptation is the organization's primary response to changes in the environment or changes in the organization itself that threaten those goals (Hedlund, 1980: 9; Davidson and Oleszak, 1976, 1971; Zaltman et al., 1973: 63; Mueller, 1971).

The impetus for adaptation can stem from either external changes in the environment impinging upon the organization's capacity to fulfill the demands placed upon it, or internal organizational changes that affect levels of output or satisfaction of organizational members (Cooper, 1977:

153-154). External environment changes include such factors as new or different levels of external demands; changes in the organization's relative power position; technological change in other segments of the environment; changes in the availability and importance of decision-making resources such as time and information; and the growth of new and competing organizations that threaten to take over the traditional reason for the target organization's existence. Internal pressures for change include the arrival of new personnel with new backgrounds and new expectations of what the organization should be doing and how it should be doing it, and the development of either formal or informal structures and behavior patterns within the organization that threaten organizational performance (see Zaltman et al., 1973: 56; Davidson and Oleszak, 1976: 39; Hellriegel and Slocum, 1979: 556; March and Simon, 1958: 183).

Individual goals can precipitate organizational change even when the organization as a whole does not feel threatened by imminent demise or decline. Students of legislative change and reform have found that individual aspirations and policy goals lead to the proposal of procedural and structural reforms, which are then often justified publicly by admonitions of organizational needs (Welch and Peters, 1977: 7).

Despite the general pressures on organizations to adapt to changing environments and internal pressures, not all are successful. The dustbin of history overflows with the hulks of former organizations that failed to recognize their incapabilities or responded with too little or inappropriate responses too late to make any difference. Since organizational change requires the active support, or at least the tacit approval, of organizational members, they must perceive the performance gap in the organization's capacity before much will be done. The insiders' perception of the problem is much more important than the imposition of outside criteria of failure by external observers (Knight, 1967: 483). Outsiders tend to evaluate performance in absolute terms, matching actual performance with some ultimate standard of peak output. Insiders evaluate current performance relative to past levels of success, which, if not ideal, was at least satisfactory enough to maintain the organization and satisfy its members down to the present time (Cyert and March, 1963).

Above and beyond the felt need for organizational change lie some basic preconditions that must be met before the process of innovation will begin. The organization must exhibit at least a minimal consensus on organizational goals. These goals will at a minimum serve as the basis for public justification of the effort involved in change, and may be important enough to motivate the promoters of change (Laudon, 1974: 77). The innovative organization needs to acquire expertise for implementation and the economic ability to take advantage of adaptive innovations (Zaltman et al., 1973: 87).

CORRELATES OF INNOVATIVENESS

The threshold precipitating consideration of change seems to vary widely across organizations. Some organizations will not organize unless there is a crisis (Wilson, 1966: 208), while in other organizations "the momentum of a new technology seems to impel its utilization and make less likely other possible courses of action" (Bereano, 1976: 9). The majority of organizations seem to fall somewhere between the extremes of last-minute crisis management and the commitment to change for change's sake. Students of organizational innovation have found the propensity to seek out and adopt new approaches to be related to the characteristics of the organizational membership, the nature of interpersonal relationships fostered within the organization, organizational structure, and the setting.

Characteristics of Organizational Membership

Individuals inhabiting various organizations differ in terms of skills, awareness, and commitment. Organizations composed of professionals with cosmopolitan contacts with outside reference groups exhibit more innovativeness than organizations whose focus is local and whose awareness of new approaches is limited (Wilson, 1966: 206-207). For more technological innovations, organizations utilizing technically competent individuals in managerial roles reduce the potential that faulty translation from technicians to administrators will impede innovation (Bigoness and Perrealt, 1981: 75-78). In general, the more diverse an organization's inputs from the environment and the more competent its membership to see the potential applications and impact of new approaches, the more likely innovation is to occur. Diverse inputs increase under conditions of continuous influx of new people from a variety of backgrounds and when such individuals must continually justify their performance to outside evaluators (Eveland, 1977: 24).

Interpersonal Communications and Relations

Innovative suggestions rarely bear fruit when potential innovators fear the reactions of their organizational colleagues. The willingness to pursue innovations increases in organizations exhibiting trust, mutual respect, openness, the ability to confront conflict, and tolerance of the freedom to criticize superiors (Shepard, 1967: 474). Although cutthroat competition often leads to the conservative strategy of not taking any chances, an atmosphere of benevolent competition, in which creative thinkers are rewarded, provides an added motivation for taking the lead to innovate above and beyond the intended results of the innovation (Rowe and Boise, 1974: 287).

Innovation requires extensive communication from outside and within the organization. Individuals doing similar jobs need to share their frustrations and requirements for change. Particularly in the area of technological innovation, superiors need to feel secure enough in their positions to be able to learn from technical experts whose status in the organizational structure is not commensurate with their own. Technical experts and the actual users of the innovations they design must communicate to assure that the final product fulfills the needs of the user, and not just the image of the technical purist.

Organizational and Task Structure

While most theorists of innovation posit the importance of organizational structure as a factor determining the innovativeness of organizations, the findings tend to be complex, confusing, and often paradoxical. Perhaps the clearest finding is that decentralization and a nonhierarchical organizational structure facilitate innovation in those cases where cooperation and coordination are not a key element in the desired innovation. Decentralization develops competition among organizational units, which then seek out innovations to give them a competitive advantage. Such systems facilitate numerous settings for entrepreneurships and allow initial innovations to be tailored to the specific interests of the more homogeneous needs of a particular subarea. Organizational leaders may encourage decentralization as a method of lowering the cost and potential risk of innovations. Failures are limited to a narrower realm, and other units can learn from the mistakes of the initial risk takers (Ingram and Ullery, 1980: 672; Zaltman et al., 1973: 88; Danziger, 1976: 19).

Wilson (1966: 200) argues that organizational diversity in the form of a complex task structure involving numerous organizational activities, a complex incentive system, decentralized units, and a membership with many extra organizational affiliations and associations leads to increased innovation proposals and initiatives, but decreases the likelihood of final adoption. The diversity increases the communication with outside sources of information and increases the likelihood that a proponent can find an ally for almost any proposal within the organization. Since most innovation proposals are at least partly accepted or rejected on political grounds, the emergence of a proposal with a differential impact on different parts of the organization will spawn new counterproposals and thus feed the pool of potential options for change (Wilson, 1966: 201). Despite the more than adequate supply of innovation proposals in a diverse organization, that same diversity tends to thwart adoption. Organizational members are less familiar with the jobs and needs of people in other parts of the organization and have little feel or empathy for the changes they propose. Diverse incentives mean that leaders do not control everyone in the organization and it becomes harder to force change. In a diverse organization differing perspectives, needs, and perceptions of impact make the bargaining to achieve consensus much more costly (Wilson, 1966: 203). The greater the degree to which all components of a diverse organization have some say in the final decision process on innovation, the greater the difficulty in coming to a decision.

The only situation in which a decentralized organization increases innovation is in those cases where subunits can independently adopt an innovation. Compared with a diverse and fragmented organization, a homogeneous subunit can move rather quickly, since the number that must be accommodated is small.

Analyzing the adoption of urban information systems, Laudon (1974: 70) added some proof to the diversity assumptions when he found that innovation was more likely in homogeneous organizations in which everyone was cognizant of others' needs and in which there was considerable agreement on existing problems and desirable solutions. He also found that where organizational units exhibited extensive interdependence there developed more communication, informal norms of cooperation, and a willingness to embark on collective ventures.

Work patterns also seem to have some impact on innovativeness. In business, Shepard (1967: 474) found that organizations with some periodicity involving "on" time and "off" time innovate more. Organizations whose members are constantly running pell-mell to meet the next deadline will tend to "put out brush fires," rather than solve problems. The organization that can step back from the fray once in a while to evaluate current performance, look around for options, and plan ahead is much more likely to get involved in innovative adaptation.

Organizational Setting

Analysts attempting to trace the spread of a particular innovation across a set of organizations have tended to search for aspects of the organizational setting to explain different levels of adoption. The rationale for using environmental variables stems either from the argument that settings vary in their receptivity to innovations by organizations within them, or the argument that environmental variables are indirect measures of need for change.

Studies of electronic data processing (EDP) innovations among local governments have shown that propensity to innovate is related to socio-economic status differences (Danziger, 1976: 11). Whether this is due to an ethos theory implying that individuals with higher socioeconomic status are more favorable toward computers, a theory based on slack resources, or some other explanation has not been determined. A similar ethos theory arguing that jurisdictions with "reformed" political structures would similarly support the more rational computerized approach to information storage and gathering has not been borne out (Dutton and Kraemer, 1976: 19).

The assumption that political units most in need of EDP would be more innovative was tested by using population size and growth rate as a surrogate measure of need (Danziger, 1976: 13). Although need so defined was related to innovation, such an external measure of need may not fully capture actual need, particularly as perceived by individuals internal to the organization.

While environmental hostility to innovation may be a factor in retarding innovation, acceptable measures of environmental attitudes are difficult to discover. Similarly, assessments of organizational need have limited utility unless they to some degree tap the need as perceived by those who will be making the decision whether or not to innovate.

Stages in the Innovation Process

Innovation is not a single action, but a series of steps, which, if successful, lead to a change in traditional operating procedures. Most students of innovation either implicitly or explicitly assume a set of stages that can be applied to most innovations (see Table 3.1). Table 3.1 is drawn from many sources, most of which showed considerable overlap in the

TABLE 3.1   Stages in the Adoption of Innovations

Problem
    Recognition of discontent with the status quo
    Problem definition

Assessment of Options
    Searching for alternatives
    Proposal of an alternative

Adoption
    Emergence of change agents
    Development of resistance
    Development of critical mass of needed support
    Definition of resistance
    Implementation of change strategy (offering inducements for support, compromis-
        ing proposal to thwart resistance, persuading opponents with information, or
        the like)
    Adoption (agreement on the general concept and plan for change)

Implementation
    Assignment of responsibility for implementation
    Gathering of necessary resources
    Establishment of an organizational structure
    Acquisition of necessary physical resources
    Staffing through outside hiring and/or internal retraining
    Restricted trial through pilot projects
    Adjustment of original plan based on evaluation of pilot projects
    Full implementation of innovation availability
    Diffusion to all units in the organization

Evaluation
    Evaluation of impact
    Changes in organizational governance to account for new procedures
    Recognition of existing problems that may potentially lead to further innovation

SOURCES: Adapted from Hedlund (1980: 10); Eveland et al. (1977: 10); Rowe and
           Boise (1974: 286); Yin (1981: 21-22); Becker and Whisler (1967: 466);
           Chartrand and Staenberg (1978: 14); and Mueller (1971: 51).

stages they expected. No one should be misled into believing that this or
any other listing applies in exact detail to all innovations or organizations.
In a particular case the ordering may vary, stages may be skipped or added,
and the process may be thwarted at any stage (Yin et al., 1977: 7-8).
Although such a list implies more rationality and planning than is the case
for many innovations, it does serve the purpose of alerting potential
researchers to developments of which they should be aware.

CHANGE AGENTS:
THE CLARIONS OF INNOVATION

Focusing on organizational change should not mislead us into taking an anthropomorphic view that somehow organizational entities act on their own. Organizations are made up of individuals who serve as the active components and the potential driving force for change. Most studies of innovation point out the important role of "change agents," "champions," "sponsors," or "entrepreneurs." These persistent proponents of a particular innovation bring information to the organization reflecting the need for change and pointing out the applicability of a specific course of action (Maidique, 1980: 60).

Although change agents can be external to the organization, internal change agents have much greater success, particularly in independent organizations (Laudon, 1974: 80). Outside forces can urge reform, but the actual change must originate within the organization (Rieselbach, 1978: 2). Internal change agents are more likely to have detailed knowledge of the problem to be solved and the respect of their colleagues, whose formal or informal support must precede adoption. While change agents might have to rely on outside experts for technical advice, they cannot delegate the initiation of change to those experts. Technicians tend to sell what they have available, rather than what is needed. "Supply-push" innovation attempts lead to proposing inappropriate solutions to possibly ill-defined and ill-recognized problems (Chartrand and Morentz, 1979: 152). In the computer realm, one congressional staff member commented, "Computer jocks design beautiful systems which don't fit our needs. One needs to know an institution and its needs before designing solutions. Legislative expertise is more important than computer skills." Aside from improving the quality of the proposed solution, an internal "demand-pull" process is more likely to involve influential and trusted individuals who have the power to bring about change (Worthley, 1977a: 424; Knight, 1967: 490).

While many types of individuals take on the role of change agent at particular times, certain types of individuals tend to predominate. Relatively new organizational entrants are more likely to have had recent outside experiences with which they can compare current performance of their new organizational affiliation. Newer and younger members also lack the commitment to standard operating procedures and do not reveal the staleness associated with acceptance of the status quo.

Individuals with professional career commitments are more likely to have the motivation to improve their organizations and are more likely to have links with an outside network of ideas (Yin et al., 1977: 78). Individuals whose organizational tasks involve limited programming have the freedom and time resources to commit some of their effort to the advocacy of innovation (Sapolsky, 1967: 498). While chance encounters with new approaches may convert an advocate of the status quo into a true believer in innovation (March and Simon, 1958: 183), certain personality types seek out broadening experiences and show particular receptivity to change in the abstract. While these personality characteristics are difficult to catalog and measure, they include such things as high tolerance of risk, an inquiring mind, and an optimistic outlook that for every problem there is a solution that hard work and human creativity will eventually discover.

The factors that motivate change agents run the gamut of potential incentives. Publicly, innovations are justified on the basis of "transcendent rhetoric." Values such as efficiency, fairness, and productivity, which transcend partisan and personal values, are used to justify the proposed change, while narrower goals initially serve as the factors that activate most change agents. Innovations often allow the individual to gain personal power, facilitate desired decisions, or simply make life easier or more pleasant. After studying the whole realm of legislative reform, Rieselbach (1978: 3) concluded that legislators promote reforms to enhance and protect their present positions; the changes they introduce reflect their short-run interests.

If the motivations of internal change agents are at best a mix of public welfare and private goals, the pattern is even stronger for external proponents of change. Few individuals take the time to pursue change on the basis of theoretical niceties. Proponents of technological change generally have either an economic or psychic interest in having their technology adopted. The clear lesson is that although change agents perform an important informational and activating function, other members of the organization must be wary of reformers bearing gifts.

RESISTANCE TO INNOVATION

While "kainotophobia" (the general fear of change) gives a label to the well-known phenomenon that "human nature appears to prefer struggle with a familiar problem rather than the use of an unfamiliar solution to the problem" (Johnson, 1976: 86), understanding resistance to innovation requires a more specific inquiry into the individual and organizational factors stifling potential innovation.

Individual Resistance

Individuals who make decisions about innovation must be seen in terms of their needs and their interpretation of the organizational purpose and history (Laudon, 1974: 30). These needs and perceptions vary, both across organizations and among individuals within a particular organization.

A basic human need is to feel comfortable within the organizations with which one must interact. A fear of the unfamiliar can thwart change, particularly when the proposed change involves the introduction of new technology. In the long run, the human capacity to adapt relatively quickly to change distinguishes us from other components of creation; but in the short run, before we exchange one set of fears for familiarity, the residual fears can lead to immobility. In Kanter's (1967: 100) homey example:

> Great grandfather drove a horse but feared the automobile; Grandfather drove an automobile but feared airplanes; Father flew piston planes but feared jets; now all of us ride jets, but many of us are scared to death of horses.

Much of the resistance to technological innovation stems from more specific practical fears. Individuals see the introduction of new technology as threatening the security and desirability of their lives and jobs. The initial fear of office automation in the private sector was for job security (Laudon, 1974: 27). Individuals either felt that their jobs would be dispensed with or that they would not be able to live up to the new demands.

The adoption of an advanced technology may depend on the familiarity of potential users with more basic technology. The keyboard of a computer terminal did not intimidate most office workers or even executives in the American system since they could transfer their skill from the typewriter keyboard to the terminal with little difficulty. The adoption of computer terminals in the British setting suffered from the fact that typing was seldom taught in British schools and was not expected for most jobs (Franklin, 1976: 66).

Even if a job itself is relatively secure, technology may affect its quality. Parole officers required to work with a computerized administrative system saw it as a way to monitor and evaluate their performance (Albrecht, 1979: 271). Such monitoring was felt to threaten their professional autonomy, judgment, and skills. Individuals whose sense of self-worth stems from their unique contribution to their job often find the introduction of technology to do even a part of that job a tremendous blow to their egos.

"Any change is likely to run counter to certain vested interests and territorial rights" (Shepard, 1967: 470). Technological innovation tends to throw incumbent power holders onto completely foreign ground (Zaltman et al., 1973: 86). Power and status based on familiarity with traditional procedures, or on access to the results of those procedures, are clearly threatened. Protecting one's turf becomes a never-ending game. In organizations, "turf" is a zone of control from which individuals derive their power, status, and reason for existence. Individuals and organizations alike seek to protect their turf from outside encroachment and look for ways to expand its scope. The motivations are not so much collective as stemming from the primal personal goals of protecting, if not enhancing, one's power and therefore one's security. The "territorial imperative" drives many decisions that on the surface seem unreasonable and poorly conceived. In assessing the sources and resistance to technological innovation, one should first look at who personally will gain and who will lose from the change.

Although power losers oppose specific innovations and gainers support them, determining the likelihood of change is not simply a matter of counting up the winners and losers. A number of mediating factors intercede. Not all of those affected will realize their stake in the decision. Not all of those affected begin with equal power resources and the skill to use them. The decision to innovate will be played out according to the rules of the old state of affairs, not in anticipation of a new power game. Some losers will rise above their parochial interests and opt for the broader advantages, while some potential gainers will look at the material, personal, and organizational costs, and eschew their potential gain. As in most human situations, the active minority will have an influence well beyond their numbers (Downs, 1967: 209). And, while the actions and reactions of individuals play a large role in determining whether resistance will successfully thwart innovation, organizational factors also play a role.

Organizational Resistance

The very concept of "organization" is inimical to innovation. Organizations exist to bring about reliability through established procedures

(Shepard, 1967: 470). By its very nature, innovation threatens to upset the established patterns. It takes particular effort for an organization to provide fertile ground for change.

Most innovations involve costs and run counter to the "sunk çosts" already invested in current procedures. Above and beyond the need to acquire the material aspects of the technology, costs accrue in the form of new personnel and retraining of the old. In a more ephemeral but no less important sense, organizations as well as individuals attempt to protect their reputations by not admitting that past decisions were inferior. A major sunk cost in current operating procedures is the trail of decisions for which current organizational members still feel responsible.

Even if the organization might be receptive to innovation, it may never become aware of potential options. Organizations and their memberships exhibit "selective attention" in relating to the information in their environment (Hedlund, 1980: 29) and may not receive potentially useful information on many topics. Even if the basic information is available, technological innovation is likely to be expressed in terms of jargon that is foreign to the potential target. Such a "coding scheme barrier" may mean that the technological proponents talk past, rather than to, those who must decide to innovate (Zaltman et al., 1973: 86).

In organizations where decision-making power is divided among many individuals or subgroups, comprehensive innovations often fall prey to decimation by a series of "concurrant minorities" (Davidson and Oleszak, 1976: 48). While each decision-making unit may approve of the general plan and have no trouble with most components, intense opposition by subgroups to the segments that affect them may lead them to oppose it completely. Also, individual organizations are not independent of other organizations. Interorganizational agreements, such as labor contracts with unions, may make it impossible to adopt seemingly beneficial innovations (Hellriegel and Slocum, 1979: 552).

Strategies

The first line of defense against undesired technological innovation lies in thwarting or delaying initial adoption. If this does not work, individuals forced to use a new innovation against their will can attempt subtle sabotage that might lead to inadequate performance and eventual removal. Office workers forced to work with new EDP applications have been known to overburden the system or point out the inaccuracies emerging. Probation officers chafing under the adoption of a new computer system advocated by the judiciary mounted a counterattack, suggesting that similar advantages could be reaped by adopting such a system in the judicial branch itself. Faced with the prospect of gathering data on case loads, variations in recidivism for each judge, and the like led to the judges joining the probation officers' major argument that quantified data does not tell the whole story of work performance (Albrecht, 1979: 274).

Most often the adoption of a new system involves such a long-term commitment that early reversal is unlikely. In innovations dealing with information, the common strategy follows the dictum, "If you can't lick'em, join'em." Individuals formerly opposed to the adoption see the handwriting on the wall and begin to plot ways in which they can control the system. Putting oneself in line for determining data entry and access policies may ameliorate the anticipated power loss associated with the original innovation.

Innovators should anticipate the emergence of resistance on even the most innocuous proposals for change. If resistance does not appear, the innovators might reconsider their proposal, for the lack of resistance probably implies that the innovation makes little difference.

PLANNED CHANGE

Kurt Lewin saw change not as an event, but as a dynamic balance of forces working in opposite directions. The status quo is an equilibrium between resistance to change and the pressure for it. The potential innovator must "unfreeze" the equilibrium by increasing the pressures for change, reducing resistance, or changing the direction of resistance into support (Hellriegel and Slocum, 1979: 555-556). Innovation is seldom natural or unaided. Careful planning at all stages of the innovation process determines whether and how the entire scenario will be played out.

Proposing Acceptable Innovations

If proponents of innovation do not have an acceptable product to sell, there is little likelihood of adoption. The size of a proposed innovation is important. It cannot be so small and insignificant that no one is willing to see the effort through. On the other hand, extreme change spawns both specific opposition and a more general fear of the potentially massive impact. Committee reform in the House (the Bolling Plan) was rejected partially because it was "too drastic, [and] it went too far too quick" (Davidson, 1979: 31).

The quality of innovations generally increases when the eventual users are involved at the planning stage. Particularly in the area of information technology, technical designers lose touch with the needs of the users and provide a system that fails to reach its potential (Amara, 1974: 82; U.S. Congress, Senate, Committee on Rules and Administration, 1977a: 27). The involvement of eventual users not only increases the likelihood of a match between what is delivered and what was wanted, but also sets up the possibility that potential opponents will be coopted into supporting a system they helped design.

Particularly, but not exclusively, in the political system, the likelihood of adopting an innovation increases when the proponents clearly take into account the political costs and payoffs. While decision makers often do not like to be reminded publicly of their narrower political motivations, ignoring such factors when developing a coalition for change and anticipating resistance will not make such factors go away. Even the users "will not accept or effectively use such help unless it is offered to them in a way that takes their own interests into account" (Downs, 1967: 210). Downs (1967: 210) applies this directly to the implementation of modern information systems:

> The ways in which public (and private) officials use automated data systems will be determined just as much by their perceptions of the resulting shifts in personal power as by their desire to reap technical benefits for the public interest.

Promoting Reform

Adoption of an innovation just does not happen. Initial resistance must overcome through active promotion. Successful proponents "grease the skids" for adoption through both formal and informal channels of communication (Maidique, 1980: 60). Promoters of EDP in local government have employed the traditionally successful strategy of focusing on the success of a single comparable system, not mentioning failures, and avoiding discussions of real human and financial costs. In order to maintain long-term credibility and not threaten future innovation initiatives, internal change agents must also avoid overselling their proposals and thereby setting up the possibility of frustration.

Experience with diffusion of innovations in developing countries applies in a wide variety of settings. Training and informational seminars provide relatively low payoff. Demonstration projects with active involvement by others whom the innovation target respects carry a great deal more weight (U.S. Congress, House, Select Committee on Committees, 1973b: 312).

Timing

Innovation looms more likely during periods of perceived crisis. Proposals emerging concurrently with external or internal threats to the organization fall on much more fertile ground than proposals entering an organization when both organizational and individual goals are being met satisfactorily and the future shows little sign of disruptive change (Shepard, 1967: 473). Crises can be defined in terms of substandard performance relative to some absolute standard or anticipated by observing developing trend lines. Innovation prospers when timed for consideration when the present conditions are grim and/or the future promises decline rather than improvement.

Innovation can also be facilitated by timing the introduction to coincide with the arrival of a significant number of new organizational members (Davidson, 1979: 31). New organizational participants have less awareness and commitment to the status quo and have less to lose by admitting past organizational mistakes or upsetting traditional power relationships. Far from opposing change, new members might welcome it as a tactic for improving their power status by putting everyone in the same position of learning new rules of the game. While it is conceivable that new organizational entrants might aspire to take advantage of the traditional procedures, it is much more likely that existing organizational members will fight more fiercely to maintain a system with which they have become comfortable.

Timing is also important in terms of phasing in innovations. While some innovations by their very nature might require systemwide application in finished form, the strategy of phasing in initial applications through pilot projects reduces costs and potential risks (Hellriegel and Slocum, 1979: 562; Meyer and Lodahl, 1980: 37). Through a pilot project, initial bugs in the innovation can be worked out without jeopardizing the entire organization. Careful choice of the pilot project site based on the enthusiasm, visibility, and status of the initial users can increase the chances of a successful application and allow the pilot setting to serve as a showcase for change. Since being singled out for special treatment can lead pilot project participants to work harder and compensate for shortcomings of the innovation, proponents must anticipate that the final full-blown application may not exhibit all the positive characteristics observed in the pilot project. Once the decision occurs to implement either a pilot project or an organizationwide innovation, it is important to get it off the ground quickly, before enthusiasm wanes or personnel changes (Meyer and Lodahl, 1980: 62). Cooperation is more likely when the participants feel that they are on the cutting edge of significant change, rather than that they are the last to try a new approach.

Timing may also be important in terms of the work cycle of the organization. In organizations that operate in terms of cycles of heavy demand and relative calm, innovations designed to lessen or even out the work schedule will find more support when a "crunch" is on. While considering an innovation adds to the workload, the immediacy of the problem can propel it along. Organizations that keep empirical performance records provide fertile ground for change since the timing and degree of need is verifiable.

Inducements

"Technological innovation is a social and in some respects a political process that occurs in organizations" (Laudon, 1974: 29). Organizations include individuals who pursue "collective benefits," which contribute to total organizational goals, and "selective benefits," which apply more narrowly to subunit or individual goals. As Olson (1965: 15) argues, selective benefits provide a significantly more potent motivation to act than do collective benefits. In organizations where the decision to innovate requires the formal or informal approval of many participants, individuals and subunits can most easily be "bought" into the approving coalition through methods that take into account their more narrow interests.

The very act of being involved in the early stages of innovation may be enough of a selective benefit for some. Wise change agents draw high-status organizational members and even potential opponents into the planning stages of innovation in the hopes of coopting them (Shepard, 1967: 472). For the change agent, bringing such people in early and giving them a stake in the final outcome can deflect resistance and may even allow the innovator to use the status of the coopted participants to influence the willingness of others to accept the innovation. For the coopted individual the payoff comes in the form of the status and potential advantage of being on the ground floor of change. Participants in the initial planning stage are also often the ones chosen to have first access to technological innovations.

In some cases supporters must be lured through the use of tangible benefits that may or may not have anything to do with the innovation per se (Davidson, 1979: 31). The nongermane benefits could involve almost anything the change agent has access to that is desired by one of the decision makers. Compromising on the innovation itself often takes the form of limiting access and/or applications so as not to disadvantage certain individuals or subunits, and at a maximum to give them special advantages. Some bargaining goes on concerning the placement of the innovation within the organizational structure. Individuals may wish to avoid control over a new technological innovation or, more likely, to have it added to their turf. Research into bureaucratic innovation reveals that administrators may support an innovation solely to get a new line item and a higher total in their budget (Yin, 1981: 27).

The discussion of bargaining over the adoption of innovations should not imply that the contributions of the innovation are irrelevant. The adoption of an innovation is much easier when previous experience in other settings or in pilot projects clearly reveals that the innovation will deliver what is promised. The outside observer, though, must be aware that the effectiveness of innovations must be proven in practitioner terms, which often involve different criteria than those employed by external evaluators (Yin, 1981: 26).

Shortcuts

While the adoption of a major innovation usually involves extensive effort and a long time period, some approaches have proven to be useful in speeding the process and assuring that the momentum for change increases and reversals are avoided. For example, getting the early approval and conspicuous support and usage by existing power holders intimidates potential opponents and makes the support of innovation less risky and more acceptable.

At times it is possible to make innovation a *fait accompli* (Shepard, 1967: 471). Secretly instituting an innovation without going through formal channels is a risky business, but can pay handsomely if the new approach proves its utility unmistakably. Such an approach is likely to result in opposition on the basis of principle alone unless the perpetrators can show that their actions did not fall into the category of being specifically denied, but were at least in the gray area between disapproval and acceptance.

Innovations are more likely to stick and not be reversed by later decisions if the old system is completely removed after the new system is in operation (Yin, 1981: 26). This is clearly evident in the adoption of modern information technology. If traditional mechanical records exist side by side with the machine-stored records, the cost of rejecting the new approach is lessened. When the new approach is the sole depository for needed information, the sunk costs of change shift from the traditional system to the innovation. Those who wish to "revert" (a good negative verb) to the old system inherit the burden of proving that the costs of the initial shift and the necessary updating of the traditional records are justified.

POTENTIAL PITFALLS
IN THE INNOVATION PROCESS

The various hurdles at each stage of the innovation process imply that the successful innovation must win many battles, while supporters of the status quo must only block the proposal at one point. Adopted innovations are not secure until they have completely proven themselves to a vast majority of the organizational members. Danger looms not only from the adoption of poorly designed systems but also from those that fail to match capabilities with necessities. Bargains struck to rush a proposal into adoption may reemerge and come unglued. Innovations may fall victim to the fact that the problems they were designed to correct were really symptoms of a larger problem not dealt with (Hellriegel and Slocum, 1979: 563). Innovations adopted with little concern for the social setting of change often wake up to the rude reality that enthusiastic and supportive users can compensate for a multitude of errors, but reluctant users who feel forced into using an innovation that works against their interests can find a multitude of ways to reduce the effectiveness of a seemingly ideal system. Unless the human component of change is anticipated, the potential problems may be ignored until it is too late.

While users of a new technology must be sold on its benefits, the dangers of overselling are just as dangerous (Kraemer and King, 1975: 2-15). Tales abound of innovations that failed to match the most optimistic promises of their ardent proponents. When the promised millenium does not arrive immediately, users feel tricked and can take it out on the innovation itself, even if it is performing up to a reasonable standard. In the Canadian Parliament a computerized text editing system was summarily removed after it failed to live up to the promises of its advocates, and in the process the general use of computer services was set back a number of years (Worthley, 1976: 139).

In general, the greatest threat to adopting innovations is the unanticipated or inadequately articulated consequences that develop. Innovations that either reduce the overall effectiveness of the organization or, more importantly, reduce the power or job satisfaction of the individuals within the organization are unlikely to continue unscathed. Their vulnerability increases if it can be shown that the original decision was faulty or misguided and therefore worthy of change.

CONTROLLING INNOVATION

No clear answer exists as to who should control a particular type of innovation and where it should be placed within the organizational structure. Both the utility and likelihood of a particular placement depend on such factors as organizational traditions, goals, and power distribution.

While a great deal has been written on the impact of innovations on the organization, some attention should be paid to the impact of the organization on the shaping of the innovation (see Laudon, 1974: 5). Innovations impinge on organizations with existing organizational and behavioral patterns within which the proposed innovation will eventually be subsumed. Organizations with a concentration of power at the top are likely to locate innovations perceived to have major impact on power at the top, while more diffuse organizations will allow more subunit control. Innovations therefore will at least initially reinforce organizational patterns rather than upset them. This is not to say that in the long run, or in cases where decision makers do not take organizational traditions into account, that structural decisions do not make a difference. On the contrary, an organization's choices as to where an innovation fits in the authority structure, were it is physically located, and who is allowed to use it will affect its acceptance and impact.

The organization has the basic choice of installing a technological innovation at the top or allowing subunits to experiment and control innovations that they develop. The pyramidal installation "provides integrated control to benefit overarching organizational goals as opposed to chauvinistic divisional objectives" (Spector et al., 1976: 9, Section 3). In a divisional installation of an innovation, one might lose the organizationwide perspective and control, but it is possible to design an application for special needs and cut the scope of potential risks should the innovation prove ineffective. Division adoption of innovations is usually easier since interests are likely to be more homogeneous and communication of benefits and procedures less burdensome

If organizational traditions and power structure do not dictate which of these sets of arguments on innovation placement prevails, the nature of the innovation will determine the placement of an innovation in the organizational structure. Innovations that require extensive cooperation and coordination lead to placement at a level within the organization that can bring to bear enough power to make them work.

CONCLUSION

As can be seen by the catalog of separate if not conflicting factors associated with the adoption of innovations by organizations, it is clear that the theory of innovation is still at the relatively primitive stage of looking for variables and assessing their individual impacts. Virtually all observers of innovation point out that the process of innovation adoption begins with linking a perceived need to an innovation championed by a change agent. The factors that make some organizations more receptive and the optimal strategies for overcoming initial resistance are less precisely defined. Underlying much of this chapter is the assumption that individuals within organizations who must make decisions on innovations are motivated by organizational as well as personal goals, and that, if anything, the personal goals predominate. While considerable evidence of this assumption exists, it is not totally verified. Despite the potential ambiguity in theory, the next chapter, which focuses on the adoption of a particular technological innovation by Congress, will emphasize personal goals over those of the organization.

4 THE ADOPTION PROCEEDINGS

Legislatures have been among the few institutions to resist the uncontrolled rush to computers [Worthley, 1977b: 17].

Technologies do not "impact" on organizations like two ships colliding at sea. Instead, technological innovations are filtered through the organization's traditions, constraints and resources [Laudon, 1974: 30].

As an organization, Congress adopted computerized information services in a slow, halting, and fragmented manner. Reminiscent of the old joke that says a camel is a horse designed by a committee, the odd-shaped information system that emerged from Congress looked little like the ideal information system a specialist would design. It is in fact incorrect to talk about "the" decision to adopt computerization, since there were a whole series of decisions made by subunits of Congress that were unaware or unconcerned about what other subunits needed or were doing. Congress was like other realms in that "EDP innovation is best conceptualized as a flow of implementation through time rather than as a single decision to adopt computers" (Danziger, 1976: 2a). The pressure for innovation built up slowly, and then began to move rapidly almost of its own accord. The key to understanding Congress's move into the computer age lies not in discovering the nature of modern information systems, but rather in delving into the nature of Congress as an organization.

ORGANIZATIONAL SETTING

Viewing Congress as an Organization

Until recently, organization theorists have paid little attention to Congress, and congressional scholars have ignored much of the work of the organization theorists (for an exception, see Cooper, 1975, 1977). The mutual ignorance has not served either group well.

Congress exhibits many of the characteristics of business and bureaucratic organizations such as size, multiplicity of functions, and the common problems of recruiting personnel, processing information, and making decisions. The organization theory literature is rich with discussion of technological innovation processes, as was seen in Chapter 3. The commonalities between Congress and other organizations encourage the attempt to apply these theories from other realms to innovation in Congress. An understanding of the differences between Congress and other organizations serves to stimulate specific hypotheses that might apply to Congress alone and helps us understand those areas where more traditional organization theories do not seem to apply to the Congress.

Uniqueness of Congress as an Organization

Organizational goals and motivation

Perhaps the most important difference between a governmental unit such as Congress and most organizations in the private sector has to do with the factor of profit. Private enterprises operate under the pressure of profit and have a concrete measure of their success or failure in their balance sheets. In one congressional staff member's words:

> While the introduction of computers in business was accompanied by some inefficiency, there was always a bottom line of profit or loss. No one in Congress thinks in terms of costs.

Much of the research on technological innovation focuses on industrial firms, which must accept new technology or lose their economic viability (Laudon, 1974: 29). Gaining acceptance for innovation in government is more difficult. Governmental units do not directly compete with each other for profits in the normal sense. In government, nothing is owned and no proceeds are retained. No one has any claim on the increase in value a technological innovation might bring. Governmental units deal with public goods, which are difficult to measure and hard to motivate people with (Roessner, 1975: 345-346). Most individuals are primarily motivated by those private goods that give them a selective advantage or benefit.

Private organizations compare themselves with their competitors in the marketplace and expend a great deal of effort in borrowing, copying, or adapting approaches proven beneficial for others (Laudon, 1974: 29). Congress sees itself as a unique organization that can gain little by comparing itself with "inferior" or at least different state and foreign legislatures. In fact, the image of uniqueness goes even further: Members of the House and Senate see little similarity between their needs.

Profit-seeking organizations see efficiency as the route to more profit, and technological innovation is sold on the basis of its contribution to efficiency. Government organizations do not necessarily see efficiency as a primary goal. In fact, slowness and inefficiency serve as a strategy for governmental decision makers opposed to particular courses of public policy. Although he was speaking about state and local governments, Feller's words apply with equal force to Congress. He suggested that governments are

> superbly equipped to do tomorrow what they did yesterday. But that governments are not designed to be highly efficient, responsive, flexible or innovative. . . . New programs and ideas move slowly and fitfully in a climate that is essentially hostile to them [Feller and Menzel, 1978: 470].

Starting from different perspectives, organization theorists, economists, political scientists, and other students of innovation have come to the conclusion that "public organizations are less efficient, and probably less innovative, than private organizations" (Roessner, 1975: 350). Since it is a governmental organization, we should perhaps be surprised that Congress innovated at all, rather than critical that the national legislature lagged behind state legislatures and considerably behind the business world in adopting computerized information services.

Organizational membership

The nature of the individuals who inhabit the halls of Congress affects the speed and nature of technological innovation. A central dilemma of those who wish to improve Congress through the adoption of innovations is that the careers of individual legislators are separated from the collective product of the institution. "Performance is collective, but accountability is individual" (Davidson and Oleszak, 1977: xiii). Individuals often run for Congress by running against Congress. Members are accountable to external groups of constituents and special interests and find it easier to use the congressional organization as a scapegoat, rather than improving its organizational capability. The rewards for the organizational innovator are minimal.

The high rate of personnel turnover and the ever-present insecurity brought on by approaching elections lead to legislators with rather short time perspectives and limited willingness to embark on long-term projects with deferred benefits. Those innovations most likely to gain acceptance in the congressional setting involve low risk and quick payoff (Roessner, 1975: 349). In the public sector, officials will often eschew probable large improvements for assured limited risks, since bad performance is generally penalized rather than good performance rewarded (Feller and Menzel, 1978: 470).

The individual propensity to pay little attention to organizational innovation is reinforced by the seniority and personnel system of Congress. The seniority system rewards those who "keep their fences mended" externally and "keep their noses clean" internally. Members move up the leadership ladder largely on the basis of the ascriptive character of their entrance date rather than on the basis of their organizational achievement. Organizations that promote from within lose the potential innovation stimuli of hard chargers entering laterally and bringing with them new ideas (Feller and Menzel, 1978: 471). The more senior members inherit the positions of power; they are the most committed to the status quo since it was the system that secured their position. The proposed benefits of technological innovation must guarantee increased power and/or status with little potential for risk before senior members will threaten their current positions.

If the motivations and receptiveness to innovation are dulled among the membership of Congress, a similar influence exudes from the staffs. By and large, congressional staffs are not recruited openly with selection based on achievement characteristics. Individual members of Congress control personnel fiefdoms and put "their people" in key staff jobs. The more senior members, with less motivation to upset the status quo, control most of the staff positions. For a staff member, the key to job security and longevity is to reflect the interests and wishes of his or her sponsor. It is not at all uncommon for congressional insiders to refer to a staff member as "so and so's man." The staffs therefore do not serve as a continuing force for dramatic change.

Power structure

The power structure of Congress is nonhierarchical and fragmented. While fragmentation of power mitigates against overall decisions on innovation, it is easier to get the "critical mass" of support on the committee or subunit level. The competition among individuals, committees, and other subunits for control over such a crucial element as information and the autonomy of congressional subunits should set the stage for limited innovation applications placed under the control of the initiating subunit.

The potential for adopting an integrated congressional information system is much more limited. In Janda's most positive scenario, the transition from manual to automated methods must inevitably be gradual. The pace may even seem frustratingly slow to the technically competent, who see clearly what should be done next. But Congress constitutes a system with integrated parts as much as an information processing system that the information specialists would impress upon them (U.S. Congress, House, Select Committee on Committees, 1973a: 276).

Congressional decision-making and the role of information

The discussion in Chapter 1 pointed out the crucial role information plays in Congress. This fact alone influences the potential for the introduction of modern information technology. Previous studies of such innovations have dealt with organizations that used information for some other purpose. For government, information is both the output and the "core technology." Introduction of a totally new method of processing information is analogous to the introduction of mass production in industry (Laudon, 1974: 4). We are not dealing with some marginal change to increase efficiency or output, but with a change that has the potential for totally changing work styles, establishing new power relationships, and revising the policy choices of Congress.

In order to be acceptable, the information technology adopted must provide the desired kinds of information to the right people, in a format that is understandable and usable. Providing the desired information will require expanding computerized information to help provide politically relevant information. Determining the right people to receive the information will lead to extensive battles over access in a setting where the participants rightfully view access to information as a power resource. Providing useful information in an understandable format will require developing information systems that take into account the unrelenting work pace of members of Congress, the never-ending deadlines, and the fact that Congress is made up of a group of individuals oriented toward action and verbal media more than reflection and in-depth personal research (Worthley, 1976: 165).

Congress is not an easy organization to provide with information. The participants have conflicting goals and use information as a power resource. Since Congress is a collegial decision-making body with numerous decision stages, the variety in desired information formats increases the task. The collegial nature of decision-making on substantive issues also means that the decision to innovate will be made collectively. Previous research has shown that diverse organizations such as Congress are good breeding grounds for innovative ideas, but that such organizations have more difficulty setting innovations adopted than homogeneous, hierarchical organizations (Wilson, 1966). In a hierarchical organization, the leader can activate innovation down through the chain of command. In a diverse and fragmented organization such as Congress, technological innovations must be sold in such a way as to provide some benefit to a wide group of decision makers.

The congressional decision-making system is very fluid compared to that of a hierarchical organization. Hierarchies are developed to filter information and options and avoid information overload for those at the top. Congress is designed to be a much more permeable information environment. The Congressional information system developer never reaches closure. Final decisions are rare. Not only does the information change throughout the process, but so do the options to be considered. The process can be compared to an automobile manufacturer changing model styles as the cars pass through the assembly line (Thompson, 1976: 45).

DEVELOPING MOMENTUM FOR CHANGE

Congress certainly failed to step out as an innovative leader in adopting the computer to handle its information problems; on the other hand, it was not a complete laggard, looking the other way when change became possible. A number of factors came together in the late 1960s to push the Congress tentatively and hesitatingly over the threshold and into the computer age. While none of these factors alone might have been a sufficient cause for change, the combination activated some change agents and eventually unfroze the status quo.

Stimuli for Change

Growing need for information

The information needs of Congress as a whole and of individual members (outlined in Chapter 1) became particularly overbearing by the late 1960s. Larger constituencies and increased communications from constituents overburdened staffs and members alike. The complexity of problems with which Congress had to deal cried out for new and better information. The competitive advantage of the executive branch in providing information became clear, especially to the Democrats, when they had to deal with a divided government controlled by a president with policy interests divergent from that of the congressional majority. It is not so bad to have the executive branch overwhelm you with information when they are generally on your side, but it becomes particularly galling when the information advantage is on the other side. It is no mere coincidence that the Nixon years in the White House, with expanded executive powers and partisan information control and usage, saw numerous reforms in Congress (Jones, 1976: 257). The concern with White House information control did not simply start with inauguration day 1969. The last years of the Johnson administration were marked by distrust and growing restiveness on the part of the Congress.

Increasing time pressures

At the very time that a seat in Congress became a career goal, the demands to perform and the time pressures of the job were also increasing. Someone once said to Hubert Humphrey, "Senator, if you could just give me an hour," and he replied, "Hell, If I had an hour I'd take a nap, I wouldn't give it to you" (Chartrand and Morentz, 1979: 47). Members of Congress desiring to stay in office, but dissatisfied with the time pressures, were ripe for any suggestions that would cut down the workload. The increased staffing begun by the 1964 Legislative Reorganization Act was not sufficient. One Senate study during the period found that Senators were spending over 50 percent of their staff funds dealing with mail, and the figures for the House would be even higher.

The time and information pressure was exacerbated by the broadening nature of the congressional job. One staff member observed that prior to World War II, the average member of Congress "had only two interests, what was good for his district and matters before his committee." Now a member is expected to be a generalist, with a well-formed opinion on everything.

Increasing awareness and feasibility of using computers

By the late 1960s computers were well established in the business world and in some state legislatures. The computer was no longer seen as a toy and the more ominous projections of negative consequences had not occurred. Individuals were coming into Congress with computer "literacy" from business, state legislatures, and academia. In a number of cases, new members of Congress with state legislative experience with computers expressed outrage at the primitive state of information technology on the Hill (U.S. Congress, Senate, Committee on Rules and Administration, 1980: 19).

The costs of computers had also come down and emphasis was being put on increased ease of usage. Computer vendors had tapped the business application field quite deeply and were now willing to attempt to crack a tougher nut. The availability of machine-readable information as a by-product of automated photocopying systems, the development of commercial data and bibliographic packages, and the potential for adapting legislative information packages developed on the state level made computerization look like a better bargain.

Increasing influx of new members

The 1960s saw a dramatic change in the personnel of Congress. Previously typical members who were schooled in the pre-World War II form of party loyalty politics was being replaced by younger, more aggressive members who had personally fought their way into Congress and felt less indebtedness to party leaders. Such new members were unwilling to rely on the "old boy" network of information sharing and deference to the supposed expertise of senior members. If changing the information system would make their jobs more pleasant and potentially give them a more even footing in the decision-making process, they were not going to let traditions get in their way.

The stage was set for change. The latent dissatisfactions and fears echoed through the halls of Congress. All that was missing was a set of actors to solidify the definition of the problem, suggest options, and build support.

Congress in Comparative Perspective

During this period, Congress did not stand alone among national legislatures in looking toward computerization, but its unique character forced it to take the lead. Because Congress is more independent of the executive branch, has less disciplined parties to develop policy positions, and deals with more legislative proposals in a more complex manner than is the case with most other legislatures, deeper concern for improving its information capabilities arose. The U.S. Congress began computerization earlier and still surpasses other national legislatures in terms of breadth and depth of computer usage (Clayton, 1979: 8).

CHARACTER AND MOTIVATIONS OF CHANGE AGENTS

The pressure for moving Congress into the computer age emerged from both internal and external sources. While the internal change agents did not fit a single mold, they tended to be relatively senior members who were committed to the Congress, knew its limitations, and had credibility that added weight to their suggestions.

Hubert Humphrey was the first member of Congress to speak out in favor of computerizing some of Congress's information sources. In a 1964 speech before a computer convention, and in other statements in the *Congressional Record* (1964: 9075), Humphrey took the words of his science advisor, Howard Wink, and popularized the idea that Congress could use computers. Humphrey's contribution to this area was similar to that in other areas he touched. He was an idea man, with little taste for the mechanics of implementing his ideas. That task was left to others.

Over in the House, Robert McClory, deeply influenced by a staff member, introduced the first legislation calling for a congressional information system in 1966. This was to be only the first of over 40 pieces of legislation promoting computers for Congress introduced by different members between 1966 and 1975. John Brademas (D-IN), a former Rhodes scholar and emerging House leader with considerable foresight, had seen the need for a national data center and joined the fray. Wayne Hayes (D-OH), chairman of the House Administration Committee, became a believer in computerized information systems for more practical reasons.

He saw the area as a power void into which his committee could move and expand its purview to more important things than the House elevators and barber shops. Although his arrival in 1972 postdated initial moves toward the adoption of computers, Charlie Rose (D-NC), an unmitigated "gadget freak," used his position on the House Administration Committee to become "Mr. Computer" on the Hill, and still serves as the prime spokesperson for pushing computer applications to their ultimate end.

In the Senate, the change agents seem to have been affected by their previous experience and were more interested in computer applications that would allow their offices to run efficiently than in providing services to the entire Senate. Charles Percy's (R-IL) experience as president of Bell and Howell, one of the first corporations with a computerized management system, led him to use his own money to study Senate applications and apply them to his office. Senator Mark Hatfield (R-OR) came to the Senate with an executive orientation after experiences as a businessman and governor. He was used to saying, "Let's do such and such," and having it get done. According to his staff, "He was frustrated with the antiquated information-processing procedures in the Senate and wanted to try and move it into the twentieth century." The offices of these two senators served as models for their colleagues who wanted to consider computerization. On the Senate side there have been fewer champions of general computer applications. Comparing the Senate with the House, one staff member complained:

> Absent, however, has been any catalyst to motivate Senate computer users to examine the computerized resources available and either accept or reject them. Some individual should fill this catalytic role for the Senate (U.S. Congress, Senate, Commission on the Operation of the Senate, 1977b: 128).

While the members themselves began to discuss the applicability of computers to Congress, similar discussions began among the staff and staff agencies. In the Senate, young activist staff members of northern liberal Democrats, who saw the potential of the computer for shifting the power balance in the Senate, began to meet in the late 1960s to discuss computer applications. Edward Beach, director of the Senate Republican Policy Committee, familiar with computers from his days as a nuclear submarine commander, was influential in bringing the Republicans along (Glass, 1970: 1155). Robert L. Chartrand arrived at the Legislative Reference Service (now the Congressional Research Service) of the Library of Congress as a specialist in information sciences in 1966 after seven years' field experience with IBM and TRW (Schloss, 1970: 42). Chartrand immediately began writing articles, preparing testimony, holding seminars, and bending the ears of anyone who would listen about the need for computerization. The publication of his study, "Automatic Data Processing for the Congress" (Chartrand, 1967a), was the first of many overall analyses and paved the way for eventual computer adoption (Hopkins, 1972: 455). His prolific writings and his role as a coalescing force, bringing together individuals from the various subunits of the congressional system, continue today.

W. Pat Jennings, a former member of Congress and clerk of the House during the late 1960s, sought to improve Congress's performance and increase his turf by making the Clerk's Office the administrative unit for congressional information technology. He dazzled the House with a demonstration of computer capabilities, but pressed his claim for jurisdiction too far and eventually lost out in a power struggle to the House Administration Committee (Glass, 1970: 1151).

In the Library of Congress, computerization was spurred on by the library professionals more than by the researchers in the Legislative Reference Service. Contact with sophisticated computerized bibliographic capabilities convinced the librarians that the future lay in computers. In Chartrand's (1976c: 329) words:

> The Library of Congress avoided computerization as long as possible, was intimidated into exploration, suddenly realized the potential, became fascinated and wildly hopeful, received the icy shock of reality, and is now grimly trying to make it work among those day to day procedures where it seems to be genuinely appropriate.

Outside of Congress, independent researchers and consultants commissioned by Congress were joined by commercial vendors to develop a chorus of support for the applicability of a computerized information system for the Congress. In 1965, the American Enterprise Institute published *Congress: The First Branch of Government,* which included three chapters on the role of information for Congress (de Grazia, 1965). This was followed a few years later by seminars and further publications (Chartrand et al., 1968). The Brookings Institute began a series of seminars a few years later, under the direction of Robert Chartrand, which attempted to bring together individuals who might move Congress toward computer adoption. In the hope of developing wider awareness, NBC

commissioned Arthur Little and Company to do a management study of
Congress. The findings were presented on a television special and published
under the provocative title *Congress Needs Help* (Donham and Fahey,
1966). Among the conclusions was that Congress's analytical problems call
for flexible manipulation of massive data in many different arrangements
and that, at the time, "Congress takes too little advantage of modern
electronic equipment to facilitate its work." In the academic realm,
Davidson and his colleagues (1966) surveyed Congress and found that one
of the most frequently articulated problems was the lack of useful information. Saloma (1969) predicted that the new politics of Congress would
include heavy utilization of modern information technology. The computer industry, not about to be left behind, also got into the action. The
Association for Computing Machinery attempted to increase familiarity
through seminars on the Hill, while individual computer vendors talked to
individual members.

While the Congress began a dialogue about the potential for computers
in the legislative realm, many state legislatures had turned speculation into
reality. True to arguments supporting federalism, the states served as the
testing ground for new approaches and were on the average far ahead of
Congress in considering computerization (Chartrand and Staenberg, 1978;
Worthley, 1977b). While the states did not do much active promotion,
their existence as a model and the influx of state legislators with computer
experience served to spur Congress to action.

While each of these outside groups spoke only to specific audiences, the
combined impact was to increase the awareness of the information problem and the potential for computers among a major segment of the
interested population. These change agents represented many differing
views and were motivated by everything from a commitment to improving
Congress to more narrow personal power goals. In Chartrand's (1976c:
315-320) words, 1965 to 1970 constituted the "Years of Anticipation."
The change agents set the stage for eventual chamberwide decisions.

Proponents' Arguments

While the actual motivations of the change agents included personal
goals, the debate over computerization largely employed "transcendent
rhetoric" that linked the adoption of computers to values upon which
most participants agreed.

Redressing the power balance with the executive

By far the most common theme in the debates over computerization proposals involved comparisons with the executive branch and its information-handling capacity. While some of the proponents simply compared the number of computers in the executive branch agencies with the lack of such resources in Congress, more thoughtful analyses discussed the actual impact of such an imbalance. No one said it better than Robert McClory (R-IL) during his initial call for computerization in 1966:

> The balance in the relationship between the executive branch and Congress has been in jeopardy because of the demands upon the energies and time of legislators. . . . We must use every mechanism to insure that Congress executes its traditional responsibilities. . . . We must move to harness the technological forces that can provide us the wherewithal to function more effectively as public servants [Congressional Record, 1966: 27824].

While McClory was at least partially concerned with the ability of the computer to relieve legislators of the demands that reduce their effectiveness, John Brademas (D-IN) borrowed from Lord Acton to strike at the heart of the power stakes when he argued that "lack of information tends to weaken Congress, and absolute lack of information will weaken Congress absolutely" (Brademas, 1972: 152). In the Brookings seminars one of the congressmen expanded on this theme:

> Computerization of legislative data is an absolute necessity if any legislative body is to continue to make a meaningful contribution to the governmental process in today's complex world. Without the technological advantage of automated research, our prime purpose as a law-making body could very well come to a standstill [Congressional Record, 1970: 28893].

The congressional feeling of information insecurity compared to the executive branch received early support from Joseph Califano, a former participant in White House decision-making. He argued that "Congress has ignored the revolution in analytical technology," with the consequence that Congress had "second-class citizenship" among the three branches of government (Califano, 1971: A18). Congressman Charlie Rose (D-NC) broadened the feeling of information inferiority when he argued, "When others such as interest groups and the executive branch have computers and I don't, they have power over me and own me."

By 1971, it was particularly clear in the budget realm that Congress could not compete without computers. The Office of Management and Budget could not prepare the president's budget without a computer, and Congress was beholden to the office for data. Proponents saw the computer as a way to redress the balance of power with the executive branch, which had been yielded in the budget area after passage of the 1921 Budget and Accounting Act (Glass, 1970).

Improving the decision-making process

Proponents of computerization emphasized that modern information technology would improve the quality and speed of congressional decisions. In his early clarion call for computerization, Hubert Humphrey sounded a theme that eventually became the conventional wisdom:

> The legislative branch should itself take the lead [in computerization]. Few groups of men and women need more, better or more varied information. . . . [They need] pushbutton, preferably display-type access to specialized banks of information. . . . When Congress has better access to the answers it needs, it will be in a position to ask still better—more useful—questions [Congressional Record, 1964: 9075].

Computerization came to be associated with better information, and better information was seen as leading to better decisions. Robert McClory, in his original call for computers in the House, echoed this theme by arguing that Congress needed computers because "decisions are ideally made on the basis of that information which is timely, accurate, complete and relevant," and the computer would help assure such information (Congressional Record, 1966). A bit later in the adoption process, Representative Charlie Rose intoned that computers are needed because they "make Congress smarter and faster"(Reilly, 1979: 78).

Computers for Congress were touted not only as the source of more and better information, but also as a faster and more efficient source. Jack Brooks (D-TX), one of the early proponents, attested that "in a world where circumstances change with breathtaking suddenness . . . we [Congress] must have a budget and appropriations system capable of immediate reaction," and the computer was looked to for the solution (Congressional

Record, 1969). Senator Hugh Scott (R-PA), justifying broader computer applications, compared the Congress with other parts of government and proposed that "no single technological advance in recent years has contributed more to the efficiency and effectiveness of government operations than the development of EDP equipment" (Congressional Record, 1966: 27824).

Improved representation of citizens and therefore better decisions also were included as part of the litany to computer contributions. Alfred de Grazia, in testimony before Congress, used a body analogy to argue that Congress's intelligence system linking members to their constituencies was

> like the network of nerves in the body that transmit information to the brain. Without a continuous, reliable stream of communications of correct signals as to what is happening in the remotest part of the organism, the human organism will become aimless, flabby, non-responsive and finally collapse [U.S. Congress, House, Select Committee on Committees, 1974: 52].

Chartrand, considered "the" expert on information technology, was no less eloquent or hopeful:

> The state legislatures, along with the Congress, may correctly hold great expectations in regard to the future contribution of information technology. The resources required, together with the necessary empowering legislative authorization, can result in an unprecedented responsiveness by the legislatures to the needs of the citizenry and a surer dilineation of policies ensuring future stability and prosperity [Chartrand and Staenberg, 1978: 32].

Representative Charlie Rose predicted that computerization would not only "establish a new sense of communication with those we represent," but pave the way for a system of government that is more than participatory, by moving it to a new level of being anticipatory of the needs and desires of the citizens (Chartrand and Morentz, 1979: 108).

Cost savings

Not only were computers hailed as redressing the power balance between Congress and the executive branch and improving the quality of decisions, but all this was promised as part of a package for cutting costs. Jack Brooks (D-TX), who took the lead in promoting computer utilization throughout the government, attempted to speed up the process in Congress and allay some fears by asserting that

> we must take advantage of these new techniques [computers] as soon as possible rather than wait until circumstances force them upon us. Tens of billions in public funds can be saved and a significantly higher efficiency in government operations can be achieved if we move forward now [Schloss, 1970: 43].

The push for a computerized electronic voting system defined cost in human terms. Manual roll call voting took up one-fifth of the House's time in session during 1965, which amounted to over 90 hours for the members who stayed on the floor for all votes (Congressional Record, 1972: 36006-36011). However, the large price tag on computers served as a particular impediment in Congress since the supposed advantages of better decisions and cost savings would take a considerable time to realize, while the costs would have to be justified to the public before the results were in (Schlappe, 1974: 13).

Improved public image

The adoption of computers also became part of Congress's attempt to spruce up its public image. Both the general move toward computerization and specific applications were seen as proving to the world that Congress was an efficient and modern institution. Frank Thompson (D-NJ), a senior member of the House Administration Committee, termed it an "embarrassment" that the House was "so far behind in modernizing itself with computers" (Congressional Quarterly Weekly Report, 1971: 2382).

The proposal to install a computerized electronic voting system in the House was touted as not only saving a considerable amount of time for members, but also "signaling the American people that we [Congress] are determined to modernize (Congressional Record, 1972: 36011). For the citizens who came to visit Congress, electronic voting was promoted as reducing the monotony and confusion surrounding votes and quorum calls, therefore making visits to the chamber more interesting and enjoyable.

True to the pattern of innovation rhetoric in other realms, the public rationale for computerization in Congress was heavily infused with linkages to transcendent values such as efficiency, cost-effectiveness, better public policy, and the reclamation of the proper balance of power between Congress and the executive. These values are "transcendent" in the sense that in the abstract everyone agrees with their pursuit. Beyond being transcendent, the values pursued publicly were "collective" in the sense that should they be reached everyone would gain relatively equally.

In less public discussion, emphasis was given by the proponents to the "selective benefits" of computers that might apply to individuals and provide them with different levels of benefits. The steady stream of transcendent rhetoric had an undercurrent of narrower personal desires to adopt computers that were separate from, if not in conflict with, the more widely touted goals. These selective benefits of computerization served as more potent activators for computerization and also set into motion resistance from those who saw computerization as a selective "detriment."

The range of selective benefits that could accompany computerization runs the gamut of personal desires. For the average member of Congress, the computer promised to increase the efficiency of office operations and get the mail out more quickly and with more options. While the proponent using transcendent rhetoric might justify this in terms of increasing the representativeness of Congress or freeing the members' time to give more in-depth consideration to legislation, the individual member may well have seen it in terms of his or her selective goal of reelection. Although the management of constituent communications is one of the most relevant applications for computers, it tended to get bypassed in the adoption debate. In Chartrand's early treatise on the role of computers in the legislative process, only one short paragraph in a three-page insert dealt with this aspect (Congressional Record, 1967a: 1801).

The selective benefits of increasing one's power and gaining one's objectives are seen as too unseemly and selfish to broadcast widely, but that does not mean that they are any less important. In Grumm's (1979: 3) words:

> Often the purpose behind many intentionally initiated changes is simply the redistribution of personal power of individual members, or the achievement of some particular policy objective.

A modern information system for Congress looked much better to junior members who lacked adequate information. The desire for an efficient Congress assumed that one's policy preferences would be promoted by action rather than inaction. A resurgence of power by Congress through improved information only looks desirable if one wants to challenge the executive branch and not facilitate its desires. At times the personal power motives can be quite narrow. Wayne Hayes (D-OH), as chairman of the House Administration Committee, spoke eloquently in favor of electronic voting using virtually every transcendent value possible to support his case, but it is probably a better bet that his prime motivation came from the fact that the introduction of such a system selectively endowed him with more than 40 additional employees to supervise and put him in control of what was then the House's only computer (Ornstein, 1975: 204).

Before we go too far in assuming that computerization came to Congress either because of a need to reach some transcendent values or because of petty avarice, it is important to realize that at times the reasons for employing technology are quite simple. The prime reason the Senate adopted a computerized mailing system was not to improve the representative performance of democratic government or to satisfy the desire for some fiefdom builder, but rather because of a very practical problem. The weight of the metal addressograph plates used to send out senatorial mailings was so great that there was a danger that the floor of the Senate office building would buckle and the rest of the Senate would physically fall in around it (Chartrand, 1980: 11-12).

Assessing the importance of both the public and private arguments for computerization is quite difficult since it involves delving into the innermost thoughts of Representatives and Senators who have a stake in not revealing their baser natures. While members vary in terms of the arguments that affect them, reading between the lines leads one to believe that computer proponents made more points when they were able to convince individual members of the selective advantages of computerization than when they were justifying the action on the basis of the transcendent, but not particularly galvanizing, values. The transcendent values are important to look at, however, because they did motivate some members and because they were important as the ammunition in a stylized public debate over computerization.

EMERGING RESISTANCE

If it is difficult to determine whether proponents of computerization were won over on the basis of collective or selective benefits, little of that problem exists for discovering the motivations of the opponents. While opponents were generally forced to frame their debate in the form of competing sets of transcendent values with collective consequences, most opposition stemmed from perceived selective benefits that would make certain individuals less comfortable or powerful.

Individual Resistance

To a large degree, it is probably not legitimate to emphasize the resistance to computerization in Congress as much as the lack of interest and awareness. There was not much opposition to computers or technology in the abstract, only when particular applications were seen as negatively affecting a particular individual or group. Quite early it became clear that computers would eventually come to Congress, and the battle shifted from one of stopping their arrival to thwarting particular application plans and fighting for control of the accepted systems (Glass, 1970: 1150).

Most members of Congress had limited perspectives on the potential of computers to go beyond simple data processing tasks. A pool of experts did not exist that combined sophisticated knowledge of both computer applications and congressional needs and procedures. Neither the congressional recruitment process nor the staffing procedures facilitated the orderly entrance of such individuals into the process. Legislative politics and computer science existed as two separate worlds seeking a translator to begin conversation. Such people eventually emerged, but not before a great deal of time was lost. Even when such people were available, it was not always possible to get the message through. As one staff member who played this role commented, "We had to deal with very busy people. Members just do not have the time to sit down and discover the options. Once we could get their ear, they were quite receptive, but we often could not get to first base."

General opposition to change

Individuals in all positions become comfortable in patterns that have worked moderately well for them in the past. Generals fight the last war and members of Congress are captives of the past decade. The congressional lifestyle is not one that facilitates operating at the cutting edge of new technology. Change is threatening, and in an institution where power is most likely to go to those who have had the most time to absorb the traditions, those with the power to change have the least motivation and the greatest fears.

Congress entered the computer age with two handicaps. It entered the field late, and the field was incredibly fast moving. In the computer world, "hardware is five years ahead of software," and the software capabilities are "five years ahead of the willpower" to use them (Congressional Record, 1964: 9075).

Computers engender particular fears not associated with other technologies. A 1973 national survey indicated that of the twelve technologies studied, computerized information banks were perceived as being least useful and most harmful (Dutton and Kraemer, 1976). Most individuals have a love-hate relationship with computers. We are impressed and awed by what they can do, but we each have a story about a computerized billing system that went haywire. We often express our fears in our humor, and early on, computers on the Hill were used as a scapegoat. One of the less reliable elevators in a House office building sported a sign for a number of months, "Forgive the delays, this elevator has been computerized." A well-posted cartoon on the Hill during the early days expressed the fear of dehumanization by showing a member's computer communicating directly with a constituent's computer, without the aid of any human.

Even after the introduction of computers, the distrust remained. Representative William Natcher (D-KY), who had many years of roll call voting behind him, could never quite trust the electronic voting system. He would go from one voting station to the next, voting repeatedly just to make sure he was recorded (Perry, 1978: 33).

Power stakes of innovation

If the leaders of Congress were not fond of power, they would not have entered politics to pursue it. Perhaps we are all fond of it, but it is in the nature of politicians to hunger for it, to work, conive and scheme to get it, and having got it, they simply are not going to give it away [Donham, 1966].

Modern information technology challenged the power of key members of Congress. "The power of certain chamber functionaries or committee chairmen (and sub-committee chairmen) is vested, quite often in the information which they control" (Chartrand, 1970: 183). Veteran committee chairpersons dependent on resident information and expertise to supplement their formal position feared that open access to information would weaken the seniority system and make the "diligent freshman representative as knowledgeable on some subjects as his superiors in the hierarchy" (Congressional Quarterly Weekly Report, 1969: 525). Just as improved information was intended to change the power relationship between the Congress and the executive branch, the introduction of computers could reach down into the Congress and redistribute internal power. The threat was not only from fellow members. Some members of Congress feared that they would become more dependent on their staffs, particularly the technical experts who designed and ran the information systems.

Congress does not exist in a vacuum. As with other organizations, external bodies can thwart internal change. Plans to automate the *Congressional Record* fell victim to the territorial claims of the Government Printing Office and ran counter to government contracts with printers' unions. The Congress was forced to back off politely.

Once the advantages of computerization for incumbents became obvious, Republicans in Congress began to have second thoughts about accepting those applications that would give the majority Democrats another tool for staying in office (Bemer, 1975). A technological innovation had proven to be a factor in the partisan power struggle.

Fear of external reaction

Members of Congress keep the ballot box and their constituents' views at the forefront of their consciousness. Members were concerned that their constituents would not understand if they assigned each one a number and communicated in a supposedly more impersonal way through computer-generated letters (Chartrand, 1980: 11). Some members feared the loss of anonymity should voting data, bill sponsorship data, and expenditure data be computerized and more readily available to the public.

Staff opposition

While members of Congress harbored vague fears as to the potential negative impact of computerization, staff members were more specific. The most basic fear was for their jobs. When vocal assurances were finally accepted that no one would lose their jobs on the Hill due to computers, the fear turned to concern over the quality and nature of jobs in a computerized environment. For many staff members, the requirements of computerized data meant that jobs would become more routine, tasks more repetitive, and the role of creativity and insight less important (U.S. Congress, House, Select Committee on Committees, 1974: 109-110). Staff members performing research roles feared that they would lose the middleman status of gathering and interpreting information for their bosses, who could not get direct access to information. Researchers exhibit some of the most conservative work habits of any group. Once they have developed an approach that works, they do not like to tamper with it (Sanfield, 1979: 115).

Staff members who could not see themselves coexisting with the computer age showed their full share of resistance to learning new skills (U.S. Congress, Senate, Commission on the Operation of the Senate, 1977c: 187). They feared losing power to the technicians and did not look forward to the physical intrusion of terminals, which take up precious space and give off heat and noise.

Cost

Not the least of the reasons to oppose computerization was the cost factor. Fiscal conservatives used the large price tags on computers to oppose them, but were also less interested in information systems in general, which serve to increase the problems that can be dealt with and the changes that can be made. Interest in particular computer services available to individual members of Congress was quite high until it is proposed that they pay for the services, and then the interest waned. Proponents of change saw benefits in personal terms, and intimated that the costs would fall on the organization (Wilson, 1966: 208). The more ambitious proposals for Congress creating a one-for-one equivalency for information resources held by the executive branch fell by the wayside under criticisms such as that leveled by Robert Byrd (D-WV):

> The need for computers can be exaggerated. The computers in the Defense Department operate just like those on the Hill would. We can get the same information from their computers [Cohen, 1973: 385].

Resistance to computers was not universal, nor was it as important as ignorance and indifference. Computerization was simply not a hot issue to more than a handful of members of Congress. Specific proposals drew spirited praise and criticism, but on the whole the issue of adopting computers got lost in the multitude of issues members must face. The relatively low priority of computerization frustrated the technical experts, one of whom commented:

> In many areas there have been inordinate delays in implementing important information systems. No one was willing to bite the bullet

and authorize a system. They were afraid of the political opposition, concerned about stepping on someone's toes and paranoid about the possibility that current technology would be superseded before the new system was in place. But at some point you just have to get the show out of New Haven.

Organizational Resistance

The introduction of computerized or analytical techniques must be done as far as possible in support of, rather than in competition with, the existing principles, concepts and procedures that now frame the legislative and administrative functions (U.S. Congress, House, Select Committee on Committees, 1974: 69).

The organization of Congress encourages some types of innovation and thwarts others. As a diverse organization with multiple power centers, it is an ideal place in which to spawn innovations, but those very same characteristics make it difficult to get organizationwide innovations adopted (see Wilson, 1966). Subunits of Congress protect their turf against outside encroachment and put roadblocks in the way of change. When Senator Hatfield (R—OR) wanted to get wall phones installed to free some desk space for terminals, it took considerable effort and required the approval of the Senate Rules Committee in order to change the standard operating procedure (Jost, 1979: 50). The Congress is so diverse that proponents of change have had to come to the conclusion that for many applications they are not dealing with Congress as an entity, but must look at it in terms of 535 separate and unique organizations (O'Donnell, 1980: 71-72).

On top of the basic organizational structure is the hectic nature of congressional life, which mitigates against long-term planning. A sort of Gresham's Law of planning develops, in which daily routine drives out planning. When an individual is faced both with highly programmed and highly unprogrammed tasks, the former tend to take precedence (March and Simon, 1958: 185).

Despite the active resistance, passive indifference, and organizational barriers to technological innovation, Congress did eventually move into the computer age, but did so in its own way. The story of the move is really a set of stories happening within each separate branch of Congress and its subunits.

MILESTONES AND STRATEGIES IN THE HOUSE

While it has been a truism that the U.S. House of Representatives and the U.S. Senate are different institutions, the processes of their adoption of computers bear out these differences. It is necessary to deal with each chamber separately. Table 4.1 summarizes the adoption milestones applicable to each chamber and the Congress as a whole.

Robert McClory's (R–IL) pioneering legislation in 1966 calling for a congressional computer system designed to provide budget and legislative history information (Congressional Record, 1966: 27824) fell on fallow ground, but the soil was fertilized with a continuing stream of new proposals and worked with diligent effort by numerous individuals and groups during the next few years. Robert Chartrand from CRS produced numerous studies on the benefits of computerization, and external research organizations and scholars began writing about the applications of computerization for legislative tasks (see Chartrand, 1976c, for a chronological bibliographic essay). Chartrand played a key role in broadening the span of support among members and staff through testimony, individual briefings, and conferences. A total of nineteen congressmen responded to personal invitiations by McClory to meet at the Brookings Institution with Chartrand and other information specialists for extended discussions of computer applications for Congress (Chartrand, 1976c: 316). These individuals were coopted into becoming some of the "movers and shakers" in the move toward computerization. Chartrand was a master at asking marginally committed members to join him in speaking to outside groups on computerization. Once he got their behavioral commitment, their supportive attitudes and willingness to work toward computerization increased. In Chartrand's words, he "threw the net out and involved potential supporters through conferences and speeches."

Growing interest in computerization coincided with the initial hearings on the Legislative Reorganization Act, which finally passed in 1970. Significant portions of the 1967 hearings dealt with Congress's information needs (for example, see the Congressional Record, 1967b: 3732). At various points in the legislative process, the proposed act contained two significant items to upgrade congressional information. A proposal for a Joint Committee on Data Processing, with a broad grant of authority to acquire information-processing equipment, made it through the Senate, but was defeated on the House floor (Hopkins, 1972: 473-474). While the Legislative Reorganization Act backed away from formally moving Congress into the computer age, it did urge Congress to consider "new sources

TABLE 4.1   Milestones in Congressional Computerization[a]

Year	Key Decisions on Computers	New Computerized Services
1966	First bill to create congressional computer facility (HSE)	
1967		CRS automates *Bill Digest* Clerk's data processing office estab- (HSE)
1968		CRS computerizes first House calendar capability Computerized mailing lists (SEN)
1969	Passage of Brademas Resolution (HSE) Activation of Select Committee on electrical and mechanical office equipment (HSE)	
1970	Passage of legislative reorganizational act Subcommittee on computer services created (SEN)	LOC conversion of bibliographic control system to ADP
1971	House information system created (HSE)	
1972	Electronic voting approved (HSE)	Automated campaign expenditure system developed
1973		LOC SCORPIO system developed CRS acquires commercial services such as JURIS, MEDLINE, NYT Info Bank Electronic voting system operational (HSE)
1974	Congressional Budget Act passed House select committee on committees recommends more use of computers	
1975	House committee order 23 authorizes transfer of $1000/month from office funds (HSE) Senate provides terminals for offices that desire them	Pilot member information network (HSE)
1977	Policy group on information and computers established (HSE) Policy coordinating group for technology development established	Pilot member office support system established (HSE)
1978	Rules changed to allow members to freely transfer office funds	

(continued)

TABLE 4.1   Continued

Year	Key Decisions on Computers	New Computerized Services
1979		LOC converts card catalog completely to computer Geographic reporting system data base operational
1980		Correspondence management system fully operational (SEN)
1981	H.I.S. funding slashed and autonomy reduced (HSE)	

a. This is a selective and expanded version of the chronology developed by Robert Chartrand and presented in a number of his publications (Chartrand 1976a, 1978 and others).
ABBREVIATIONS: HSE = House of Representatives; SEN = Senate; CRS = Congressional Reference Service; LOC = Library of Congress; ADP = Automatic Data Processing.

of information and research including the development of automatic data processing" (U.S. Congress, House, Select Committee on Committees, 1974: 55-57). The newly created Joint Committee on Congressional Operations was charged with considering potential EDP uses, and an encouraging climate for information innovation was established.

As the Legislative Reorganization Act was wending its way through the legislative process, Representative John Brademas became restive. After seeing the defeat of numerous bills designed to provide computer support to Congress, and frustrated with the slow and unsure progress of the Legislative Reorganization Act, Brademas got the endorsement of the Democratic Study Group and eventually the entire caucus to support the following resolution: "Resolved, that the Committee on House Administration be fully supported by Democratic members in efforts to improve the efficiency of operations of the House of Representatives, and we urge that these efforts include, but not be limited to, the use of computers and of a centralized mail processing system" (Hopkins, 1972: 456). On the basis of this resolution, the Speaker instructed the House Administration Committee to take action, which responded to the mandate by referring the matter to its Special Subcommittee on Electrical and Mechanical Office Equipment, chaired by Representative Joe D. Waggoner (D-LA). The subcommittee created a Working Group composed of Chartrand, from the Legislative Reference Service, Edward J. Mahoney, from the General

Accounting Office, and Thomas E. Ladd, from the Clerk's Office. The preparation of the Working Group's report series established official credibility for the role of information science in the Congress (Chartrand, 1976c: 317).

By an unexpected quirk of fate, the mandate to the Special Subcommittee on Electrical and Mechanical Office Equipment doomed the establishment of the Joint Committee on Data Processing as part of the Legislative Reorganization Act. In a typical case of protecting one's turf, Waggoner saw the development of a new committee as a threat to his committee's jurisdiction. The role of personal pride also evidenced itself in this battle. Waggoner was particularly piqued that Senate Majority Leader Mike Mansfield (D-MT) had never responded to a letter from the chairperson of the Committee on House Administration. Mansfield indicated that he should be communicating through the Speaker, but in the House, which exhibits a continuing fear of being viewed as the "inferior" body, such a supposed slight to one of its leaders was just enough to convince them that, in Waggoner's words, "if we cannot communicate any better than that, there is no way under God's blue canopy of heaven that a joint committee can succeed" (Hopkins, 1972: 457). While Waggoner's disgust might have been real, it seems to have been more of a smokescreen to bolster his attempt to protect his subcommittee's turf.

While the political battles raged, the Working Group on Automated Data Processing under the Special Subcommittee on Electrical and Mechanical Office Equipment began pumping out reports and encouraging future research. The first annual report (U.S. Congress, House, Committee on House Administration, 1969) promoted the need for a highly integrated system and documented the largely housekeeping current uses of computers in the House. In 1970, the Working Group sent out a survey to all members to assess information needs. While the survey did not pick up much new information, it was part of a typical change agent strategy to coopt potential users by making them feel part of the decision-making process and establishing a positive attitude toward change (U.S. Congress, House, House Information System, 1979b: 594). Once their internal research was completed, the Working Group turned to the Stanford Research Institute to coordinate a group of nine consulting teams writing reports on various segments of potential legislative computerization.

Despite the mass of research findings, politics is seldom left far behind in Congress. While the Working Group was studying, Clerk of the House W. Pat Jennings was acting. He expanded his administrative uses of computers and saw his office filling in the void and serving as the locus for a full

House computer system. His plans fell victim to a damning evaluation by the Systems Research Corporation, which concluded that the clerk's data processing system was not cost-effective and not living up to its capabilities (U.S. Congress, House, Committee on House Administration, 1971). This set the stage for Wayne Hayes (D-OH), Chairman of the House Administration Committee, to make a play for his aspiration of being the House computer "czar" (U.S. Congress, House, House Information System, 1979b: 9). Hayes had the power and merged his information staff with that of the clerk's, in effect creating what was to become the House Information System (H.I.S.), a new staff group under the Committee on House Administration. The creation of H.I.S. was motivated as much by power motivations as organization theory. Hayes wanted to control all computer applications. As one staff member said, "It was a classic political blood bath in which a high ranking staff member (Jennings) lost out to a higher ranking committee chairman (Hayes)." H.I.S. was initially "a little vendetta" started by Wayne Hayes as a power battle with the clerk over data processing (Holmes, 1977: 7).

With the creation of H.I.S., computerization for the House not only had champions in the form of change agents emerging from the chamber itself, but now there was a bureaucracy that had a stake in expanding its power, resources, and purview. H.I.S. learned the strategies of bureaucratic turf building early. Its budget justifications (always for an increase over the previous year) praised H.I.S.'s own past efforts as monumental, but always pointed out that there was much to do to reach the goals widely held by the members of Congress who would be voting on the appropriation. For example, in its 1977 budget request, H.I.S. mentioned the great progress made during the last year, which, although all that could be expected, was not enough "in comparison with the enormous challenge" involved in reestablishing congressional prerogatives and providing a beneficial check and balance over executive branch actions (U.S. Congress, House, Committee on House Administration, 1977: 5). H.I.S. was definitely speaking the language of the legislators themselves.

Very early, H.I.S. rejected creating a total information system for the Congress, and instead promoted an incremental approach based on continuous selling and the creation of computer-based products in which the "service or cost-benefit [was] so apparent that a resource commitment . . . [could] be made with confident expectations of positive results" (U.S. Congress, House, Select Committee on Committees, 1974: 75). H.I.S. leaders and their overseers in the House Administration Committee realized that members of Congress were unprepared to understand the advantages and disadvantages of computerization, and that it would be hard to sell a full-blown system requiring multiyear budget commitments involving large initial dollar amounts. House insiders realized that they could avoid potentially dangerous changes in the chamber rules that would be required for the introduction of a total system by making computerization decisions piecemeal. Many of the important decisions on new computer applications never came to a formal vote on the floor because they were buried in the appropriations process (Electronics, 1971: 41). Incrementalism proved to be very effective in that it

> helped to temper the concerns of those opposed to mounting increases in costs. . . . It was also undoubtedly the best strategy of introducing members of Congress to the benefits that could be derived from computers [Norton, 1980: 11].

Beyond moving slowly and cautiously, H.I.S. realized early that members of the House had different needs, aspirations, and working styles that a general information system could not satisfy. As one H.I.S. staff member put it:

> We consider each office to be like a small business with unique needs and interests. It would be very difficult to come up with a "majority system" which would satisfy enough people. Even if we went to a centralized system we would always give members a choice.

Representative Charlie Rose, one of the active proponents of computerization, expressed the same sentiment in slightly different words:

> Each Congressional district is a unique part of America. The people elected are a unique reflection of their constituents with unique habits and views of their job. There is no advantage to try and impose one identical computer system on everyone.

The initial product emanating from H.I.S. was a bill status system used for monitoring where legislation was in the process. Again showing a cautious, incremental approach, H.I.S. did not give members direct access to the system: Initially, there was a telephone number that could be called. H.I.S. was afraid that users would not understand how to use the system or would not understand when the system was down. An expert intermediary could cover up for the limitations in the technology. As interest in the bill status system grew, the system became so overloaded that most people just got a busy signal. With such success, it was necessary to move to direct access by members.

In 1975, the H.I.S. task broadened and took on a different nature when the House rules were changed to allow individual members to use up to $1000 per month from their staff funds for computer services. H.I.S. was being called on by members to advise them on the choices of equipment from outside vendors, and also saw this as an opportunity to spread the computer "gospel" and provide a mechanism by which they could "showcase" their wares. Individualized funding grew from the recognition that congressional offices were just not willing to be put into a mold, and no one really knew enough about both congressional needs and the characteristics of available equipment to prove the utility of one system over another. A wide variety of equipment was introduced in a number of different formats. Some offices bought into time-sharing systems, others secured stand-alone word processors with limited memories, while others contracted with outside firms to handle mailing lists and computer-generated letters from remote locations. The variety of applications and approaches meant that virtually every congressional office could see some use fitted to their needs, and resistance was reduced (Dodd and Schott, 1979: 197). H.I.S. service representatives began going around to offices and pointing out potential uses, comparing available products, and generally heralding the coming of the computer age to anyone who would listen. In a number of cases, H.I.S. became a consumer advocate when offices had difficulties with vendors, because the offices often did not have the expertise to deal with technical problems. In at least one case, H.I.S. put a vendor on probation and they quickly shaped up.

H.I.S. was not alone in its role of promoter. Computer salespeople converged on Capitol Hill and the availability of 435 potential new customers spawned new data handling packages as well as some completely new companies. Not all of the outside vendors found the Hill a hospitable place. Congressional customers tend to be demanding, unique, and unwilling to accept the normal excuses for why the terminal is not working or the system is down. A number of companies that quickly jumped into the congressional market beat a hasty retreat when they found that the potential profits were not worth the hassles.

As more members obtained terminals and more data packages came on line members of Congress and their staffs began to "wow" their colleagues in other offices. Charlie Rose and others have been known to take portable terminals to the cloakrooms off the floor, to committee meetings, and out to their districts to search for information and impress anyone who happens to be around (Gregory, 1980: 43). Congressional offices have been equally willing to show off their office systems to colleagues and their staffs.

One of the most common change strategies in the House during the mid-1970s was the use of pilot projects. A pilot project allows the testing of a new data base or approach on a group of users who are already somewhat supportive of an application. As offices began to get their own terminals, they desired access to the data bases created by H.I.S. and the Library of Congress. In 1976, the Member Information Network (MIN) gave 21 offices (17 member offices and 4 committees) access to 6 data bases (U.S. Congress, House, Commission on Administrative Review, 1977b: 219). The same year, 6 offices became part of the Member Office Support System (MOSS), which gave them access to programs for letter writing, correspondence tracking, and mailing list creation programs through access to a time-shared minicomputer (U.S. Congress, House, Commission on Administrative Review, 1977b: 214-215). The pilot projects not only helped test out various approaches, but also served as "payoffs" to the members of the House Administration Committee who had been carrying the ball for computerization. By using such people, it was assured that they would bend over backward to prove the systems useful. The availability of enthusiastic trend setters gave other members something concrete to look at and compare to their office operations. The pilot projects worked well, but were not without their problems. The distribution of free services to only a few members engendered some bad feelings further down the road. As Representative Bill Frenzel (R-MN) expressed it:

> There are a large number of members who have a computer terminal who haven't paid for it. . . . If you happen to have been on Jack Brooks' committee, on the House Administration's proper subcommittee or whatever, you have a free terminal [U.S. Congress, House, Commission on Administrative Review, 1978: 101].

The utility of computer applications for managing one's office, doing legislative research, and dealing with one's committee and leadership responsibilities went a long way toward having computers sell themselves. Computer proponents were fortunate in that they received some early support from some of the very people who were most likely to oppose such changes. In one member's words: "For reform to happen, you need conservatives: for the same reason only a Nixon could go to China. It adds legitimacy to the effort" (Ornstein, 1974: 5). As we will see in Chapter 6, conservative Republicans coming to Congress with computer experience in the business world jumped at the chance to use computers once they were in office. Computerization also gained credibility when two of the most senior committee chairs, Wright Patman (D–TX), of the Banking and Currency Committee, and Emanuel Celler, (D-NY), of Judiciary, embarked on committee applications such as preparing legislative calendars. They were quite proud of the system and by showing it to others helped convince some of the more hesitant members. As one of the most deeply involved staff members said:

> We were in clover when we had the support of two such real veterans. No one could charge that these were just two young turks who did not know how the system worked.

Research in a number of realms has shown that getting the support of top-level participants, and particularly the active involvement of top leaders, is a key element in implementing computer systems (Kraemer and King, 1975: 4-2).

Computerization in the House also benefited by riding on the coattails of broader reform efforts. The computer fit in well with the deep "American faith in structural solutions to complex problems" (Davidson and Olezak, 1976: 38). The only real battle involving a large-scale computer application erupted over the introduction of an electronic voting system for the House in 1972 and 1973. The question of utilizing a computer was tangential to the debate, with the most important arguments involving the broader issue of changing traditional voting procedures. Electronic voting was nothing new. Thomas Edison was granted a patent for a mechanical voting system more than a century before Congress even considered the possibility. The initial recommendations to use a mechanical system in Congress emerged in 1914. By 1973, 36 state legislatures had well-established electronic voting systems, most supported by computers (Nation's Business, 1973: 70).

Proponents of electronic voting stressed the fact that Congress wasted a great deal of time on roll call votes and quorum calls. With an oral calling of the roll, each vote took close to 30 minutes. For an average year this meant over 90 hours of chamber time, or one-fifth of the time in session (Congressional Record, 1972: 36009). An electronic system would not only reduce the time required for voting, but would also increase accuracy and create an information base for the leadership, the members, and the press.

Opponents countered with a series of specific dire predictions and a general fear of unanticipated consequences. They took on the argument of saving time by arguing that the current time spent on roll calls was not wasted but served an important function, since members could use that time to communicate personally and pick up the necessary information to vote wisely (Janda, 1968: 446). While some opponents objected to the projected costs (Ornstein, 1975: 204-206), most opposition predicted negative consequences for the leadership and the individual members. With a shortened time period for voting, some feared a dramatic loss in the leadership's ability to hammer out compromises and strike bargains. Members could dash in, vote, and dash out without any chance for leadership influence (Congressional Record, 1972: 36010; Hopkins, 1972: 503).

On the other hand, the proposal for the leadership to have terminals by which they could monitor ongoing votes and pinpoint deviating party members, and the plan for public display boards led some opponents to argue that individual members would lay themselves open to increased leadership pressure. One academic critic even suggested that such a system might lead to voting boards in the White House or interest group headquarters, with instantaneous orders going out to Hill operatives to have negative votes "corrected" (Robinson, 1966: 284).

The electronic voting system that went into operation in 1973 took some substantive changes and clever selling. The system was promoted as a voting system rather than as an information system, to allay the fears of increasing leadership control and increasing the publicity on congressional votes. Access to terminals on the floor was restricted and members were guaranteed that historical records of their own individual votes could only be released to them personally (Porter, 1972: 20).

The introduction of electronic voting went rather smoothly. At first H.I.S. staff members were stationed around the floor to help the less mechanically oriented members insert their plastic identification cards into the voting stations and press the desired buttons. Although the system worked almost without a hitch, lingering doubts about the reliability of computers surfaced in 1979. The votes of two members showed up on the vote printouts when the members were in fact back in their districts at the time. The first reaction to this "ghost" voting was that the equipment had failed. A full-scale investigation, including an FBI investigation of the voting cards, computer simulations of the votes in question, and statistical analysis of voting patterns, concluded that it was definitely not a machine error, but a case of unauthorized proxy voting (U.S. Congress, House, Committee on Standards of Official Conduct, 1980). The electronic voting system had passed the test and assured its future in the House. The utility of monitoring voting for members interested in affecting the outcome of particular legislation led to increased access through the introduction of terminals at the back of the chamber, where any member can monitor some aspects of ongoing votes.

Other broad-based reform efforts, such as the House Select Committee on Committees (Bolling Committee), encouraged the use of computers in support of committee information needs (U.S. Congress, House, Select Committee on Committees, 1973a, 1973b). The Congressional Budget and Impoundment Act of 1974 dramatically updated the need for sophisticated data (Public Law 93-344). Section 202 of that act urged the Congressional Budget Office (CBO) to make full use of up-to-date computer capabilities. The Budget Act put a great deal of pressure on the authorizing committees. They were charged with producing cost estimates early in the budget consideration, but often did not know all the budget areas under their purview. One of the first tasks of the CBO was to develop a computerized classification system for each committee. The law also required the creation of a "parliamentarian's report," which would be used by the House parliamentarian to determine whether specific legislation is subject to a point of order because it would breach a budget resolution. The development of the Congressional Budget Office staff brought into Congress a group of high-powered economists and budget analysts, many of whom came from the executive branch and were well versed in the utility of computerized data banks, and all of whom expected that Congress's ability to do sophisticated financial analysis independently of the executive branch would be provided by congressional computers. The House Commission on Administrative Review, formed in 1976, accumulated a great deal of testimony on the need for expanded computerized knowledge in the House, and ended up with a strong report urging that H.I.S. provide every member a free terminal with direct access to all the data bases that had been included in the pilot Member Information Network program (U.S. Congress, House, Commission on Administrative Review, 1977b: 682-683). While this step was not taken, the strong stand on computerization bolstered the developing conventional wisdom that computerization was the way to go for Congress.

In 1978 the House Rules were changed so that members could spend as much of their office allowances as they wanted on computers. By 1980 any member with a terminal who wanted to be part of the Member Information Network simply had to request it. Compared to the better publicized House reform attempts of the 1970s, such as committee reform, the introduction of computers was accomplished much more smoothly. Committee reform was presented as a large interlocking package subject to the disapproval of concurrent minorities, and it was perceived as a zero-sum game in which winners took their booty out of the flesh of losers. Computerization, on the other hand, was done incrementally and ad hoc, with a "distributive" policy orientation in which there were few real losers and everyone could get a bit of benefit (Davidson and Oleszak, 1976: 63).

As we will see later, H.I.S. continued to produce more products and expanded its purview over personnel and budgets until it got caught in the post-1980 election budget-cutting frenzy. By the late 1970s, even though there had not been a single milestone decision to enter the computer age, the question was not, "Would Congress computerize?" but rather, "How far will the trend go?" and "What are the limits?" Unlike the executive branch and the business world, which rushed headlong into the use of computers, the slow evolutionary approach of the Congress reflected the nature of the House and had a salutary effect. From a staff member's perspective:

> The cautious approach used by Congress was fitting. Computerization was a bipartisan effort to attack devious problems. Services were provided after testing and in a context where one could reasonably predict success. There just have not been any major failures to turn people off.

While incrementalism does not provide dramatic steps forward, it also limits the magnitude of the regressive steps. Given the fragmented nature of the House and the different perceived needs of members, it is hard to imagine that a total information system could have been instituted any faster. In less than ten years, starting in 1971, the House essentially changed from an organization marked by computer ignorance and illiteracy to one providing, through a combination of centralized and individual systems, access to massive amounts of computerized information and manipulation systems. The computer age has arrived for the House.

COMPUTERIZATION IN THE SENATE

The move toward computers in the Senate reflected both the different atmosphere and different demands of that chamber. The correspondence load in the Senate threatened to damage the physical structure of the

Senate office building and turned many Senate staffs into little more than letter writers and correspondence filers. Pilot projects in the offices of Senators Philip Hart (D-MI), Charles Percy (R-IL), and others funded either by outside vendors or the senators themselves revealed the utility of computers to handle correspondence (Chartrand, 1976c: 325). In 1968, the Senate shifted to a centralized mailing list system to replace the heavy addressograph plates, and by 1970, over one-half of the Senate offices used the computerized lists to mail their limit of 280,000 pieces per month (Glass, 1970: 1154). The mailing list system was limited to producing mailing labels for all of a senator's mailing list or for any subset specified on the ten characteristics by which each person on the mailing list could be coded. The mailing list creation was essentially "transparent" to members of the Senate, since it was done in a remote location and simply provided the same type of product they had been used to with the old system, except for the ability to pull out subgroup lists.

In 1970, attention shifted to the use of computers for legislative and administrative tasks as opposed to correspondence management. A report commissioned by the secretary of the Senate led to improvements in administrative functions and the newly created Subcommittee on Computer Services of the Senate Committee on Rules and Administration began studying legislative applications such as bill status and research files (Chartrand, 1976c: 326-327). The passage of the Federal Elections Campaign Act of 1971 (Public Law 92-225) forced the secretary of the Senate (as well as the clerk of the House) to implement computer- and microform-supported retrieval systems. Early pilot projects linked some offices with the data banks from the Library of Congress and some commercial banks as early as 1973 (Chartrand, 1976c: 329).

Unlike the House, which centralized computer control in the House Information System under the Committee on House Administration, the Senate did not develop centralized administration and direction of computers. Computer functions were divided among the Committee on Rules and Administration, the secretary of the Senate, and the sergeant at arms. The lack of a centralized policy had the effect of speeding up the process of computerization in at least one case. In 1975 the Appropriations Committee, after hearing about the various data files available, was frustrated that it could not get access to them. Without going through the computer subcommittee, the Appropriations Committee produced legislation that granted each office a computer terminal without charge (U.S. Congress, Senate, Commission on the Operation of the Senate, 1977c: 182). While some offices were ready to utilize computers, others accepted the gift and stashed the terminal away, almost forgetting it was there. It was not until more staff became aware of computer applications that terminals "came out of the closet."

A major impetus toward computer utilization was the development of the Senate Correspondence Management System, which began with a pilot project involving eleven offices and became fully operational in 1980. This sophisticated system updated the early mailing list creation application and added new features such as mail tracking and more sophisticated retrieval of specialized mailing lists (Chartrand, 1980).

Electronic voting was never seriously considered for the Senate. The smaller size of the Senate made the time commitment for roll call voting significantly less important. The heavy demands on senators' time means that they need even more information from their colleagues as to the proper course of action. As one staff member explained it:

> Electronic voting would reduce the importance of roll call votes. The primary purpose of a recorded vote is to get people together to find out what is being voted on and to horsetrade on the floor. With or without electronic voting, that time would still be needed.

HOUSE AND SENATE APPROACHES

While the Senate jumped out ahead of the pack in initially employing computers for nonadministrative tasks (mailing list creation), it has not kept pace with the variety of applications available through the House Information System. The Senate still provides more centralized computer support for handling correspondence, but is far behind the House in other applications (Flato, 1977: 255). As late as 1977, the Commission on the Operation of the Senate (1977c: 169-174) took its parent body to task by concluding that

> Congress generally has been comparatively slow to make use of computer technology for its operating information needs. . . . In most respects, the Senate has the least developed legislative operating information system in the national legislative branch. . . . Congress, especially the Senate, entered the computer age two or even three technical generations behind the executive branch and private business, and at least one generation behind the state legislatures.

The reasons for the relative slowness of the Senate to use computer technology reflect both the differences in the basic nature of the Senate and the processes of innovation chosen by each chamber, which, to some degree, also reflect the nature of the two bodies. With its longer terms and more developed traditions, the Senate is a less likely setting for innovation. The Senate has always viewed itself as a continuing body, whereas the House rules are open to redefinition after each election. Because it views itself as the "upper house," the Senate is less open to borrowing approaches used by "inferiors" such as the House and state legislatures. The increased turnover in the House due to the two-year terms creates an influx of new members who "bring with them innovative information ideas from their roles in business, the professions or academia" (Gregory, 1978: 100). Only lately has the Senate been welcoming new members with House computer experience.

The Senate has fewer well-placed internal change agents willing to take on the job of shepherding computerization through the chamber. As a staff member put it, "Senators tend to think great thoughts, but not pursue detail" and much of the movement in the House was composed of detailed incremental steps. The Senate subcommittee on computers tended to use a "passive-reactive approach," expecting the users to initiate demands for services (U.S. Congress, Senate, Commission on the Operation of the Senate, 1977c: 178). With the creation of H.I.S., the House had a single well-staffed organization with a stake in promoting computer usage. In the obviously evaluative words of a key Senate staff member:

> The House and Senate have approached computerizing data in very different ways. The House has taken a garbage can approach. They create numerous data bases, promote heavily and hope that they will serve some purpose. The Senate has been more parsimonious with its money and computerized only its official actions for easy search and analysis.

While the House used a laissez-faire approach of allowing each member a great deal of latitude in choosing services and approaches, the Senate chose to centralize its services (although not the administration of them) and provide them free to all members. Since senatorial offices did not have to pay directly for services, they were not about to look a gift horse in the mouth. By making computer services a direct cost for House members, H.I.S. created a much more interested and critical clientele.

One of the abiding differences between the House and Senate emerged subtly in the semantics of the interviews with information specialists in each chamber. On the House side, new information services were justified on the basis of their intrinsic utility or as services demanded by individual potential users. Discussions on the Senate side were laced with references to the leadership. Either "the leadership took great interest in this area and mandated its adoption," or "the leadership does not have much interest in this area so we won't proceed." This impression bridges the change of party control in the Senate and implies that the difficulty of the House leadership to get cooperation on substantive legislative issues reflects a much deeper problem, with roots in the underlying nature of the two institutions.

Although all computer applications for Congress are paid for from public funds, the general grant of total access to all Senators and the focus in the Senate on constituent correspondence applications have put the Senate in line for more criticism. Common Cause has a suit pending against the Senate in regard to the franking privilege that pays special attention to the ways in which the Correspondence Management System can be used for supposedly political purposes (Common Cause, 1981). One of the results of this situation is that the Senate computer operation has traditionally been shrouded in secrecy. Visitors, especially those from the press, are politely turned away. No public records are kept of the specific computer costs; they are included in the lump-sum appropriation of the sergeant at arms (Glass, 1970: 1154). The House Information System, as an active promoter of computerization, encourages publicity and sees outside acclaim as one more method of encouraging use by member offices.

The centralized dictation of policy concerning specific computer applications in the Senate has paid off for particular types of applications. In areas fraught with political considerations, the laissez-faire approach of the House facilitates opposition and sabotage. For example, both the Senate and the House needed help in scheduling myriad committee meetings. Committees and their staffs do not like to lose control of their meeting spaces and the strategic advantage of scheduling meeting times. On the Senate side, the use of a scheduling program was made mandatory and has worked very well. On the House side, committee chairs were given the choice as to whether to use it. As a result, a senior staff member explained,

the COMIS (Committee Information and Scheduling) system is a good example of a good idea which really did not get off the ground. At least ten million dollars have been spent with little impact. It is essentially a matrix system matching every member's committees to determine potential conflicts when scheduling a meeting. It never worked because it was voluntary. Every junior college in the country has successfully dealt with such a scheduling problem with computers, but committee chairmen in Congress will have nothing to do with it.

While it would be presumptuous and foolhardy to say whether the House or Senate approach was better, it is clear that choices of implementation strategy do affect the kind of product delivered. It is also evident that organizations choose implementation strategies that reflect their organizational character.

HOUSE AND SENATE COOPERATION AND COORDINATION

The Initial Breakdown

To say that the House and the Senate got off on the wrong foot for cooperation on computerization would be an understatement. The initial plan for a Joint Committee on Data Processing that was included in the early versions of the Legislative Reorganization Act of 1970 made a great deal of sense from the perspective of cost and efficiency, but it did not take into account the power stakes involved in controlling an information system, the fear in the House of becoming subordinate to the Senate, the ego of the participants, and the fact that the House was far ahead of the Senate in planning (U.S. Congress, House, House Information System, 1979b: 8-9). Joe D. Waggoner, chair of the Special Subcommittee on Electrical and Mechanical Office Equipment, was not only miffed at Senate Majority Leader Mike Mansfield for not responding to his letter on joint computer efforts, but also felt that joint committees had not been particularly successful in the past, and that in this particular case a joint effort would set back computerization in the House by two years (Glass, 1970: 1152). House Administration Committee Chairman Wayne Hayes reaffirmed this last argument in his public fight against the joint committee when he stated:

> We [the House] are ready to go. We are on the threshold, and I do not want to see us back up [Hopkins, 1972: 458-459].

While it may be true that implementing a joint computer operation would set computer applications in the House back a few years, starting out on separate tracks set any hopes for a coordinated system back a decade or more.

Once the joint committee proposal died, little discussion on cooperation or coordination occurred as each chamber went its own way. As the consulting firm of McKinsey and Company reported to the Congress, the state of the information art in Congress was "ensnarled in problems and issues resolved in the private sector over a decade ago." There was duplication of effort and a proliferation of hardware "owned by a number of competing and parochial groups." In almost every realm, one saw a parallel development of "jealously guarded applications, similar in purpose, but not compatible in concept or even design language" (Gregory, 1978: 100).

Even for the most simple applications, such as monitoring the flow of legislative decisions, the House and Senate could not agree on a single bill status system. The House opted for a simpler "quick and dirty" look at legislation, while the Senate developed a richer data base, which included the monitoring of amendments. The Senate and the Library of Congress have always been more cooperative and both used the same bill status system and shared the work. The closest thing to cooperation between the House and Senate in this realm is the sharing of computer tapes to avoid duplicate data entry. In the creative words of a staff member:

A passerby might think something funny is going on each night at midnight on Capitol Holl. A Capitol policeman makes a series of pickups and dropoffs on a regular schedule. Far from being a drug deal in process or another case of bribery in high office, it is the routine swapping of computer tapes between the House, Senate and Library of Congress which have been updated during the evening and will be ready to go on line in the wee hours of the morning.

In 1977, the Policy Coordinating Group for Technology Development was created to improve House and Senate cooperation. While coordination had improved on the technical and programming level, little cooperation was evident in terms of policy. Senior staff members from the House Administration Committee, Senate Rules Committee, and the Congressional Research Service were appointed to "coordinate the development of a technology-supported information system" (U.S. Congress, Senate, Policy Coordinating Group for Technology Development, 1978: 1). They proceeded to create a series of task forces made up of technical experts to study coordination on particular applications. While one of the members of the coordinating group, Boyd Alexander, director of H.I.S., optimistically predicted that "all of Congress is finally starting to look at itself as a whole in the areas of information and computers, and that is where I think the future is" (Flato, 1977: 256), little concrete progress has been made toward improving cooperation. Each chamber looks at the other with a bit of amusement and fear—not the kinds of emotions that engender cooperative effort.

COMPUTER ADOPTION IN OTHER REALMS

The Library of Congress

While the House and the Senate went their separate ways in computerization, the Library of Congress and its subunit, the Congressional Research Service, were also on the move. The initial impetus came from the professional librarians, who foresaw the applicability of computers for bibliographic record keeping and developed the MARC (Machine Readable Card) System, which led to the development of SCORPIO (Subject/Content Oriented Retrieval Program for Information On Line) and a group of bibliographic data bases for selectively retrieving bibliographic data on books, articles, and convention papers. When this system came on line in 1980 the traditional card catalogue became an inefficient anachronism. Until 1979, the Library of Congress used a duplicate bibliographic system, filing a physical card in the card catalogue and entering the information in the computer. After that time the computer record became the only one available, and there was no turning back.

The Congressional Research Service really rode on the coattails of the Library of Congress. Once the machinery was available, CRS looked around for applications. As pointed out by a CRS staff member:

> We at CRS first applied computers to the ongoing activities which were just too hard to do without mechanization. By law we had to publish the *Digest of Public Bills*. We applied the computer to this arduous task as a sorting and composing tool.

> It was not until 1973 that CRS went beyond using the computer to automate traditional bibliographic functions. The Senate Rules Committee asked for a set of brief reports on key issues. After a fifteen month development period, Issue Briefs went on-line. Only six Senate offices were in the pilot project and had terminals in their offices, but the Issue Briefs soon became "best sellers." When the Senate was ready to move and put terminals in all offices, we had a real product to sell.

Structural and staffing changes in Congress imposed by the Legislative Reorganization Act of 1970 put new pressures on CRS that stimulated computer applications. In a key staff member's words:

> Selective dissemination of information began as an in-house project to keep the CRS experts up on their fields. Journals would be scanned and handwritten 3 by 5 cards would be delivered each week. With increasing numbers of journals, the task became more and more difficult, but it was not until the Legislative Reorganization Act of 1970 tripled the CRS staff that providing the service was impossible without a computer to search, store, sort and print targeted bibliographies each week.

CRS has played an important role in training potential users and making computer utilization easy and convenient. Staff members are encouraged and cajoled into attending training sessions. One training expert with experience both in Congress and on the outside pointed out that

> compared to the business world there was a real attempt to get user feedback and confusing systems were simplified to make the user more comfortable. Users were constantly queried as to the utility of various information products and at times products were revised to better fit user needs. We tried to make the users a part of the development process.

In order to encourage use, particularly by offices without their own terminals, the Library of Congress installed terminals in their various resource centers scattered around the congressional office buildings and staffed them with experts who could "hold the hands" of reluctant users.

Congressional Committees

While congressional committees were treated much like individual members of their respective chambers in terms of computer utilization, some committees began creating data bases and manipulation techniques of their own. The Joint Committee on Internal Revenue and Taxation sought out and finally received direct access to a series of Internal Revenue Service simulations that allowed them to project the consequences of various tax proposals. The creation of the Congressional Budget Office in 1974 stimulated the creation of new data bases and the acquisition of a series of commercial economic simulation models and eventually the creation of an in-house model.

ADMINISTRATION OF COMPUTERS IN CONGRESS

Any group that designs and runs a computer system in Congress, also has the potential to shape the legislative process [Glass, 1970: 1150].

The battle to determine where computer facilities fit into the organizational structure is more than an academic discussion of the niceties of various organizational options. While a centralized system is touted as providing better control and cost savings due to economy of scale and decentralization supposedly gives better service to users (Kraemer and King, 1975: 4-11), the underlying consideration in the placement of computers is political. On the state legislative level, the pattern has been to assimilate computers rather informally by placing control so as to accommodate existing legislative power interests (Worthley, 1977b: 160). In Congress a similar pattern emerged. On the House side some jockeying occurred among the Government Operations Committee, House Administration Committee, Rules Committee, Appropriations Committee, and the clerk of House for ascendency over control, but the Committee on House Administration was more aggressive and won out (Hopkins, 1972: 459). The House Information System was created to handle the day-to-day promotion, development, and administration of computers in the House, while the Committee on House Administration and its subunits retained control over policy.

H.I.S. is staffed with a combination of technical experts and political administrators. As with much of the staffing in Congress, the administrators are the personal representatives of the chair of the oversight committee. Frank Ryan, the initial director of H.I.S., was clearly Chairman Wayne Hayes's man, and when Hayes left the House, Ryan was replaced by Boyd Alexander, new Chairman Frank Thompson's (D-NJ) man. Other staff members also found their jobs in jeopardy when their patrons lost power. Although current House Administration Committee Chairman Augustus Hawkins (D-CA) did not drop Alexander, considerable "housecleaning" took place at lower levels.

The actual oversight of H.I.S. has gone through a series of transformations. Until 1974 the H.I.S. director reported directly to the chair of the

House Administration Committee, but once he had secured computer services under his committee, Chairman Wayne Hayes showed little interest in day-to-day administration. Between 1974 and 1976, an Ad Hoc Subcommittee on Computers emerged, only to be replaced by the more formal and better staffed Policy Group on Information and Computers in 1976 (U.S. Congress, House, Commission on Administrative Review, 1977b: 208). Under the chairmanship of Charlie Rose the Policy Group took an active role in studying computer applications, promoting usage, setting policy, and actively overseeing the day-to-day operations of H.I.S. (U.S. Congress, House, Commission on Administrative Review, 1978: 462-463).

The Policy Group suffered from lack of interest and too deep an involvement in everyday decisions. Three of the members seldom came to meetings, and Rose essentially became the committee. He began to lose interest in the details also. When Hawkins took over as House Administration Committee chairman, he was much more interested in H.I.S. than his predecessor and felt that the Policy Group had become too much of an advocate of computers and H.I.S. interests. He wanted more control over H.I.S. centered in the committee. Acting on the wishes of Hawkins, the Policy Group lost its staff and oversight functions and only retained the right to make policy recommendations and long-range planning suggestions. H.I.S. is now clearly under the control of the House Administration Committee as a whole and faces a more critical and hetergeneous group of masters.

Senate computer operations are managed by a troika composed of the Committee on Rules and Administration, the sergeant at arms, and the secretary of the Senate. The Senate Computer Center is a department within the Sergeant at Arms Office and does not exhibit the independence or promotional tendency of H.I.S. The sergeant at arms takes primary responsibility for computerized mailings under the correspondence management system. The secretary of the Senate manages computer applications related to the public record and the Rules and Administration Committee is responsible for overall policy. Although the Senate chose not to centralize administration, the Senate's approach has always been one of determining what senators need and centralizing the provision of services to all members. Chartrand (1976c: 320) concludes that the division of responsibilities for various services had "sometimes prolonged developmental undertakings."

Neither the House approach of centralizing policy making and providing users a great deal of freedom in choosing services nor the Senate approach of dividing policy making concerning computers and centrally providing set packages of services seems to stand out as better, more efficient, or more appropriate. Little realistic discussion occurs about the possibility of creating a congressional computer center to supersede the existing organizations. No one is willing to take on the power battle and no firm evidence exists as to how such a center should be organized. Members of Congress and their staffs have become accustomed to the current state of affairs and would be reluctant to give up a familiar system with which they are generally satisfied for an unknown quantity.

PATTERN OF COMPUTER GROWTH

Growth in Availability

The availability of computers in society in general and in Congress in particular has shown rapid growth during the last decade. It is projected that computers will be as common as telephones throughout American society by 1990 (Laudon, 1977: 6). Table 4.2 reveals that no matter what measure one uses, access to computers has steadily grown since 1970. In Congress, what was once a novelty has become a standard operating procedure. While availability does not dictate either the quantity or quality of use, the lack of availability rules out usage (see Chapter 5 for data on usage patterns).

Rules concerning the availability of computer terminals in the House and Senate have been increasingly loosened. In the Senate, general provision of terminals to all offices was followed by providing terminals to committee staffs and then by allowing each senator to have up to four terminals in his or her state offices funded by the Senate. In the House, members continue to have the choice of using some of their office funds for terminals, and have been increasingly allowed to join the Member Information Network (MIN), which gives them access to Library of Congress, H.I.S., and commercial data bases. While members may hesitate to use computers for a number of reasons, lack of availability is no longer one of them.

Funding Computerization

Funding is the life blood of computer services. Budgetary commitments indicate membership support and determine the kinds of development that

TABLE 4.2   Indicators of Computer Availability in Congress and in Society in General

	1971	1972	1973	1974	1975	1976	1977	1978	1979	1980	1981
Societal Measures											
Number of terminals per 1000 Americans[a]		.5					5			10	
Number of computers in federal government[a]	5300					9648	10282				
State Legislatures											
Computerized bill status[b]		25					36		36		
Electronic voting[b]		35					44		45		
Library of Congress											
Number of terminals[c]	6	32	44	138	304	711	1149	1711	2120		
Number of computer staff[d]											
Funding (thousands)[d, e]	$1253						$13734				
Congress House											
H.I.S. staff (authorized)[e,f]	1	31	122	134	161	226	210	225	195	210	203
Number of offices with terminals[g]					30	195	208	243	300	326	
Member Information Network[h]						30	170	266			

(continued)

TABLE 4.2 Continued

	1971	1972	1973	1974	1975	1976	1977	1978	1979	1980	1981
Congress/Senate											
Senate Computer Center staff[c]											185
Terminals in offices[i]				45	68	80	98				

SOURCES: a. Laudon (1977: 6).
           b. Chartrand (1976a: 27).
           c. U.S. Congress, Senate, Committee on Appropriations (1979: 63).
           d. U.S. Congress, Senate, Policy Coordinating Group for Technology Development (1978: 27).
           e. Chartrand (1980).
           f. U.S. Congress, House, House Information System (1981b, 1979b: 11).
           g. Clerk of the House Reports (quarterly).
           h. U.S. Congress, House, Committee on House Administration (1979c).
           i. U.S. Congress, Senate, Commission on the Operation of the Senate (1977c).

can be planned and products delivered. By and large, funding for computers was generous and relatively easily secured during the first decade (see Table 4.3). The computer-related aspect of the budget was lost in the general appropriations for the legislative branch and little conflict emerged. H.I.S. took a small cut in its healthy growth in 1979, but few took much notice. Senate computer funding was harder to isolate since it appeared in three budget categories and was the subject of even less debate.

In the House, particularly, the winds began to change in 1981. A number of factors came together to put a real scare into H.I.S. and potentially hamper its future growth. After the 1980 elections, almost everyone was a born-again budget cutter. The newly elected Republican Senate set the pace by cutting its operating budget by 10 percent. Budget-conscious Republicans in the House sought to dramatize excessive federal spending by focusing on spending in their own backyard (Arieff, 1981b). H.I.S. was an easy target. Over the years, its appropriations had been included in those of the House Administration Committee. With a budget of over $9 million, it dwarfed its parent committee and spawned jealousy from other committees with much more modest funding. Because it had such a large budget, a percentage cut from H.I.S. would also make much more of a dent in the legislative operating expenses than would accrue from a similar cut from other committees. Cutting H.I.S. meant delaying equipment purchase and the development of new services, but not laying people off, as would be the case for most committees whose primary budget category is salaries. In Representative Charlie Rose's words:

> Computer applications were a safe area to cut. If you cut people, they scream and vote differently. If you cut a computer off, it just sighs and the fan turns off.

Underlying the desire to cut the budget was a growing concern about H.I.S. and computers in general that had been muted until linked with the budget issue. Representative Bill Frenzel (R-MN), ranking minority member on the House Administration Committee and in line to be chairman should the Republicans gain control of the House, took the lead in criticizing the aggressiveness of H.I.S. in selling its products and the rapid growth in services:

> I am nervous about undertaking new adventures in H.I.S. until we learn to control and understand the old adventures and decide which of them are working and which are not [Groban, 1981: 5].

TABLE 4.3 Funding Levels for Computer Utilization in Congress

	1971	1972	1973	1974	1975	1976	1977	1978	1979	1980	1981
House											
Authorized H.I.S. funding level (thousands)[a]*	$434	$1,500	$2,400	$3,089	$4,500	$6,729	$7,980	$10,995	$9,889	$9,881	$7,509
Change from previous year		245%	60%	29%	46%	66%	19%	38%	-10%	-.01%	-24%
Authorized H.I.S. funding corrected for inflation						$6,729 (base year)	$5,707	$7,327	$6,075	$5,570	$3,286
Senate											
Authorized Senate Computer Center funding level (thousands)[a,b]						$2,461	$8,099	$10,672	$14,515	$14,048	$13,939

SOURCES: a. U.S. Congress, Senate, Policy Coordinating Group on Technology Development (1978); see also U.S. Congress, House, House Information System (1981b).

b. Chartrand and Borrell (1981); U.S. Congress, Senate, Committee on Appropriations (1979).

*These figures only reflect H.I.S. expenditures, not those for services contracted by individual House offices and congressional committees. Including such expenditures would add over $5 million to the total computer expenditures.

While much of the criticism came from Republicans, even majority leader Jim Wright (D-TX) joined the fray by exclaiming:

It seems to me that it [H.I.S.] has just run amuck. . . . Gone completely out of control, [and] resisted efforts of Congressional oversight [Groban, 1981: 5].

Other members echoed that "H.I.S. has displayed a penchant for pursuing programs of questionable value and limited applicability" (U.S. Congress, House, Committee on House Administration, 1981: 168). Another member argued that H.I.S. had a penchant for "answering questions no one had asked." Attempting to strike while his victim was down, Representative James Collins (R-TX) introduced a resolution to disband H.I.S. completely since its services were readily available from the executive branch and the Library of Congress (Congressional Record, 1981a). While H.I.S. was in no danger of demise, the budget battle unleashed considerable anti-H.I.S. sentiment.

The H.I.S. budget fight in 1981 revealed a repeated political pattern. Arguments and decision formats in a political setting are much like bullets on a battle field. Proponents and opponents would like you to believe that their arguments are consistent and immutably true, while in fact they change to fit the situation. Just like the advancing army that picks up and uses the ammunition of the retreating forces, political adversaries are not above using the same technique in a political fray. Both the Republican proponents of drastically cutting H.I.S. funding and the Democrats who wished for much less severe cuts revealed inconsistency in their overall arguments, but consistency in their selective use of arguments for strategic purposes.

In their attempt to pass President Reagan's overall budget, Republicans in the House argued that the budget had to be viewed and voted on as an integrated whole, but when it came to voting on the legislative appropriations package, which is not part of the president's budget, they wanted to use a committe-by-committee approach because it would give them a better chance of inflicting deep cuts in H.I.S. The Democrats, who in the past had pushed for committee-by-committee appropriation votes for internal expenditures and liked to look at the president's budget (at least when he was a Democrat) as a unified package, proposed dealing with the Reagan budget piece by piece but fought to consider the legislative appropriations as a total package where they could better protect H.I.S. (Arieff, 1981b; Congressional Record, 1981: H1092-H1114). The humor

of such transparent inconsistency was not lost on Representative Bob
Eckart (D-TX):

> I can not help but be reminded about the story by a famous
> midwestern prohibition violator who said that when he sells liquor it
> is called bootlegging, but when his patrons serve it on silver platters
> in mansions, it is called hospitality [Congressional Record, 1981:
> H1114].

While the opposition to H.I.S. brought together fiscal conservatives and
members with deep concerns about H.I.S., some members saw a partisan
underpinning to the battle. Representative Jack Hightower (D-TX) looked
at the fight over computer funding and exclaimed,

> I can only assume that this effort is a partisan one, designed more to
> hamper the effectiveness of a House still with a Democratic majority
> [Congressional Record, 1981: H1092].

With their majority in the House, the Democrats won the battle to have
the legislative appropriations bill dealt with as a whole and fought back a
Republican challenge to cut the overall committee appropriations even
more than the 9 percent they favored (Arieff, 1981a). H.I.S. led the pack
in cuts, having its appropriation cut by over 20 percent.

Aside from having over $2 million cut from their budget, H.I.S.
received some additional bad news in 1981. They were given a staff limit
of 203 and lost some of their freedom and autonomy. From now on,
formal approval by the Committee on House Administration will be
required for all new projects, and their aggressive outreach program was
dropped (Groban, 1981: 5). In many members' minds, according to a staff
member, H.I.S. had "just become too eager. Whatever a member asked,
they did. Now there will be some evaluation and prior approval of
projects."

Charlie Rose, one of the most important change agents, took a double
beating in 1981. His Policy Group on Information and Computers was
stripped of its staff and oversight functions and the H.I.S. budget was
slashed. Despite the seeming reversals, he took it rather philosophically:

> The cuts and changes don't really discourage me. The ground has
> been well watered. Perhaps we need to let it sink in a bit before we
> begin expanding again.

The Adoption Proceedings   143

TABLE 4.4   Legislative Branch Computer Expenditures[a]

| | 1970 | | 1980 | |
	Budget	Percentage of Legislative ADP Expenditures	Budget	Percentage of Legislative ADP Expenditures
House of Represen- tatives	$ 434,000	9	$11,381,000	19
Senate	$ 298,000	6	$14,048,000[b]	23
Library of Congress	$1,253,000	26	$15,587,000	25
General Accounting Office	$ 907,000	19	$ 6,350,000[c]	10
Government Printing Office	$2,004,000	41	$ 9,849,000	16
Congressional Budget Office	$1,208,000[d]	–	$ 3,383,000	6
Office of Technology Assessment	–[e]	–	$ 214,000	.3
	$4,896,000		$61,279,000	

SOURCE: Chartrand and Borrell (1981: 14).

a. Budget figures provided by relevant legislative personnel include equipment, personnel, and contracting services. The option for each House member to spend $15,000 annually on computer services from clerk-hire funds is not included.
b. The Senate figure has declined from $14,515,000 in 1979 due to the purchase of ADP equipment.
c. U.S. General Accounting Office (1980).
d. Figure is for year of CBO's first formal budget (1976) and is not part of 1970 total. For 1980 figures, see U.S. Congress, Congressional Budget Office (1981). (CBO's policy is to use existing House and Senate computer facilities wherever possible; 73 percent of 1980 costs were for commercial services and 27 percent were for reimbusement to House and Senate computer centers.)
e. The Office of Technology Assessment spent $100,000 in fiscal year 1979 for the use of time-sharing services and peripheral equipment to access the system. This figure is .002 percent of the total legislative ADP expenditure percentage; 1980 ADP funding is taken from U.S. Congress, Office of Technology Assessment (1980).

Perhaps his optimism stems partly from the fact that the H.I.S. cut may not be all that it seems. In the past H.I.S. provided all its services free, but had begun to use a system of reimbursements from other committees to cover services provided. These amounted to $1.5 million in 1980 and approximately $3 million in 1981. With this growth and plans to charge individual members for some services, H.I.S. may well show that it received a symbolic cut, but will suffer few ill effects. Perceiving this trend, Representative John Rhodes (R-AR) predicted that the Democrats would soon push for increased individual office accounts to pick up the slack (Congressional Record, 1981: H1116).

Not only have the total expenditures for computers in Congress changed over the years, but so has the distribution of funds among congressional agencies. In the early period, computers were primarily the domain of the Library of Congress and the support agencies such as the Government Printing Office and the General Accounting Office. More recently, the concentration of computer expenditures has migrated back to the chambers themselves (see Table 4.4). This shift indicates a change in accounting responsibilities, but, more importantly, it indicates a shift in functions. While the initial locus of computers reflected more mundane administrative applications, the current pattern implies a shift toward applications associated with policy making and representational functions.

CONCLUSION

The process of computer adoption in Congress seems to have reached a plateau. After a dramatic decade in which Congress went from computer illiteracy to what has been called "the world's largest concentration of policy-makers using on-line systems" (Gregory, 1979b: 1), the pace of development has slowed. Members of Congress at first resisted computerization, then a few change agents stepped out and showed the way. Rapid adoption followed and now immediate access to information through computerization is the expected norm. A new equilibrium has developed. Most members of Congress and their staffs are comfortable with computerization and satisfied with what is available. The process of moving Congress into the computer age was relatively quick and painless. There were no major disasters to slow down the process. New computerized products generally delivered what they promised without evident and clearly negative unanticipated consequences. However, while availability is important, it does not tell the whole story. Before we can understand the ultimate importance of computers in Congress, we need to know exactly what is available via computer, who is using it, and for what purpose.

5 APPLICATIONS AND USAGE PATTERNS

BY THE TIME that Congress was equipped to use computerized information resources, considerable development had occurred at the state legislative level and among commercial vendors. The question for Congress was not so much how computers could be used, but rather which of the vast array of options should be embarked upon first. As with the states,

> the norm in legislative use of EDP has been to take a rather narrow, cautious approach, limiting applications to procedural needs such as bill status [Worthley, 1977b: 7].

Computer applications for Congress fall into two general categories. In one group are those applications that apply to the aggregate role of Congress as a legislative decision-making unit, while the second group includes those applications used by individual members of Congress in managing their offices and dealing with the demands placed on them by the electorate. A third group of purely administrative applications, such as payroll and inventories, are nonpolitical and have no impact on policy making; these will not be discussed. Proponents of computerization in Congress emphasized the legislative applications and gave short shrift to those applications with primary concern for individual offices. The dividing lines between categories are not absolute, but are generally accepted by users and observers alike.

SYSTEMWIDE LEGISLATIVE APPLICATIONS

Monitoring and Tracking Legislation

Congress deals with thousands of pieces of legislation each year. Public records as to the disposition of each bill or resolution must be kept accurately while individual members of Congress need to monitor what has been introduced and anticipate required decisions. Prior to computerization, researchers in Congress and outside relied on such paper products as the House and Senate Calendars and the *Digest of Public General Bills and Resolutions.* These resources were cumbersome to use and often not as timely as would be desired in a fast-moving political environment such as Congress, where finding the correct information immediately is critical.

The decision to adopt a bill status system as the first major computerized effort by Congress was a natural reaction to the need for speedy and accurate information on legislation. While the House, Senate, and Library of Congress developed their own systems, continual enhancement of each and diligent attempts to avoid duplication of effort have led to systems with very similar capabilities. The LEGIS (Legislative Information System) supplies basically the same information to each chamber. All bills and resolutions can be traced by bill number, sponsor, cosponsor, and subject matter. A chronology of the bill provides information on committee referral, types and dates of action, and current status. The file is up to date within a few hours of action. Sophisticated searches of the file allow the combining of categories. For example, it would be possible to produce a list of all legislation introduced by a particular member on a specified subject. The data base for the Senate is a bit more detailed and allows for the tracking of amendments and their purposes, presidential messages, nominations, committee scheduling, leadership floor scheduling, and the provision for a keyword search (U.S. Congress, Senate, Committee on Rules and Administration, 1980: 1; see Figure 5.1)

Although the existence of separate data bases in the House and Senate may seem inefficient, key staff members argue that, once the duplicate data entry problem was removed through the sharing of computer tapes, the current approach has an advantage. As one put it:

> Having three computer systems is useful since a Senate user can be switched to the House system if the Senate computer is down. Redundancy in communications systems is an advantage, whereas duplication is not.

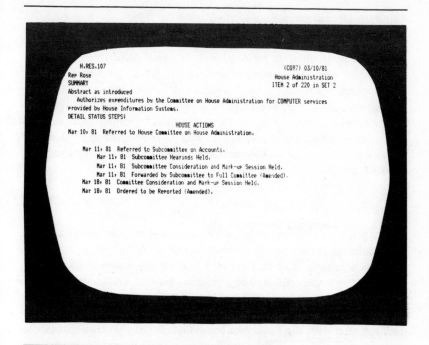

```
        H.RES.107                                               (CG97) 03/10/81
    Rep Rose                                                 House Administration
    SUMMARY                                                  ITEM 2 of 220 in SET 2
    Abstract as introduced
        Authorizes expenditures by the Committee on House Administration for COMPUTER services
    provided by House Information Systems.
    DETAIL STATUS STEPS:
                                    HOUSE ACTIONS
    Mar 10, 81  Referred to House Committee on House Administration.

        Mar 11, 81  Referred to Subcommittee on Accounts.
            Mar 11, 81  Subcommittee Hearings Held.
            Mar 11, 81  Subcommittee Consideration and Mark-up Session Held.
            Mar 11, 81  Forwarded by Subcommittee to Full Committee (Amended).
        Mar 18, 81  Committee Consideration and Mark-up Session Held.
        Mar 18, 81  Ordered to be Reported (Amended).
```

Figure 5.1   Bill Status File (CG97): Bill Summary Option

Scheduling

Much of the real work of Congress goes on in committees. With members of Congress serving simultaneously on a number of committees, scheduling committee meetings to fit the optimal number of members is difficult. Traditionally committee chairs unilaterally scheduled meetings, while in recent years some of this power has been shared with some or all of the committee members. Both the House and Senate have developed committee scheduling programs that work on the basis of a matrix. The person scheduling a committee or subcommittee meeting can see what conflicts occur on a specific date for members of that committee. On the House side, the COMIS (Committee Information and Scheduling) System ran into a great deal of opposition and has remained a voluntary system with incomplete data and limited usage (U.S. Congress, House, Commission on Administrative Review, 1977b: 208). In the Senate committee scheduling participation was required, and the system is used extensively.

Committee Assignments

The party leadership in the Senate is faced with the task of filling committee positions after each election. The final decision on committee assignments must take into account not only the preferences of the senators, but also Senate rules concerning allowable combinations of committee assignments. The committee assignment system is used heavily after each election to check out the implications of various appointments. The system allows the leadership to test out the potential impact of changes in party ratios on the committees and the cumulative impact of a series of assignments.

Decision-Making Information

The process of making policy decisions in Congress involves a series of information-gathering steps. Problems must be identified and defined. Potential solutions must be canvassed and the consequences of choosing various alternatives defined. The legislation must be drafted and a record kept of the final outcome. The legislative leadership plays a crucial role in shepherding bills through the process and lining up votes. Policy making does not stop with the passage of legislation. Legislators must oversee the application of the policy they pass and be prepared should new problems arise. At each stage in the process, the computer has been harnessed to provide more comprehensive information more quickly.

Problem-definition information

Bibliographic searches. Until a few years ago, legislative assistants or congressional speech writers depended on personal contacts with committee or outside experts, reading lists of mass media or specialized journals, or their own ingenuity in going through the Library of Congress card catalog or periodical indexes to become aware of new research or arguments concerning their areas of public policy. Members of Congress used even less comprehensive search patterns and depended on staff or constituents and interest groups to make them aware of what information should be consumed.

The introduction of computerized bibliographic data bases by the Library of Congress made more comprehensive and efficient bibliographic searches possible. The Library of Congress has computerized three bibliographic data files. The Library of Congress Computerized Catalog (LCCC) contains the card catalog information on all English-language books added

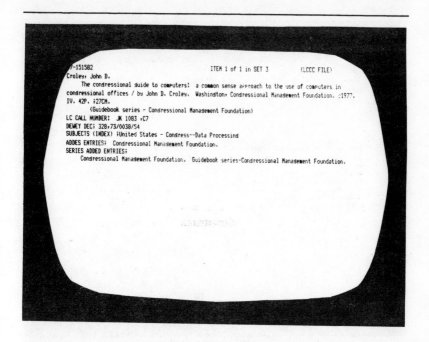

Figure 5.2   Library of Congress Card Catalog File (SCORPIO/LCCC File)

to the Library since 1969. It can be searched by author, title, or subject, as is the case with all the bibliographic files. A person can update previous searches by looking only at the new material. The Bibliographic Citation File (CITN) includes bibliographic citations for current periodicals, convention papers, interest groups, and lobby groups, plus a brief synopsis of current periodicals, academic journals, convention papers, interest group publications, government documents, and United Nations periodicals on topics of concern to Congress. The National Referral Center Resources File (NRCM) contains a collection of more than 10,000 organizations and individual contacts qualified to answer questions on virtually any topic in science, technology, and the social sciences (see Figures 5.2, 5.3, and 5.4).

While the computerized bibliographic services provide easy access to a multitude of potential sources for defining public policy problems and searching for their solutions, their use requires the initiative and effort of members of Congress and their staffs. In an attempt to make it easier for congressional offices to update themselves on topics of interest, the Congressional Research Service (CRS) maintains a Selective Dissemination

Figure 5.3   Library of Congress Periodical File (SCORPIO/BIBL File)

of Information (SDI) program. Each week over 3000 scholarly reports, popular press articles, and interest group publications are summarized, sorted, and distributed to members and their staffs. The individual recipient fills out a "menu" card, listing the topics on which he or she wishes information, and each week receives a stack of bibliographic slips to pursue if he or she wishes (U.S. Congress, House, Commission on Information and Facilities, 1975b: 45-46). This service promises to keep Congress more aware of current developments and thinking, and to serve as a major conduit for outside analysts into the Congress; however, as a bibliographic process, it is no better than the sources it cites, and depends on the interest and perseverance of its users to have an impact.

Issue briefs. In its role as the research arm of Congress, the Congressional Research Service prepares concise, objective reports on major issues facing the Congress. These issue briefs define the issues, provide background and analysis, and outline the chronology of events that brought the matter to congressional attention, plus note action taken by the Congress. The issue briefs are designed for instantaneous retrieval on computer

Figure 5.4 National Referral Center Data Base (NRCM): Example of Listing Under the Term "Office Automation"

terminals or they can be ordered in hard copy from CRS. In most offices, the computer is used to review specific briefs quickly to determine their applicability before the hard copy version is ordered. Close to 200 issue briefs make up the current file at any one point in time. CRS attempts to keep the material exceptionally timely and relevant (U.S. Congress, House, Commission on Information and Facilities, 1976a: 44, 55). While the computer is not an absolute necessity for creating or disseminating the issue briefs, it does increase efficiency. The interest in issue briefs remains high; CRS handles over 20,000 requests per month for hard copies alone (see Figure 5.5).

Commercial bibliographic data banks. Rather than duplicate the efforts of outside bibliographers, Congress contracts with a series of commercial data banks for specialized bibliographic searches. Some are available to all members of Congress, while others are limited to searches initiated through CRS or particular committees.

IB74105   For Further Info Call 287-5700   ISSUE UPDATED: 01/19/82
Privacy: Information Technology Implications
BACKGROUND AND POLICY ANALYSIS: ITEM 1 of 2 in SET 3
     Disclosures of the extensive nature of Government surveillance and abusive record keeping
activities have increased public concern that there is a need to provide controls to ensure personal
privacy. Improving management and controls of Government information have emerged as important
goals. In general, the growth of record-keeping operations and the widespread use of computers
and communications technology have stimulated the demands for more effective controls and regulations
to ensure protection of personal privacy in a free society. Recent attention has focused on
balancing the legitimate need for information and personal data with the protection of personal
privacy...

Figure 5.5   Congressional Research Service Issue Briefs File (Partial Text)

(1) The *New York Times* Information Bank. The *New York Times* computerized Information Bank abstracts *New York Times* articles from 1969 to date and selected material from over 60 other periodicals. The file grows by over 20,000 abstracts per month and is extensively subject coded for rapid and precise retrieval. The file is quite popular for basic research and speech writing.

Most members like the *New York Times* Information Bank as a data base to get things from, because more likely than not they give some credibility to what is found in the *New York Times* [Chartrand and Morentz, 1979: 131].

(2) Justice Retrieval and Inquiry System (JURIS). JURIS, created by the Department of Justice, allows keyword or subject searches of the U.S. Constitution, U.S. Code, Supreme Court decisions, and briefs and memoranda from the solicitor general and the Tax Division. Checking such

sources to determine what is on the books and the constitutional constraints that might apply is the first step in writing new legislation.

(3) MEDLINE. MEDLINE was created by the National Institute of Health and provides access to bibliographic citations from over 1200 journals in the fields of medical research and public health. Data can be retrieved by subject or author.

(4) NEXIS. Mead Data Central's NEXIS provides full text retrieval of material from major newspapers, magazines, wire services, and the *Federal Register.* Data files can be searched by date, subject, or author [Chartrand and Borrell, 1981: 11).

Social indicators information. Defining public policy problems is more than a matter of access to bibliographic sources. Ideally, the starting point for legislative remedies to social problems would be a universally accepted comprehensive set of social indicators, which would serve as a baseline with which to compare the ideal state of affairs. When the current situation varied significantly from the ideal, Congress would move in to correct the situation that the social indicators verify as a current or impending crisis. In some realms, such as the economy and national defense, widely accepted baseline figures on such things as unemployment or missile superiority can be garnered from the executive branch. The lack of comparable time-series data in the social realm has spawned a so far unsuccessful drive for government-collected social indicators (Gross, 1969: 7). The result is that Congress often does not jump into the policy process until others on the outside have defined the crisis, often on the basis of limited or biased data. The few exceptions to Congress's weakness in this area tend to highlight its limitations rather than indicate a promising trend.

(1) EDSTAT. Through EDSTAT, Congress has access to the National Center for Educational Statistics data drawn from the annual Higher Education General Information Survey. These institution-by-institution statistics on enrollment, expenditures, and degrees granted have some utility for Congress, but fall far short of the social indicator goal of monitoring the actual delivery of the educational system.

(2) The Domestic Information Display System. Using current census data, the Domestic Information Display System, created by the National Aeronautics and Space Administration (NASA) and the Bureau of the Census, provides color-graphic presentations of census data down to the standard metropolitan statistical area (SMSA) level. The system allows combining of data sets and color coding of the results (Bulletin of the American Society for Information Science, 1978: 23). For example, it would be possible to generate a map of the United States differentiating

areas of high average income and low minority residence, high income and high minority residence, low income and low minority residence, and low income and high minority residence. Such a presentation would graphically reveal the economic deprivation of minorities in America. By controlling for a third variable such as education and creating a broader color classification, it would be possible to assess the validity of possible causes.

Canvassing solutions and comparing alternatives

Traditionally, the congressional search for alternative solutions comprised a haphazard mixture of borrowing from other jurisdictions, intuition, research, and creative luck, while evaluations of proposed options stemmed from the accumulated hunches and experience of the members of Congress as influenced by staffs, constituents, colleagues, and outside interests. The computer is unlikely to have much impact on such a process unless it can increase the efficiency of the search, help uncover new material, or provide hard data indicating the unassailable value of one option over another.

Improving the efficiency and comprehensiveness
of information searches

The bibliographic data banks discussed above provide the diligent researcher with both the problems and solutions proposed by outsiders and their evalutions of probable impacts. The LEGIS system keeps track of all the proposed solutions formally introduced by members of Congress.

The computerized *Congressional Record* file maintained by the Library of Congress provides the capability of keyword, subject, and author searches of the *Congressional Record* for material inserted since 1977. A member can search out the arguments and data on a particular bill or subject matter area. Since members of Congress are often looking for information to bolster an intended decision, they might search for statements by fellow members with whom they tend to agree most often (see Figure 5.6).

Decision-facilitating information:
projecting consequences

Members of Congress enter the legislative decision-making arena with policy goals and biases reflecting their individual perspectives and political needs. They need information that will help them decide the most favorable courses of action given these goals. The intuitive projections of others

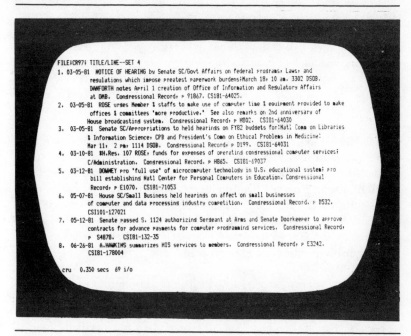

FILE:CR97; TITLE/LINE--SET 4
1. 03-05-81 NOTICE OF HEARING by Senate SC/Govt Affairs on federal programs, laws, and
             regulations which impose greatest paperwork burdens;March 18, 10 am. 3302 DSOB,
             DANFORTH notes April 1 creation of Office of Information and Regulatory Affairs
             at OMB. Congressional Record, p 91867, CS181-64025.
2. 03-05-81 ROSE urges Member & staffs to make use of computer time & equipment provided to make
             offices & committees 'more productive.' See also remarks on 2nd anniversary of
             House broadcasting system. Congressional Record, p H802, CS181-64030
3. 03-05-81 Senate SC/Appropriations to held hearings on FY82 budgets for:Nat'l Comm on Libraries
             & Information Science, CPB and President's Comm on Ethical Problems in Medicine:
             Mar 11, 2 pm; 1114 DSOB, Congressional Record, p D199, CS181-64031
4. 03-10-81 &H.Res. 107 ROSE, funds for expenses of operating consressional computer services;
             C/Administration, Congressional Record, p H865, CS181-69037
5. 03-12-81 DOWNEY pro 'full use' of microcomputer technology in U.S. educational system; pro
             bill establishing Nat'l Center for Personal Computers in Education, Congressional
             Record, p E1070, CS181-71053
6. 05-07-81 House SC/Small Business held hearings on affect on small businesses
             of computer and data processing industry competition, Congressional Record, p D532,
             CS1101-127021
7. 05-12-81 Senate passed S. 1124 authorizing Sergeant at Arms and Senate Doorkeeper to approve
             contracts for advance payments for computer programming services, Congressional Record,
             p S4878, CS181-132-35
8. 06-26-81 A.HAWKINS summarizes HIS services to members, Congressional Record, p E3242,
             CS181-178004

cru 0.350 secs 69 i/o

Figure 5.6 Congressional Record Abstract File (CR97): Listing of *Congressional Record* Insertions Indexed Under the Term "Computers" (Partial Listing)

have little more credibility than their own and are difficult to prove right or wrong before action is taken. Legislators search for hard data on which to base their decisions. A variety of simulation models have been developed to help project the consequences of various congressional decisions.

Simulation models are simplified representations of complex processes that attempt to assess the consequences of various decisions. Simulations come in two basic forms. Logic-based models predict the future through deductive reasoning. Assumptions with some degree of verification in the real world are linked together through mathematical or logical equations to predict an outcome. Actual data may serve as the basis for some of the equations, but the heart of the model is its assumption about human behavior. Data-based or "feed-forward" models base their predictions much more heavily on data from previous decisions, with minor alterations to account for new decisions (Laudon, 1977: 35). The heart of a feed-forward model is its historical data base rather than its sophisticated internal logic. Congress relies on both types of models and reveals the strengths and weaknesses of each.

Simulation models are touted as making legislators more aware of the full range of impact of their decisions, potentially yielding counterintuitive predictions and moving Congress away from its typical short-range solutions to a concern for long-term problem solving. Simulation models also allow the decision maker to ask "what if" questions in which controllable factors are set at various levels or uncontrollable factors take on specific values (Kornbluh, 1977: ii-vii).

Simulation models do not lead to automatic decisions, however. As a simplification of reality, each model must make some assumptions and use limited data. Legislators disagreeing with the conclusions of a model will attack its assumptions and the data it uses. Model outputs get caught up in the politics of the situation. When competing models exist, legislators choose those conclusions that best fit their own values. Even if members can agree on the assumptions, they may not act on that basis. As one staff member involved with modeling explained:

> Some congressmen get very upset with the assumptions which serve as a basis for our projections. It is not so much that they disagree but they can't afford to accept them politically. We won't compromise our assumptions, but will be glad to run our data using another set of assumptions.

Or, as the CRS expert on socioeconomic models argued:

> The career of socio-economic models is likely to be shaped by the organizational and political environment in which they are used [Kornbluh, 1977: 50].

Logic-based models. Congress and its various units have contracted with a number of commercial firms to provide computer-based, large-scale econometric models of the U.S. economy. Models created by Data Resources Inc. (DRI), the Wharton School, and Chase Manhattan Bank can be used interactively to predict GNP and other economic indicators based on the model assumptions or by entering one's own assumptions at key points in the model to receive altered consequences. The growth of model availability has been largely a defensive strategy on the Hill.

Although the Congressional Budget Office has created its own model, in which it has the most faith, it compares its projections with those used by the executive branch. During the 1981 legislative battle over President

Reagan's tax and budget proposals, each side trotted out that set of economic projections which bolstered its particular case and questioned the assumptions and therefore the validity of the models used by the opposing side. The Reagan projections were considerably more optimistic than those of the CBO, which was dominated by economists with less confidence in the "supply-side" economic assumptions on which Reagan based his program. Supply-side economists believed that the Reagan budget would break the self-fulfilling prophesy of continued inflation, while the CBO experts and most of the private forecasters did not build such assumptions into their models (Towell, 1981: 681-682).

The logic-based models are most subject to political entanglements since they are extremely complex and based on a number of abstract assumptions. They tend to get tagged very quickly as "supply-side" or "demand-side" models or become known for their optimistic or pessimistic projections. The large-scale econometric models attempt to project simultaneously a whole series of consequences that combine to cause a final effect. With such wide societal disagreement on economic assumptions, it should be no surprise that no one model has become universally accepted. One recent analysis, for example, took the Congressional Budget Office model to task, arguing that its assumptions favored expanded government spending and involvement in the economy (Miller and Rolnick, 1981). During the 1981 battles over the budget and tax cuts, the conflicting assumptions came to the forefront. OMB Director David Stockman admitted changing the assumptions of his model so that the figures would come out "right" politically (Greider, 1981).

Feed-forward models. Given the political nature of Congress, the simpler and more straightforward the simulation model, the more likely it is to avoid partisan sniping. The feed-forward projection models, which attempt to predict the "first-order" impacts of policy choices based on past data on similar choices, have more utility to members of Congress. These models assume that people will behave the same under a new set of decisions as they did in the past and only attempt to predict the consequences of different distributions of resources or distribution formulas.

The Individual Income Tax Estimation System developed by the Department of the Treasury simulates the 1040 tax form. Using data from previous years on such things as number of dependents and charitable deductions, it projects changes in tax revenue based on changing laws concerning tax liability for categoric groups of taxpayers. By knowing the number of deductions taken in previous years and changing the amount of the deduction allowed, it is possible to project the overall revenue implications of such a change. The model assumes that everything affecting taxes, except for the tax laws, will remain constant from the previous data collection point. A similar model exists for projecting the consequences of changes in corporate tax laws.

The Social Programs Model developed by Applied Urbanetics, Inc., provides a projection of federal fund distribution under various proposed formulas for social programs such as education, assistance to the aged, crime prevention, and child care. Expected funding can be determined for states, counties, or local jurisdictions (U.S. Congress, House, Committee on House Administration, 1976). Under this system a member of Congress can immediately determine the impact of various funding formulas on his or her district.

The Transfer Income Model developed for the Department of Health, Education and Welfare estimates the changes in federal programs in terms of entitlement costs aggregated by income class and geographic area (U.S. Congress, House, Commission on Information and Facilities, 1975a: 46). The model describes the steps a social worker would use in determining eligibility for public assistance and estimates the number of people eligible. By combining allowable payments with census data it is possible to determine the amount of funds that would be expended under various sets of distribution rules (U.S. Congress, House, Commission on Administrative Review, 1977b: 233). A Countercycle Revenue Sharing Model can be used to test the effects of alternate versions of revenue sharing formulas (U.S. Congress, Senate, Committee on Rules and Administration, 1980: 10).

While the availability of projected consequences of public policy decisions does not guarantee their use, Congress is better able to determine the consequences of its decisions through computer-based simulations, should it so desire.

Further analysis tools

Committee data bases. A number of committees have established policy analysis data bases with special applicability to their substantive responsibilities. Some of the current data bases include military manpower requests and capabilities, corporate ownership and control data, consulting contract data, and specialized document indexes (U.S. Congress, Senate, Committee on Rules and Administration, 1980: 10).

Statistical analysis. Aside from simulations and bibliographic data banks, congressional computer banks make possible sophisticated analysis tools for individual members of Congress or committees to apply to their own data. The Statistical Package for the Social Sciences (SPSS) is available through CRS to provide increased analysis capacity to Congress (U.S. Congress, Senate, Committee on Rules and Administration, 1980: 10).

Bill drafting assistance

On the state legislative level, computers have been introduced extensively for the purpose of drafting legislation. Such systems reduce the steps necessary for printing and allow for direct insertion of amendments to provide an immediate clean copy of a revised bill (U.S. Congress, House, Commission on Administrative Review, 1977b: 235). Congressional developments in this area have been somewhat more modest and halting. The Senate Office of Legislative Counsel introduced a system largely designed to increase the efficiency of printing in 1978, but the system was soon overwhelmed by the volume of legislation. Enhancements and revisions are in the process of being made to expand the system's capability (U.S. Congress, Senate, Committee on Rules and Administration, 1980: 17).

Budgeting Information

One of the most obvious areas for heavy computer usage is the budget. The resurgence of congressional interest in the federal budget, exemplified by the passage of the Budget and Impoundment Act and the creation of the Congressional Budget Office, led to vastly improved computerized budget data tailored to congressional needs. Prior to the Budget Act, Congress depended on the Office of Management and Budget for its information. Coming "hat in hand," they received only that information OMB wished to share and were presented with it in the form OMB found useful. Unfortunately, Congress's information needs did not match those of the OMB. The OMB needs only static information to come up with a single budget document, whereas Congress needs a constant updating of budget information to track the cumulative impact of various budget decisions at specified points in time. In Representative Charlie Rose's (1978: 14) words:

> The budget is a living document, constantly changing as it moves. . . . The only way there can be any control of the budget is to be able to track its component parts, to find out what makes it tick. And this can only be done with the latest computer technology.

The Congressional Budget Office received a mandate to employ computer technology and moved in quickly to fill the necessary voids through in-house data packages, modifications of OMB data, and the use of commercial packages. The computer-facilitated analysis applications are numerous. For example, the Comparative Statement of New Budget Authority (CSBA) system tracks the president's budget as it goes through Congress to provide a "snapshot" of an appropriations bill at any given point in time, taking into account current committee and floor actions in the House and Senate (U.S. Congress, House, Commission on Information and Facilities, 1975b: 49-50). Prior to the budget procedure mandated by the Budget Act, Congress dealt with the budget in a piecemeal fashion and could never see the total picture. One of the purposes of the act was to change this approach, and the CSBA makes this possible.

The CBO Congressional Scorekeeping System facilitates a related goal of the Budget Act. Under the new procedure, Congress is required to pass a budget resolution setting a target for expenditures. The Scorekeeping program reveals how close the existing budget proposal is to the target set in the May budget resolution (Rivlin, 1978: 25). CBO also uses the computer to keep track of recision and deferral requested by the president and to project the costs of proposed federal programs.

The Member Budget Information System (MBIS) developed by H.I.S. provides individual members of the House with budget information on current or past proposals. The system allows the user to look at the actual expenditures for previous years and to identify patterns of surplus or deficit.

Decision-Recording Information

The large number of recorded votes in the House and the large membership make the relatively leisurely, but time consuming, calling of the role an anachronism in a chamber feeling the pressure of limited time and expanding responsibilities. The computerized electronic voting system installed in 1973 is activated by members inserting their identification cards into one of the 44 voting stations located throughout the House chamber. Each voting station allows the member to vote "Yea," "Nay," or "Present." As soon as a member votes, his or her preference is recorded on a visual display board on the chamber walls and inserted into a computer data bank. According to the chamber rules, the voting stations remain open for 15 minutes, although the Speaker has some leeway for turning them off. During the 15-minute period members may change their votes at will by reinserting their cards. Aside from the vote display on the chamber walls, consoles are available to the tally clerk, the leadership, and the general membership to monitor ongoing votes. When the vote is completed the computer prints out an official copy for the press and for insertion into the Congressional Record (U.S. Congress, House, Committee on House Administration, 1979b).

Political Strategy Information

The electronic voting system would be a rather mundane administrative application, replacing a clerk and speeding up the decision-making process and little else, if it were not for the capability of monitoring and analyzing ongoing votes. The system was designed with consoles available to the majority and minority party leadership. The consoles operate independently, but have identical capabilities. They can be programmed to sort voting preferences by such variables as party, state, region, length of service, and voting preference (U.S. Congress, House, Committee on House Administration, 1979b). While the vote is in progress the leadership can look at the voting preferences of members of their party from a particular state, for example. If they find members voting against the party and out of step with their states, they can buttonhole those members on the floor and use this information to attempt to get them to change their votes (Gregory, 1979b: 2). Although such monitoring provides the leadership with a major power resource, a staff member explained,

> the leadership made a specific decision not to use the analysis capabilities of the vote monitoring terminals to their full capacity. They were afraid of a member revolt, and therefore unleashed this resource selectively. They particularly didn't want the information to go public. Printed reports of the voting breakdowns only go to the leadership.

Despite the restraint by the leadership, other members with an interest in affecting policy decisions pressured the leadership to provide wider access. Eventually two consoles with more limited capabilities were installed in the rear of the chamber.

Success or failure in the struggle over legislative decisions often stems more from an ability to use the rules rather than from the substance of one's case. For many years, parliamentary procedure as practiced in Congress could only be learned by direct experience or a friendly discussion with the parliamentarian, who worked from a looseleaf notebook and a prodigious memory. With the retirement of Louis Deschler, long-time

House parliamentarian, efforts were made to codify his knowledge. After the publication of *Deschler's Precedents,* the Precedents Preparation System was installed to assist the parliamentarian in compiling and updating precedents.

Oversight Information

Congressional concern for public policy does not end with the passage of bills, but extends to monitoring the consequences of public legislation. Congress has turned to the computer to help in this oversight function.

The General Accounting Office Reports File

Over the years, an increasing number of pieces of legislation included formal provisions that executive agencies report to Congress on decisions, activities, findings, plans, and budgets. By the early 1970s over 1000 reports were required annually (Johannes, 1977: 35). Most executive agencies had little idea what they were sending to Congress and most committees had no systematic way of checking on the receipt of reports (Chartrand and Morentz, 1979: 135). The creation of the GAO Reports File provided such systematic information, giving committees advance notification of which reports they should be expecting and flagging impending required actions.

The Geographic Reporting System (GRS)

While members of Congress exhibit some concern for the overall implications of their policy decisions, their main concern lies in the impact on their states and districts. The Geographic Reporting System provides information on the distribution of federal funds for community services on a regional, state, congressional district, county, or city basis. To extract such information from published sources would require looking up each program under each political subdivision and accumulating the totals (U.S. Congress, Senate, Committee on Rules and Administration, 1980: 23). Using the H.I.S. IMAGE Graphics System, the data can be presented both in numerical and graphic fashion (Staff Journal, 1979: 18).

Committee applications

Aside from overall data systems, particular committees have developed specialized monitoring systems. The Program Review System allows Senate committees to establish and maintain computer data base information about the financial and performance aspects of programs within their jurisdictions and to perform comparative statistical analyses of the data. The system was initially developed for use by the Senate Committee on Labor and Human Resources and is now being used by a number of other committees. The mechanics of the program work quite well, with the major continuing problem being the unavailability or lack of timeliness of relevant data from the executive agencies (U.S. Congress, Senate, Committee on Rules and Administration, 1980: 8).

Future Legislative Applications

Congress has only scratched the surface of legislative applications. Numerous applications well established on the state level could be easily transferred to Congress, while more sophisticated systems dot the drawing boards of information specialists both inside and outside of Congress.

Improved problem definition

The most abiding suggestion for improving Congress's ability to anticipate emerging problems and better define existing ones comes from those who propose a better system of social indicators. Much of the push for social indicators comes from those who argue that politics is no longer so much the control of events as a reactive posture to events after they have happened. For those who accept the cybernetic approach, government takes on the role of steering society and reacting to the feedback from previous corrections. In such a system Congress needs to know precisely where society is off course before proper corrective steering is possible (McHale, 1976: 85-88).

While the goals of those pushing for social indicators are clear, their proposals often amount to little more than a plaintive cry for more and better data, and give little direction as to specific improvements. Elmer Staats, former director of the General Accounting Office and active proponent of social indicators, is a bit more specific than most. He argues for more comparable time-series data and a focus on direct measures of citizen welfare (such as health statistics) rather than on the indirect ones (number of doctors) on which we often fall back (Staats, 1978: 277-285). Chartrand has argued that the federal government needs to expand its data base by tapping the computerized files on the state level (in Krevitt Eres, 1980: 33).

Representative Charlie Rose, one of the most optimistic visionaries when it comes to computer applications in the legislative realm, argues that

> the computer could become an "Oracle of legislative knowledge," which could analyze and compare existing laws, discovering the relationships between existing laws and pointing out conflicts between laws. The computer could answer precise legal questions and point out legislative intent. Perhaps most importantly, an intelligent computer could make comments about the need for further legislation in light of existing laws or proposed changes. Ultimately the decision-maker would have the finest information, advice and analysis.

Decision-facilitating information

Improving representation. Some observers of politics see the computer, when combined with other information technology, as the mechanism for regaining a portion of the direct democracy we lost when the town meeting became a physical impossibility. Simon Ramo sees a future in which

> the citizens ... would be able to tune in on the highest level discussion of the big issues and take part by expressing their opinions electrically from their houses in the deliberations of Congress, state legislatures and city councils [in Adams and Haden, 1973: 397].

Proponents of such a system envision a system in which the electorate would be "primed" on the issues through televised discussions and debates one month prior to the vote. Individuals would vote simultaneously via special television sets and have their votes verified by local computers. Following the vote Congress would deal with the recommendation as it would with a proposal from a committee. A prototype of such a system, QUBE, is operational through cable television in Columbus, Ohio, and has been used to assess political as well as social preferences (Laudon, 1977: 28; Time, 1978: 47).

The projected consequences of such a system are split. The proponents argue that such systems would create a more informed public, increase citizen participation, and usher in a "renewal of democracy." The opponents present a much more sanguine view. They point out that the elite would still control the "priming" of the issue during the debate period

(Laudon, 1977: 31), and that the temptation would be to oversimplify important issues and manipulate the information presented (McHale, 1976: 80). There are also fears that a computerized plebiscite would reduce the time period for coalition building around an issue and increase the conflict level in society (Laudon, 1977: 39). Under such a system individual members of Congress would be put in a much greater quandry as to whether they should react to the national moods, on which they have precise information through the plebiscite, or to their constituents, whose views may be less apparent. Such a plebiscite might strengthen the vertical linkage between the citizens and the elite but would break down an important horizontal linkage between citizens and their elected representatives (Laudon, 1977: 31-32). In the final analysis, there would be no assurance that the views that are heard under such a system would be any more representative than those heard under the current system. As Simon (1975: 224) summarized the criticisms:

> The Genius of Democratic government is not arithmetic; it is informed consensus. . . . The most positive contribution of the computer lies in informing the public, not in counting noses.

While there is little desire among members of Congress to use a computerized plebiscite, some limited steps in this direction are being contemplated and tried out. Some members have participated in a pilot two-way video conferencing program via satellite. It would be possible to use the computer to present the conferees with decision-making data or to install the capability for a member of Congress to speak to a large group of constituents from Washington and have them register their preferences via computer (Wood et al., 1979).

Currently H.I.S. will analyze constituent surveys taken by members of Congress, and has proposed a nationwide program of opinion sampling that would provide members with adequate scientific samples of their districts (U.S. Congress, House, House Information System, 1979b: 3).

Facilitating consensus building. Coalition building in Congress takes time and effort. Representative Charlie Rose sees the computer as a method of easing the task of building coalitions:

> The computer can facilitate communication. I see a networking approach among partisan and functional groupings in Congress. The average member is overloaded with committees, caucuses, delegations and other groups which demand his attention. A member who

must physically participate in the deliberations of ten groups will evidence sporadic and low quality participation. The computer could be used to share information and analysis. Prior to meetings areas of agreement and disagreement could be sorted out. When the less frequent meetings are held, the participants could be laser sharp about the options and come to decisions quickly.

For the leadership, the computer could be used to sharpen strategies and provide influence resources to a much greater degree than it is now. Providing on-line access to voting patterns of members would allow the leadership to target those most likely to be influenced. On close votes, the leadership could program the computer to search out members whose public commitments were at variance with their votes and collar them with this information while the vote was in progress. The leadership could also use the computer to communicate more efficiently with the party members through whip notices and specialized requests (U.S. Congress, House, House Information System, 1979b: 44).

Decision-recording applications

Voting procedures. Members of Congress spend a great deal of time going back and forth between their offices and the floor to vote. Some have argued that this inefficiency would be removed by allowing members to vote from their offices with a closed-circuit television system to make sure that it was the member doing the voting (Janda, 1968). While the computer makes this technologically possible, remote voting runs up against the whole tradition of Congress as a deliberative body.

Decision recording and publishing. Congress is relatively old-fashioned in its procedures for recording its deliberations. Through computerized image processing it is possible to capture, edit, retrieve print, and publish congressional documents directly without having to go through typesetting or other time-consuming and expensive processes (U.S. Congress, House, House Information System, 1979b: 42). Not only would such a system save money and increase efficiency, but it would reduce the problems of storing and maintaining hard copy documents. However, even such largely administrative activities run into opposition. Capacity to do a task does not mean that such an approach would be accepted. As a key participant in computerizing Congress pointed out:

Change runs into many roadblocks such as threats to one's turf and benefits. It is technically possible to produce the *Congressional Record* in a much more usable format with a useful index more cheaply and efficiently via the computer, but one runs into the GPO

(Government Printing Office) and its numerous unions and comfortable procedures.

There are some potential applications which could be implemented with little effort. All committee deliberations are now captured in machine readable form, but not all are printed. This is a great data base which has potential commercial applications. Congress is so paranoid about secrecy that it took a private firm to develop its own bill status and voting data base which is being marketed commercially. Congress could have recovered some of its cost distributing these public records, but no one would make the decision.

Certain activities cry out for automation. The documents room still has five-hundred copies of each bill printed no matter what the level of interest. They run around on roller-skates looking through the reams of bills. There is no reason that machine readable bills couldn't be produced on demand, but the documents room is the repository for a number of patronage types.

Improving oversight. The complexity of governmental activities boggles the mind of even the most diligent legislator. As Representative Charlie Rose sees it:

> No human being can totally analyze and understand the breadth and thrust of the Federal government. The computer could analyze how far things have gone, determining how the parts are working, evaluationg the performance of programs and applying effectiveness quotients across government.

The computer could be programmed to notify Congress when funds are not being spent in the intended ways (Government Executive, 1977b: 48). Cross-correlating data bases (for example, running telephone book tapes against lists of taxpayers) have proven effective in other realms for providing previously unavailable data, and similar applications are available for Congress (Chartrand and Morentz, 1979: 10).

Congress does not suffer from the availability of options for using computers in its legislative task. The key decisions for the future lie in choosing those applications that promise the greatest improvement.

INDIVIDUAL MEMBER APPLICATIONS

While the rhetoric of computerization emphasized the expected improvements in policy making, the driving motivation for many members' support for change stemmed not from systemwide improvements in information processing, but from those applications that would make their own jobs easier, more enjoyable, and more secure. Former Representative David Stockman, later to gain fame as President Reagan's budget-cutting director of the Office of Management and Budget, made no bones about his extensive expenditures for computerizing his congressional office and spoke frankly about his motives and those of his colleagues:

> The spinoff is what most people want. Most members don't want a lot of information about issues. They've already made up their minds, and don't think they need it. What they want is that computer building up the lists of people they can communicate with, learning what the specific interests of those people are so they can inundate them with follow-up mail. It is a very political business. What you do is segment the electorate into what they are interested in, and then bombard them with mailings written in a way to elicit a favorable response [Perry, 1978: 1].

Constituent Communications

Handling the workload more efficiently

The mail is the life blood and the first priority of most congressional offices. It not only informs members on constituent problems and concerns, but it also is the one method of direct service they can provide for a large number of constituents. By the early 1970s the problem of "handling the mail" was inundating most Capitol Hill offices. A 1978 House survey indicated that the average House office was receiving over 14,000 letters per month (O'Donnell, 1980: 66), with Senate offices receiving significantly more. When a mid-1970s survey was done of the Senate, it found that the average senator was spending over 50 percent of his or her clerk-hire funds just to answer the mail.

Traditionally, legislative mail was handled quite inefficiently. Each letter was answered individually, made part of a mail count on the issue, and filed, either under the subject or the constituent's name. When a large number of letters on one issue came in, a form letter was created (if the member was not afraid of it looking like a form letter). Staff members spent a great deal of time composing letters, mail counts were imprecise, and the filing of the hard copies of letters limited retrieval options. Computerization allowed offices to increase efficiency by designing a standard letter on a topic with interchangeable paragraphs that could be typed out with limited use of staff time.

The House and the Senate approached the computerization of correspondence quite differently. In the House, members were allowed to use office funds to contract with outside vendors for systems that fit their needs. Some offices used stand-alone word-processing systems with limited memories. Others opted for a time-sharing arrangement with a computer company, or for batch processing for large mailings, in which the vendor would print and address mailings to long lists of constituents (U.S. Congress, House, House Information System, 1979a: 2-4). The Senate centralized its mailing capability, first through providing mailing lists and then through the adoption of the integrated Correspondence Management System (CMS; U.S. Congress, Senate, Commission on the Operation of the Senate, 1977a: 25; Burnham, 1980: 96).

The computerization of mail handling also facilitates the filing and monitoring of correspondence. Each letter can be recorded and categorized according to the stand on the issue and personal characteristics of the constituent writing. This not only improves the quality of the mail counts on an issue, which will give the member an aggregate idea of how constituents feel, but it also increases the efficiency of retrieving a particular letter or constituent's name based on a variety of defining characteristics.

Increasing the quality of communication

While the desire to reduce duplication and increase efficiency encouraged computerization for individual offices, the ability of the computer to enhance the quality of communications provided a further motivation. Constituents expect to be treated as important and unique individuals by their elected representatives. In striving for efficiency in answering a number of similar letters, the old style form letters were too general and lacked the personally typed look. Computerized letters allow personalization through carefully selected paragraphs. This is especially important for "Christmas tree" letters, letters that include whole series of questions (Jost, 1979: 50). In 1978, 78 percent of the offices using the computer for legislative mail used a process by which they could assemble prepared paragraphs into a final letter (O'Donnell, 1980: 68). Computerized letters are also personalized by typing in a personal salutation and adjusting the formality of the member's signature to fit the person writing.

Congressional offices vary in the degree of frankness exhibited in their letters. Some offices spell out the member's stand on the issue, no matter what stand the constituent's letter reflected, while others vary their responses so as not to upset the writer. If the members can be assured that their inconsistencies will not be caught and prove to be a political embarrassment, the computer makes such an approach easy to take.

Through his computerized filing system, Representative David Emery (D-ME) personalizes the contacts with constituents during district trips. Before a trip he pulls out letters from constituents in the towns he plans to visit. He then quotes from those letters and makes an attempt to meet with the authors personally (Perry, 1978: 33).

At times the desire for personalization conflicts with the potential for efficiency. Some offices have avoided the computerized laser printers, which are extremely fast, but whose letters lack the "IBM Selectric look."

Increasing the quantity of communication

Members of Congress and their staffs would like to have you think that their extreme emphasis on constituent communications and the increase in mail volume stem solely from increases in constituent demands. In reality, mail volume is also related to increased office efficiency and specific congressional encouragement. Efficient mail handling leads to quicker and more meaningful responses, which encourage repeated correspondence. Many offices develop a "pen pal" relationship with a number of constituents. The image of the office manager bemoaning the amount of mail must be balanced against the number of unsolicited mailings, direct solicitations of future communications in newsletters, and the standard closing line in much congressional correspondence, "Feel free to contact me about this or any other matter." Letters out of congressional offices beget letters coming in. One staff member reported a 50 percent response rate to an unsolicited mailing from his office above and beyond the regular mail volume (Haydon, 1980: 45).

The "average" senatorial office has 5 terminals connected with the CMS system, each capable of sending out 40 "personalized" letters per hour, for a grand total of 2500 letters per month. The Senate alone is sending out over a million personalized letters per month with the CMS system, which means that the average constituent could receive at least 2 letters a year (Robinson, 1981: 60).

Some offices have instituted a "tickler system," which alerts staff members to write a new letter at some specified time (Jost, 1979: 50). For example, a constituent who writes to express an opinion on a particular bill might receive a letter every time the legislation passes one hurdle in the legislative process. The concern is not limited to outside observers. In the words of a congressional staff member:

> There is no question that constituents are very impressed with the responses, especially follow-up letters which update them on the actions taken on the bill they originally wrote in on. In some cases it does get ridiculous though when one letter spawns nine or more responses, one for each authoritative stage in the legislative process.

Mailing list creation. Congressional offices use the computer to increase the amount of communication through the creation of strategic mailing lists and clever techniques of unsolicited mailings based on those lists. Each letter arriving at a congressional office with a computerized communications capacity can be scanned for such information as types of issues mentioned, stand on the issues, occupation, age, geographic location, sex, religion, and the like. The Senate Correspondence Management System allows each senator to have up to 2400 coding categories into which individual letter writers might be placed. As in the House, the member controls the content of the coding categories and the coding scheme for each letter (Common Cause, 1981). In the House, typical mailing lists include 20,000 to 30,000 names (Congressional Quarterly, 1979: 146), with over 100,000 not uncommon in the Senate. Mailing lists do not stop at individuals. Many offices keep coded lists of reporters, radio stations, newspapers, and corporations with whom they might want to correspond selectively.

An individual whose name shows up on a congressional mailing list may never have had any previous contact with the member. Increasingly, congressional offices reach out to their constituencies by buying or otherwise appropriating private, commercial, or governmental mailing lists. Most specialized lists, from driver's licenses to registered voters or lawyers, can be had by the elected official for the asking. An outside firm or in-house expert can be hired to "merge and purge" groups of lists to avoid duplication (Haydon, 1980: 43-44). The variety of lists available is only limited by the creativity of the member's mailing-list expert. The best lists are those that are periodically corrected (such as voter registration lists and licenses) to remove deceased and otherwise departed individuals. All such lists have the advantage of containing individuals who have an inherent interest in particular types of congressional action.

Creative communications. Members of Congress want to keep their names in front of the public as much as possible. By targeted mailings financed at public expense, the member of Congress can tailor communications to hit a receptive group. Aside from the more general excuses to communicate, such as mailing out public opinion polls, order blanks for government documents, and general newsletters, narrower targeted mailings are facilitated by coded mailing lists. The possibilities are almost endless, as the following examples indicate:

> In 1972 Senator Robert Griffith (R-MI) identified busing as a key issue. His staff created a mailing list of car owners (upper income and supposedly more conservative) in counties where he wanted to pick up votes. By dropping individuals on the list who lived in largely black census tracts he had a group of people to send his anti-busing letter who might be very receptive to its content [Arieff, 1979: 1447].

> One southern congressman created a list of over one-hundred groups of people with whom he wanted to communicate at least every three months. Realizing that he had not written to the list of citrus growers which he acquired from the Department of Agriculture, he prepared a short statement on the importance of the citrus industry to America and had it inserted in the *Congressional Record*. He used his government subsidized reprints of this speech along with his subsidized franking privilege to accompany his computer generation, "Thought you would like to know what your congressman is doing in Washington" letter. This office prided itself in sending out an average of seven-hundred targeted letters per day [interview with staff member].

> Realizing that form may be more important than substance in constituent communications, another congressman arranged his mailing lists by the amount of time it took a letter to get from Washington. He used his blank check right to send out "town meeting notices" as late on Thursday to miss the Friday delivery. The constituent going to the mail box at 11 a.m. on Saturday would be greeted with the notice that the congressman had been at the town hall from 9-11 a.m. that morning. Rather than getting mad at the congressman, the constituent would damn the inefficient postal service and chalk up one more piece of evidence that the congressman was interested in doing his job. Without having to face a horde of constituents with demands and requests, the congressman used the computer to get all the credit and none of the hassle [interview with staff member].

Many congressmen use their lists of National Honor Society members, Student Council members or simply those coded as students to send out helpful information brochures on summer jobs with the federal government, internship opportunities or announcements for the Peace Corps or service academies. Similar techniques are used to send out government brochures to senior citizens and the classic *Infant and Baby Care* books to new parents [interview with congressman].

In its investigation of the franking privilege, Common Cause found that it was not all atypical for offices to seek out opportunities to communicate and to have detailed two- and three-year mailing plans, making the best use of chamber rules and the capabilities of computer technology. In the realm of mailing, the computer makes possible strategies that would have been impossible using traditional mechanical filing and addressing procedures.

The legal and ethical questions
of computerized communications

Questioning increases in the efficiency and quality of congressional communication techniques facilitated by computers puts one on the horns of a dilemma. Everyone believes that constituents deserve as much information as possible about their representatives and congressional behavior, but there remains a nagging fear that much of the communication is designed to perpetuate incumbents in office by trickery and stealth. While some may question the ethics of using the computer to enhance the quality of franked mail, there is little doubt that the volume of mail produced by the Congress corresponds to the demands of the electoral cycle. As Figures 5.7 and 5.8 indicate, mail increased dramatically for members facing reelection battles and subsides in the off-year period. In the House, with its two-year terms, the pattern is universal. In the Senate, increased communication with constituents shows up most graphically for members who are up for reelection in a particular year.

In a system such as that in the House, where members have their own system, H.I.S., the House Administration Committee and the Ethics Committee have largely sidestepped the issue by saying that it is up to each member to abide by the rules set up for franking mail, and that anything that can be franked legally can be generated using computer funds. The franking rules say nothing about targeted mailings and focus more on when mailings are allowed (certain types of mailings cannot go out less

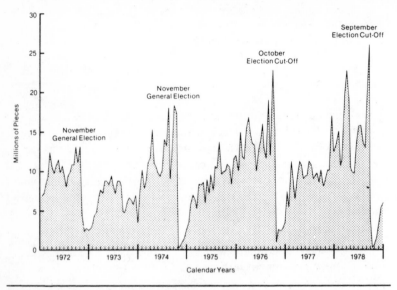

Figure 5.7   House of Representatives Franked Mass Mail

than 60 days before an election) and their content (such as limits on personal pronouns and pictures of the member). The catch phrase in the House is that a member can mail only for "official purposes," but the lack of a clear definition of these purposes means that such a definition could cover a multitude of sins. Originally House members were not supposed to store anything "political" in their files, but according to an H.I.S. official, "We have loosened up a great deal lately." As one staff member put it:

> The frank isn't a loophole; it is a black hole. If you can't do it under the frank, you're either dumb or hopelessly unsubtle.

Control in the Senate is potentially greater due to the centralized administration of the CMS system. Senators are only supposed to put people on mailing lists when they would be interested in some issue before the Senate. While this might cut out the filing of Christmas card lists, the breadth of concerns taken up by the Senate means this limits very little activity. Until 1977, senators could only purchase mailing lists with personal funds or be given the lists as campaign contributions. After 1977,

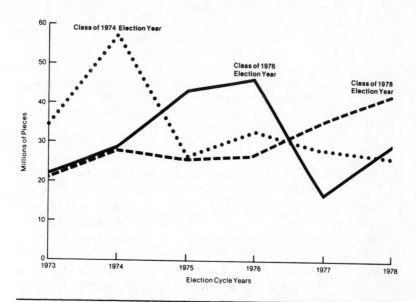

Figure 5.8   Senators in the Classes of 1974, 1976, and 1978: Franked Mass Mail

senators could use up to 10 percent of their office account money for purchasing mailing lists (Congressional Quarterly, 1979: 144).

Realizing the potential political benefits of computerized lists, the Senate passed Resolution 110 in 1978, which stated:

> Staff members may not assist a Senator to use the Senate computer facilities to store, maintain, or otherwise process lists of names and addresses identifying individuals as campaign workers, or contributors, as members of a political party or by any other partisan political designation; nor to produce mailing labels or computer tapes except for use in Senate facilities [Common Cause, 1981; Congressional Quarterly, 1979: 142).

While this sounds quite official and comprehensive, problems still exist. There are a number of gray areas, such as whether mailing lists can include members of ideological groups or party functionaries. In its suit against the Congress focusing on the misuse of the frank, Common Cause argues that the rules are honored in breach more than in reality. Since each senator controls his or her own coding scheme, what was once an identifiable "D," "R," "I" partisan coding scheme can be easily transferred into an "X," "Y," "Z" camouflaged scheme. Common Cause produced a number of memos from Senate staff members, which conclude:

> A blatantly political list ... might put the Senator in a compromising position. I suspect, however, that this sort of operation is done by all Senators. Senate people (the Senate Computer Center) did not seem reluctant, or express any concern over it [Common Cause, 1981: deposition 79].

Through interviews with Senate staff members, Common Cause found that over one-third of the Senate was using official funds and sophisticated direct-mail techniques to promote reelection. The willingness of the Senate to bow to the electoral needs of its members was seen recently when Senators Long and Cranston went to the Rules Committee to ask for permission to use official funds above and beyond their 10 percent discretionary fund for minicomputers designed for word processing and targeted mailings. Rather than change the rules completely, the Rules Committee authorized an "in service test" for five senators (Cranston, Durkin, Laxalt, Long, and McGovern), all of whom just happened to be up for reelection in 1980 (Congressional Quarterly, 1979: 145).

For the House and the Senate, one of the remaining loopholes is found in the question of who owns the mailing lists and who can transfer them to whom. After a review of congressional procedures and legal precedents, the CRS came to the conclusion that the issues had been defined quite broadly and, even though data were collected at public expense, the individual member retained proprietary rights to it (Staenberg, 1977: 22).

There are some indications that congressional insiders do not see the ethical problem as major. As one observer stated:

> Ultimately the technology will get cheap enough so that everyone will have his own computer, and the crime will likely become reduced to the stature of misusing a xerox machine.

Part of the ethical dilemma stems from the difficulty in distinguishing between "official functions" and reelection activities. As a staff member explained it:

> If you serve your constituents well, you serve your reelection purposes. The two can and should not be separated. . . . Casework and

communications are the backbone of the congressional office and who would suggest we approach these tasks less efficiently.

Despite Common Cause's challenge and other criticisms, observers, at least on the inside, see open rules on computerized mailings as more beneficial than detrimental. In a key staff member's words:

> Common Cause seems to be either naive or elitist. They complain about newsletters and then in the same breath complain that congressmen do not provide enough information to their constituents. They don't have much faith in the voters' ability to cut through the self-promotion and make a reasonable judgment.

Electronic mail

Besides communicating with constituents, members of Congress communicate with specialized groups, staff, and each other. One computer-based technology that is just beginning to be felt in Congress is electronic mail. In the House over 200 offices are linked by an electronic mail system and over 100 offices are active users of a system that allows them to communicate with each other via computerized messages. The House Energy and Commerce Committee created a distribution list of its members and communicates meeting notices and substantive information. Some Senate offices use electronic mail to speed up communications with district offices. The H.I.S. staff communicates extensively via computer-based mail files. One H.I.S. staff member spoke glowingly of the advantages:

> Electronic mail has numerous advantages: It saves time by reducing the social amenities typical on the telephone and by reducing "telephone tag," where numerous callbacks are necessary before two people can finally get together. It saves money by reducing the number of phones needed since phones are not being tied up and its unit cost is cheaper than commercial phone rates. It saves face by allowing a subordinate some "thinking time" before answering an inquiry. The subordinate does not have to admit orally that he does not have an answer. It increases efficiency by allowing options such as the creation of automatic distribution lists.

Electronic mail is certainly technologically possible, but its future is somewhat clouded. It is a good example of how Congress uses technology as an add-on, rather than as a replacement. While electronic mail is proven and available for communications around the Hill, no one wants to drop the existing page system with its patronage advantages.

Monitoring and Planning Applications
for Individual Members

Scheduling

Members of Congress lead hectic and peripatetic lives, with conflicting demands for their time and attention. Members wishing to accomplish a significant portion of their responsibilities must schedule their time efficiently. At a minumum, members of Congress are expected to cast their votes for legislation on the floor, but a slavish commitment to being present on the floor for all debates in anticipation of votes wastes precious time. In order to help members better schedule their trips to the floor, the House installed the computer-based Summary of Proceedings and Debates (SOPAD), which allows members to retrieve summaries of floor activity and current and future scheduling information for votes. When the bells indicating a vote or quorum call begin to ring, the member can quickly determine the subject under consideration and the stage in the process (U.S. Congress, House, Committee on House Administration, 1980a). While still in operation and active use, the importance of SOPAD has waned a bit since the House began televising its deliberations, giving members and their staffs a direct method of monitoring ongoing activity.

Some members have developed individualized scheduling programs, which allow them to see at a glance their schedule for the day and future commitments, both in Washington and back in their districts. One staff member explained how his office combined ease of scheduling with political strategy using the computer:

Each week when the congressman comes back from the district, he gives us a form indicating how much time he spent in each precinct. He has a plan on how he should spend his time. The computer will spit out a shaded map indicating areas where he has concentrated his effort since the last election, but we can go further than that. We have programmed the computer to give us a priority list of precincts which fit our criteria for more effort (strong Republican vote, but within which we did relatively poorly last time). By combining this data with that on time expended in that area, we get a composite list outlining areas in which we might seek out opportunities for contact.

This type of strategy did not originate with the computer. Efficient members of Congress all have strategic plans for their efforts. The difference is that rather than having the data written on a scrap of paper or vaguely filed in the recesses of the member's mind, they are precisely stored in the computer's memory. And rather than having the analysis and strategy planning performed intuitively and imprecisely by the limited human capacity, the computer takes a precise strategy plan and activates it. While the results are precise, the user must remember that the prescribed plan is no better than the human-designed strategy on which it is based.

Monitoring

Both the information requests of constituents and the legislative goals of members require the tracking of myriad legislative decisions. While the LEGIS system makes initiated searches relatively simple, continual self-initiated searches would be quite inefficient. Autotracking allows an office to express an interest in specific bills and to receive an updated status report the day following any official action taken (U.S. Congress, Senate, Committee on Rules and Administration, 1980: 5; U.S. Congress, House, Committee on House Administration, 1975a: 8).

H.I.S. provides each member a quarterly Legislative Profile, which provides a summary of all the legislation the member has introduced and updates the action taken. This report provides invaluable information for the member trying to justify his or her legislative prowess in the next election. Members of the House also have the right to use the LEGIS system to extract an Individual Vote History Analysis, which lists all of their own official action on legislation.

Filing

Congressional offices process vast amounts of material above and beyond constituent communications. Interest group communications, "dear colleague" letters from fellow members of Congress, newspaper clippings referring to the member, and internally produced material such as speeches and press releases must be reviewed and filed. A number of offices use the computer to store information about documents only once and cross-reference them for easy future retrieval. Computerized files of previous public pronouncements can easily be checked for content and consistency. When such pronouncements are created on a word processor, the filed copy can be edited and updated for future use without having to repeat the whole process of creation (U.S. Congress, House, House Information System, 1979a: 11).

Problem Solving for Individuals

The modern member of Congress is asked increasingly to serve as an intermediary between constituents and various aspects of the federal government. Far from being the onerous task it might seem, this function is seen by congressional offices as one of the few ways in which they can directly prove their worth to constituents.

Casework

Congressional offices receive hundreds of letters per month asking the representative to trace missing Social Security checks, help with hardship discharge from the military, seek a change in veterans' pension benefits, and the like. Each case involves a specific individual problem and does not attempt to solve a wider public policy problem. Although the uniqueness of each request for assistance does not lend itself to form letters, a number of offices have installed systems for tracking casework. The initial letter is coded and a "buck slip" is sent to the agency from whom help is requested. The caseworker puts a "tickler" date in the case code. If nothing has been done on the case in a specified number of days, the tickler instruction prints out the case data, and the caseworker tries a new approach to the problem. Some offices keep cumulative records on the kinds of problems faced and the success rates and speed of various agencies. Such cumulative records may lay the groundwork for broader public policy.

Grantsmanship

The federal government provides vast amounts of money to solve problems through demonstration projects and targeted grants. Members of Congress serve as conduits of information and as advocates for choosing sites in their districts for these program grants. When the local school superintendent calls the legislator to ask for help in finding federal funds to replace the burned-out science wing of the high school, the member and his or her staff want to be able to find the appropriate programs, send out the application forms, accompany the local officials when they make their pitch to the appropriate bureaucrats, publicly announce the approval of the grant, and express their willingness to cut the ribbon at the opening ceremony.

Until relatively recently, the ability of the congressional office to find appropriate grants for specific problems was a hit-or-miss operation affected by the skill and luck of staff members. Programs aimed at similar problems are scattered through a wide number of agencies. The creation of the Federal Assistance Program Retrieval System (FAPRS) by the Department of Agriculture, with cross-referenced qualification and subject classifications, dramatically improved information about such programs. In a few minutes, the congressional office can sort through myriad programs to find the handful that directly apply to a given case.

The existence of FAPRS not only improved the ability of offices to respond, but also spawned a new type of outreach. A number of members of Congress and their staffs take portable terminals to their districts and operate little "magic shows" for local officials, encouraging them to create their own shopping lists of desires. As Representative Andrew Ireland (D-FL) expressed it, "It is good business and it is good politics" (Perry, 1978: 33).

While useful, FAPRS had some limitations and is being replaced with the Grants Information Data Base. Above and beyond the search capability of FAPRS, the new system provides full text retrieval of grant programs and information as to whether funds still remain, who has received grants, and whom to contact in each agency. This is the first time that such information has been centralized in the federal government.

Public Performance Rating

Members of Congress send out questionnaires both to seek guidance for decisions and to convince constituents of interest in their views. For House members, H.I.S. provides technical advice and limited analysis of constituent questionnaires. If members wish to go beyond simple totals and relationships, they must use their own resources. In some offices, questionnaire respondents immediately become part of the mailing list, with their responses captured to provide a more sophisticated basis for targeting future mailings.

Future Applications for Individual Offices

Communications

Most observers believe that the most important future application of computers in the legislative branch lies mainly in the area of communications. Aside from increasing the efficiency of targeted mailing and expanding the spread of efficiency through sophisticated word processors, which allow for editing and letter creation, the new age will move Congress toward a "paperless" office environment. Communications will be created, edited, stored, and sent via computer terminals. While final copies to outsiders will still require hard copy, electronic mail will dominate communications within Congress and between staff members in Washington and those in the district. Cables have been installed in all congressional offices in Washington to make this technically possible (Sanfield, 1979: 16; U.S. Congress, House, House Information System, 1979b: 47). Senator Hatfield (R-OR) currently serves as the prime example of what is possible. He is down to one file cabinet to hold mail that has not been indexed, acted on, and put on microfilm, and is so embarrassed by its existence that he hides it away in a closet.

In the future, the computer will not stand alone; its capabilities will be fused with other communications technologies to create what Bell has called "compunications" (in Dertouzos and Moses, 1975: 176). A number of possibilities exist for combining television and computers for video conferences among members of Congress and constituents and among staff members (Wood et al., 1979), although concern by technicians in each of these realms to protect their turf reduces the motivation to join forces.

Scheduling

H.I.S. has proposed the creation of a centralized scheduling service, which would allow members to create their own schedules and assess potential conflicts. After events, the scheduling system could provide a summary of how and where the member spent his or her time (U.S. Congress, House, House Information System, 1979b: 50).

Constituent services

Some of the most sought-after services from congressional offices are tickets to special White House tours and other events. This distribution process could be done more efficiently with a Ticketron-type system, which would make it easy for congressional offices to determine whether tickets are available and to facilitate the trading of ticket allotments to make sure that none go unused.

In a bit more substantive realm, the computer could not only improve constituent casework, but also help move beyond the symptom to the cause. On the individual level offices vary in their skill in pursuing specific cases. A computerized guidance system, such as the Grants Information Data Base, providing information on whom to contact for particular problems, would improve the service to constituents from many offices.

On the broader question of discovering the causes of casework problems, the computer promises even more potential. The current system of dealing with casework is designed to maximize the amount of credit a member of Congress can take for solving constituent problems, but not to give an overall picture of the extent, variety, and source of problems. Each congressional office gets its own image of which government programs cause the most problems, but tend to "miss the forest for the trees." In Florida, an automated ombudsman system uses citizen complaints to monitor state government to discover areas that need improvement (Worthley, 1977b: 7); a similar system would be useful in Congress. While members are unlikely to give up the advantage of taking credit for services provided, a centralized system for monitoring problems would serve as a potent resource when Congress comes around to approving budgets of various agencies.

CURRENT PATTERNS OF COMPUTER USE

The mere availability of computer capabilities in both the legislative and individual office realms does not dictate which services will dominate, who will use them, or how they will be used. Despite the sensitivity of legislators about having anyone monitor their activities, the variety of uses to which particular computer applications can be put, and the technical problems of measurement usage, all militating against precise measures of usage, analysis of a variety of threads of evidence helps fill in the picture of how computers are being employed in Congress.

Creating Application Options

From a logical perspective, the ideal way of deciding which computer application to adopt would be to identify problems and then search for potential computerized solutions. To some degree, especially in the House of Representatives, the order of these steps became reversed in Congress. H.I.S. and other promoters felt driven to apply the computer to everything in sight, whether or not a problem was critical. The adoption of particular applications took on the character of the "Law of the Instrument," which, to paraphrase Kaplan (1964: 28), states, "Give a child a hammer and the whole world becomes a nail." Computer technology was applied in almost every conceivable area by some member, and the H.I.S. catalog of current and future applications resembles a "grab bag" of applications designed to catch the fancy of almost any potential user (U.S. Congress, House, House Information System, 1979b). The Senate has been somewhat more parsimonious in the services it supplies to members, and since all senators are part of a centralized system, the Senate Computer Center does not feel as obligated to create a multifaceted product that it must "sell" broadly in order to assure its continued existence.

Both the Senate and the House have used planning task forces to study the desirability of purchasing new equipment or providing new services. Such task forces almost invariably become coopted and develop their own vested interest in change. Their final reports typically provide a glowing rationale for the change they were asked to analyze critically (March and Simon, 1958: 10).

Selecting Computer Applications

The corollary to the "Law of the Instrument," which leads to the promotion of computerization for its own sake, is the "Law of the Least Desirable Target." Not only does the creation of a technology impel its usage, but "the first target for the child's hammer is the antique lamp and not the protruding nail head." Technological solutions tend to be applied to some of the least applicable problems first.

While there is no absolute standard by which to judge the desirability of how members of Congress have decided to employ the computer, both the internal and external change agents emphasized the contributions of computers to better legislative decision-making rather than those applications that make legislative life more pleasant and reelection more possible. For example, speaking as chairman of the Senate Committee on Rules and Administration, Senator Howard Canon (D-NM) outlined the priorities for computers as:

(1) providing information and analysis for legislative tasks;
(2) providing information and analysis for committee investigations and oversight;
(3) helping senators to respond to constituent needs; and
(4) improving congressional administration (U.S. Congress, Senate, Senate Committee on Rules and Administration, 1977b: v).

In choosing specific applications for employment, members of Congress reversed these priorities initially, and in some cases exclusively, by looking to computers primarily to solidify their political bases. A number of threads of evidence verify this observation. Until the House offered members free access to the legislative data bases through the Member Information Network, the vast bulk of members used the computer exclusively for constituent services. As we will see in Chapter 6, members with the weakest electoral bases were the first to jump on the computerization bandwagon. A recent study of computer usage by groups of Congress members on various types of committees found that members on reelection committees (see Fenno, 1973, for committee classifications) used the computer almost exclusively for constituent-oriented word processing, while members of policy committees used it more for research (Krevitt Eres, 1980: 108). Reelection-oriented computer applications caught members' attention and propelled them into accepting computers. If this gave them access to research and legislative files, so much the better.

The Use of Legislation-Related Data Bases

Determining the relative popularity of the legislative data bases is difficult. Comparable data for data bases administered by the Library of Congress, H.I.S, and the Senate Computer Center are not available. The best documented data relate to the Library of Congress data bases. Two kinds of data are available. Survey data capture the perceptions of members and their staffs as to which services they are using, but this may well be distorted. Usage-monitoring data (number of searches attempted, amount of time connected to the data base, and so on) provide empirical measures, but are difficult to interpret. Counting the number of searches in a particular data base does not differentiate between the complex search providing a large amount of valuable data and a simple search. Connect time measures inflate the usage level of inefficient searchers who must go through great gyrations to get small bits of information. Despite the limitations, however, the available data provide a rather consistent picture.

If we divide the Library of Congress data bases into those used in tracking the status of legislation (LEGIS) and those designed for issue research (all others) as in Table 5.1, we can see that for individual members the LEGIS system is used most, while the committees use the computer more for research. The figures for the House and Senate are remarkably similar.

TABLE 5.1 Computer Usage Patterns in Congress

	Percentage of Complete Searches Conducted in Each File Group (1980)[a]				Perceived Utility of File Groups by Senatorial Offices (Senate Office Sample)[b]*
	House Offices	Senate Offices	House Committees	Senate Committees	
Bill status	63	56	24	27	90
Congressional Record	15	17	23	24	not available
LCCC (bibliographic book searches)	7	10	22	21	21
Issue briefs	7	7	17	18	90
CITN (bibliographic periodical searches)	6	6	10	6	67
National Referral Center	1	2	3	2	27
General Accounting Office files	1	1	1	1	not available

SOURCES: a. Griffith (1981).

      b. U.S. Congress, Senate, Committee on Rules and Administration (1977a: 15). "Not available" indicates that the data base indicated was not on line at the time of the survey.

*Data bases rated as important by a random sample of 50 Senate offices.

Before we assume that computerized legislative information has revolutionized Congress, we must realize that the computer is just one source of information; it must compete with the more familiar traditional printed sources. The lack of computer penetration in some offices can be seen in 1981 article by a senior staff member about information needs and sources in the Senate, which catalogs a great variety of sources, but never mentions the computer (Staff Journal, 1981).

Changes in the use of various data bases occur over time. The heavily used SOPAD system dropped in importance for Washington offices with the introduction of televised floor proceedings (U.S. Congress, House, Committee on House Administration, 1980b: 12). While Washington office use dropped, district offices increased their interest in what was going on in Washington and began using SOPAD regularly.

Usage Patterns Within Offices

Who uses the terminal

Direct "hands-on" usage by most members is still a novelty on the Hill. Staff surrogates make most of the searches and provide written summaries to the members. It is not uncommon to see a member in his or her office or on the floor looking over the shoulder of the computer operator, asking questions and watching the answer appear on the screen (Gregory, 1979b: 2). As one staff member stated:

> Most senators are just too busy to get on the terminal themselves and must rely quite heavily on the printed reports generated by the computer.

A few members are computer literate and "wow" their colleagues with their ability to answer questions directly. A few of the real computer "jocks" such as Charlie Rose delight in carrying terminals into the lobbies or committee rooms and performing their brand of magic.

A recent survey of staff members outlines some examples of how the computer is used on a day-to-day level by staff members. The usage vignettes reported by active users are revealing:

> We use the legislative files most often to answer constituent questions on the status of legislation.

> We have used the computer to identify other members with similar legislative interest. For example, we were preparing a memo on

legislation for the handicapped and wanted to know what legislation had been proposed and what other members were sensitive to the subject. We searched the bill status file to find members active in this area and called their offices.

When I have to write something for the *Congressional Record* or when writing a speech for my boss, I will search the *Congressional Record* file to find citations from people I know my boss generally agrees with. In that way, I don't have to start out cold on a topic.

Our office uses the bibliographic files about equally to provide legislative background information on a topic and to help with constituent requests. We'll get lengthy requests from school kids. . . . Rather than write a research paper for them, we'll send them a bibliography.

The issue briefs are super when the crunch is on. We will print out part on the terminal to get a flavor of the issue and then decide whether or not to order the whole thing.

The computer role in the flow of decision-making

The computer has the potential for use either as a source of background information before legislative action takes place, or as an active component in ongoing decision-making. By and large, computerized information is used to brief the member before deliberations or in preparing public statement. The cases of "hot" use of the computer, where the member runs to the terminal for new persuasive information that wins the day for his or her position, are not unheard of, but are relatively rare.

The image of members using computer data during debate is based on the misleading assumption that congressional deliberations are looking for "the" truth, when in fact, truth is in the eye of the beholder. Legislative eyes look through spectacles colored by ideology, parochial interest, and personal ambition. It is seldom that there exists readily available computerized information that can overwhelm such predispositions.

Application Problems

While Congress has provided itself with a variety of computer applications, the transition to the computer age has not been without its problems. Standard computer problems of "down" time and slowness of responses has frustrated some users (U.S. Congress, Senate, Committee on Rules and Administration, 1977a: vii). The initial bill status system developed by the Library of Congress was characterized by House Administration Committee Chairman Wayne Hayes as "completely and utterly worthless . . . an amateurish job" (Datamation, 1973: 124), and led to the separate development of a bill status system by H.I.S.

In the House, some of the applications have not taken hold due to the laissez-faire approach of H.I.S. The Committee Information and Scheduling Program (COMIS) never took hold in the House because it was voluntary. The Senate waited for a rule requiring compliance before adoption.

There have been cases where information systems that were too sophisticated have gotten a member in trouble. A few years ago, Senator Birch Bayh (D-IN) was quite embarrassed by the fact that a local newspaper printed side by side two copies of targeted computerized letters in which his positions varied.

Many of the problems with office applications stem from improper expectations or lack of adequate attention. As Congressman Charlie Rose explained:

> People assume that an integrated computer system will lead to office integration. You need to start with an integrated office. Without workable office concepts and procedures, the computer either becomes non-entity or simply takes over some minor functions. I get many calls from congressmen dissatisfied with what they are getting out of their computer. They arrive with their entourage to discuss the matter. The member defers to his Administrative Assistant, who demurs to the Legislative Assistant who finally introduces the part-time computer operator to answer the questions. They obviously have not given the computer a chance. It is not an integral part of the office planning.

The computer is a tool that can be used wisely or stupidly. Availability does not predetermine the quality of usage.

Members of Congress have numerous options for computer applications, both legislative and political. For the Senate, usage is free and depends only on motivation and skill. In the next chapter we will discuss the House of Representatives, where members must make a definite choice to expend scarce resources in order to have personal access to the computer.

6

DIFFUSION OF
INNOVATIVE TECHNOLOGY

INDIVIDUAL MEMBERS of Congress were faced with two different decisions concerning computerization. On the organizational level, they had to decide whether they would support appropriations and rule changes relating to chamberwide applications. On the individual level, they faced a choice as to the degree their offices would use the new technology. Research from other realms indicates that availability of a new technology does not dictate adoption. Some individuals step forward and embrace change, while others hang back and resist new developments.

Until recently, the study of individual innovation has been largely the preserve of sociologists and anthropologists.[1] Their studies of farmers, physicians (Menzel, 1960: 704-713; Coleman et al., 1966), the military (Buhl, 1974: 704), industries (Carter and Williams, 1957; Mansfield, 1968), and consumers (Robertson, 1971: 101-104) reveal that innovators can be distinguished from noninnovators by such widely varying characteristics as perceived needs, personality characteristics, ideological outlooks, social status, social integration, information sources, and resources. For students of American political institutions, these studies have held little obvious interest since they focus on nonpoliticians and/or nonpolitical acts. Although politicians are confronted with the opportunity to adopt technological innovations in a number of realms from campaign techniques to the performance of office functions, we know little about the causes and consequences of innovation in the political realm. It is a fair assumption that forces similar to those affecting other realms are at work, but no verification has been attempted.

This chapter focuses on the willingness of individual members of the U.S. House of Representatives to adopt some form of computer application as a method of improving their efficiency and effectiveness. The analysis uses the individual member of Congress as the unit of analysis and attempts to determine whether the theories of innovativeness developed in relation to other realms of human activity are applicable to an elite group of political activists.

Rather than taking a "snapshot of a moving picture," this analysis looks at innovation at various points in time. Prospective innovators are seldom faced with a "now or never" decision. The option to accept or reject innovation looms constantly. The time at which one finally accepts an innovation will vary along the same dimensions that distinguish innovators from noninnovators. Opposition to innovation subsides as dissatisfaction and the potential dangers of change are proven to be without basis. Opposition to innovation will increase under the opposite conditions.

PROFILE OF AN INNOVATOR

By definition, innovators are among the first to step out of the crowd and use a new method of reaching a desired goal. Technological innovation requires knowledge of one's goals, the willingness and ability to take risks, and access to the skills necessary for putting the innovation to use. Since these factors are not randomly distributed throughout the population, the literature on the diffusion of innovations includes a series of attempts to discover causal and surrogate predictive variables associated with innovative tendencies.

Much of the diffusion research depends heavily on the collection of personality, attitudinal, and behavioral data from samples of innovators and noninnovators. For example, knowledge and awareness of needs and options are facilitated by regularity of communications and social interaction with a cosmopolitan group of associates. Individuals manifesting such interpersonal contact patterns tend to be innovators whether they are farmers (Rogers, 1962b), physicians, or consumers (Robertson, 1971: 95). The evidence also indicates that risk taking is more typical among individuals with certain attitudes and personalities. Technological innovators among farmers and consumers are more venturesome, self-confident, and scientifically oriented and less rigid (Robertson, 1971: 86-113). There also tends to be a consistency between perceptions and behavior in that those classifying themselves as innovative behave in the expected manner (Robertson, 1971: 92, 101). While data on personality, attitudes, and self-perceived communication and interaction behavior may well get closer to the proximate causal factors associated with innovation, the difficulty of data collection and the simplistic and tautological nature of some discovered relationships limit the utility of the effort.

Another route to discovering the antecedents of innovation involves the analysis of more temporally distant, but more readily collectable, data on demographic characteristics. Such variables will at a minimum predict innovativeness and in some cases help discover more proximate causal factors. While the lack of precision and conflicting logic of associating such demographic factors as age, social status, experience, and objective measures of needs with innovation assure weaker relationships, their self-evident validity as measures of important descriptive characteristics commend them to analysis. This analysis will emphasize such variables. If these variables do move us closer to the goal of explanation, we will be able to apply our findings to a wider group of innovation targets on whom we do not have perceptual, attitudinal, communications, and behavioral data.

The general working hypothesis of this study is that technological innovators can be differentiated from noninnovators on the basis of their higher needs for changing standard operating procedures in order to reach their goals and on the basis of their higher tolerance for risk taking.

In focusing on needs, we are assuming that the pressure to innovate increases as it becomes clear that the present way of doing things threatens the attainment of desired goals. Individuals assured of reaching their goals are unlikely to change current behavior patterns, since change would not necessarily mean improvement. This introduces the concept of risk. Concern with the risk factor stems from the recognition that neither the technological nor social consequences of technological change are always either predictable or positive. Innovators face the potential of social ostracism, technological disaster, or both. Thus innovators will come from those groups for which the social sanctions mean less or for whom the risk is necessary because of the magnitude of the need.

In determining propensity for risk taking, we will work from the hypothesis that individuals less integrated into the norms and procedures of a social organization, and thus more socially marginal, will either not perceive innovation as a risk, or be less deterred by the potential social sanctions. Social marginality stems from the lack of time for socialization into the typical behavior pattern, a lack of prior experiences from which to generalize, continued frustration with the current state of affairs, or a combination of these factors.

A corollary hypothesis is that early innovators will be more distinct from the general population in terms of needs and risks than will be later innovators. This hypothesis follows from both our assumptions about needs and those about risks. Early innovators come from those groups most in need of changing the status quo, while later innovators adopt innovations to "fine tune" operating procedures that are not in desperate need of change. As more individuals adopt an innovation, two factors reduce the risk. If the innovations have lived up to some of their promises and not led to worse fears, technological risk is reduced. The reduction of social risk accompanies the spread of adoptions. As the noninnovating group becomes more of a distinct minority, its members begin to bear the burden of uniqueness once borne by the innovators.

COMPUTERIZATION AS A TECHNOLOGICAL INNOVATION

Technological innovation in the form of computers in Congress proceeds on two levels. On the aggregate level, Congress has in recent years adopted systemwide computer application for its payroll, the tracking of legislation, bibliographic and original research through the Library of Congress and the Congressional Research Service, committee and floor scheduling, economic and tax simulations, access to executive branch and commercial data files, and the electronic voting system.

While computer-based research, bill tracking, and administrative material are available to members of Congress through free terminals scattered around the Hill, and through phone service from the Bill Status Office, the Congressional Research Service, and other data producers or managers, the real innovative step for individual members is to install their own terminals. The advantage of installing a terminal is more than convenience. Members with their own terminals can create unique data bases such as mailing lists, summaries of constituent visits, tracking of constituent requests (casework), and developing letters with interchangeable paragraphs. Although record-keeping procedures do not require members of Congress to report the exact uses to which they put their computer funds, it is clear that constituent communications and services predominate.

Unlike the Senate, where all senators were given computer terminals and received access to the centralized Correspondence Management System, members of the House face the choice of getting computer services as a resource allocation question. House members must use some of their office funds to contract with outside vendors for computer support. The individual member must decide whether such a technological innovation warrants a reduction in other office support funds.

Promotion of Individual Usage

The House as an institution has encouraged computer applications by individual members through funding, pilot projects, selective benefits, information exchange, and training. In the funding realm, House rules were changed in 1975 to allow members to use up to $1000 per month for computer-related services. Although some members complained about the limits, the average computer user in 1976 expended only about $500 per month on computers. As of 1978 the House rules were changed again to allow free use of office allowances, with no limits by categories. By 1979 computer users expended about $1000 per month on the average for computers.

In an attempt to test the utility of various computer applications, the House Information System, which oversees the chamberwide computer system, has developed a series of pilot projects giving selected members particular services to try and evaluate. Over 40 members were given access to research, administrative, and/or constituent service packages to try out before they went on line to all members with terminals. Written evaluations of pilot projects and word-of-mouth promotion by pilot project members have served to reduce the perceived threat and sell the advantages of usage. Currently, all members with terminals can get free subsidized access to most of the systemwide applications except for those relating to constituent services. Members with terminals are automatically made a part of the Member Information Network.[2] Close to 400 members have taken up this option (see Table 4.2, Chapter 4, for growth patterns).

The House Information System and the Library of Congress promote computer usage through seminars, technical advisors, and training programs. Until 1981, H.I.S. assigned each office to a service representative, whose job was to introduce office staff to computer technology and help them design applications to their specific needs. According to one of the service representatives, a common technique was to go into an office, ask what they had been working on that day, and then hope to find a computer application that would sell them on the utility of computers.

Although the service representatives were not intended to be active promoters, they fell into the role of "winning one more soul" for the computer. Even Boyd Alexander, H.I.S. director, admitted that they had emphasized too much of a "supply-push" rather than a "demand-pull" strategy in selling their wares and that they became too wrapped up in the new technology without really looking at the users and seeing what they actually needed, how they needed it, and the way they operated (Chartrand and Morentz, 1979: 24-25).

In 1981, the service representative program fell victim both to its own success and to the criticism that the representatives were pushing too much. The days of really hard selling were over with the budget cut and the change of philosophy, and H.I.S. was put into a mode of "reacting, rather than going out proselytizing," according to Hamish Murry, H.I.S. deputy director (Groban, 1981: 5). Rather than actively seeking out users, H.I.S. opened a model office in 1981 as a way of triggering interest in computers and providing members and their staffs with examples of potential applications.

H.I.S. continues to promote new services, both for their intrinsic value and as a method of encouraging computer usage in general. A staff member working on one of the newest applications, electronic mail, argued that it was

> a good eye catcher. It gets them into the system. . . . It helps get down to the little guy and encourages him to explore computerization. Many of the early systems were too esoteric for many people on the Hill.

While H.I.S. and the Library of Congress pushed from within, commercial vendors initially badgered members and their staffs to use their products, but the days of hard selling by vendors are over. As one staff member commented:

> The vendors have come a long way in a few years. At first there was a great rush to market their products. Now they realize that the congressional market is very unique and demanding. Members of Congress are not willing to accept standard excuses such as "down time." They expect action. The market on the Hill is prestigious but

rather small. Some vendors have just thrown up their arms and admitted that they can't deal with it.

Individual Resistance to Computer Adoption

Despite active promotion, acceptance of computers by individual congressional offices was not automatic. The decision to put in a terminal was often dominated by the staff, but required the approval if not active promotion of the member, who has veto power. Most members of Congress are result and not means oriented. Many offices did not seek out new means of performing various functions because the results of the traditional means were satisfactory. Other offices were selectively attuned to the emerging environment and kept themselves blissfully unaware of computers. Some offices with obvious needs and awareness of what the computer could do compartmentalized their knowledge and concluded that, while computers did amazing things, "it just wouldn't work in my office" (Hellriegel and Slocum, 1979: 549-551).

The inbred hesitancy to face the risk and inconvenience of change can be seen in the story of an office selected for a pilot project. When the terminal was first turned on, it began to smoke. Although the technician fixed the problem immediately, the staff pushed the new terminal into the closet and never used it again.

A staff member involved in training potential users gave the following catalog of reasons for avoiding the computer:

> Training potential users made me aware of many excuses for not using the computer:
>
> — Congress is very traditional and does not take to change easily.
>
> — The hierarchical structure reduces desire to innovate.
>
> — Congress is a male domain inhabited by lawyers. They like to keep their information close to their vests.
>
> — Congressmen are used to trusting personal contacts whose honesty and judgment can be tested over time. They take into account the awareness that certain sources "may be biased, but they are consistently biased and will present their case honestly."
>
> — Many personal secretaries and legislative operatives felt it would be demeaning to sit at a terminal typing in data.

— Some staff were afraid of the machine. They were distrustful
of it and feared that they would break it.

While resistance to computerization was real, and continues to affect both
initial adoption and levels of utilization, Congress moved rather rapidly
from computer illiteracy to extensive familiarity and usage.

PATTERN OF INDIVIDUAL ADOPTION

Aggregate Diffusion

The most common diffusion pattern for innovations resembles an
S-shaped curve (Mansfield, 1968: 204; Warner, 1974: 436; Feller and
Menzel, 1978: 477). When a potential innovation comes on the scene it is
an unknown quantity with potential risks and little positive experience to
recommend it. The early trial period is very tentative and momentum is
slow to build. As positive experiences mount and potential risks decline,
adoption increases at an accelerating rate. The initial caution is replaced by
a "contagion effect," where competitive pressures mount and the once
unique approach becomes the norm. The rate of new adoptees declines as
the pool of potential users becomes smaller and contains a higher percentage of individuals who have successfully avoided the innovation so far.

The diffusion pattern for computer applications by individual congressional offices resembles the predicted S curve to some degree (see Figure
6.1). Prior to 1975, computer terminals in individual offices were virtually
unheard of. By 1977, the majority of offices had a terminal, and the
adoption rate flattened out by 1980. Diffusion rates for Congress are
contaminated by the fact that we are dealing with a changing pool of
potential adopters. More than half of the members of Congress serving in
1981 were not in office in 1975, and new members in recent years have
almost unanimously adopted computer applications as soon as they
arrived. Studies in other realms focused on stable potential adopters and
would be more likely to show a more dramatic S curve, whereas the influx
of new members in Congress makes the adoption rate look more linear.

IDENTIFYING THE INNOVATORS

The decision to utilize some form of computer application and the
degree of use evidenced serve as the dependent variables for this study.

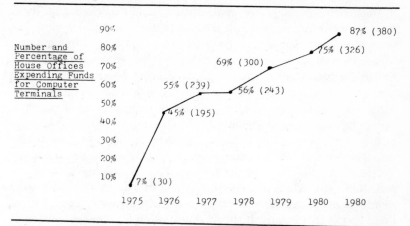

Figure 6.1 The Growth of Computer Usage by Individual Members of Congress, 1975-1981

The working hypotheses indicate the utility of looking at independent variables associated with the concepts of needs of members of Congress and the potential for risk taking.

The data for testing the general working hypothesis and the more specific ones to follow come from social background, political, and behavioral data collected on random samples of the House of Representatives from the 94th through the 96th Congresses. Information on computer usage was collected for noncampaign periods in order to avoid the potentially extensive campaign uses of computerized data files by some members.[3] Record keeping on computer usage collected by the clerk of the House is incomplete in two respects. Personal funds and those from purely campaign budgets are not included. Interview data indicate that the former is quite rare and the latter insignificant for the time period chosen. Second, there is no way adequately to identify the specific uses to which the funds were put. In particular it cannot be determined whether the funds were used for primarily legislative tasks (bibliographic research, bill tracking, substantive research, or the like) or for constituent relations (mail tracking, mailing services, political data sets, poll analysis, and so on). Although such a distinction would be useful, its lack of availability does not significantly hinder our analysis of innovativeness in the broad sense of comparing computer users with nonusers.

Members with computer expenditures for any measurement period will be defined as innovators, even though innovators were a minority group (45 percent) in 1976 and had become a majority (69 percent) by 1979.

Innovations and Needs

While some individuals get satisfaction from the innovative act itself, most technological innovation is directed at reaching specific political or substantive goals. The innovation is presented, and accepted or rejected, on the basis of its efficiency and ability to meet felt needs. Individuals reaping the benefits of the accepted way of doing things are less likely to seek out and accept innovative alternatives. Individual appeal for functional alternatives increases when goals are threatened by continuation of current behavior patterns (Barnett, 1953: 378).

In viewing members of Congress, one does not have to agree totally with Mayhew's (1974: 5) assumption that members of the House are "single-minded seekers of re-election" to accept the pervasiveness of this goal. Numerous strands of conventional wisdom indicate that the road to reelection and increased electoral security includes paying careful attention to one's constituents. It should not be surprising that the function of most initial computer applications sought out by individual members has focused on increased efficiency in dealing with constituent communications. We would expect that members with the least secure political position would most readily seek out such efficiency.

The most obvious predictor of future insecurity in reaching the reelection goal is a history of past electoral insecurity. Two measures of insecurity stand out. The most obvious measure is that of the member's previous electoral margin. While insecurity is to some degree a perceptual factor, no member of Congress can completely disregard his or her vote totals. We would thus expect members from marginal districts to be among the first to use computerized constituent services. The data in Table 6.1 reveal that members whose last electoral contest indicated relative weakness are more likely to computerize some of their office functions. In 1976 the relationship was quite strong. By 1979 it was clear that marginal members chose to use the computer more than nonmarginal members, but the relationship was considerably weaker.

A member's evaluation of his or her electoral strength is both retrospective and prospective. Incumbents can generally count on improving their margins from one election to the next.[4] Among incumbents from marginal districts in 1974, the greatest computerization (80 percent) was found among those who again faced a tough electoral challenge in 1976. Computer utilization seemed to be a way of attempting to fend off defeat.

The assumption that members of Congress adopt computers to reach electoral goals gains support when we compare members with further

TABLE 6.1   Computer Utilization and Electoral Vulnerability Among House Members, 1976 and 1979

| | 1976[a] | | 1979[b] | |
| | Electoral Margin in Previous Election (1974) | | Electoral Margin in Previous Election (1976) | |
	Marginal District*	Secure District	Marginal District*	Secure District
Computer users	27 (57%)	33 (39%)	25 (76%)	49 (65%)
Non-computer users	20 (43%)	52 (61%)	8 (24%)	26 (35%)

a. Chi-square = 4.23; p < .06; Tau b = .1763.
b. Chi-square = .7218; p < .40; Tau b = .1034.
*Less than 60 percent of the vote.

electoral goals with those lacking such motivation. In 1976 only 18 percent of the members voluntarily retiring, and thereby relieved of electoral needs, used computers in their offices, compared to the 50 percent of House members contesting a seat in the 1976 election. In 1978, 38 percent of the retirees were computer users, compared to the 56 percent of House members contesting a seat in the 1978 election.

By 1981, one staff member explained the pattern:

> The current technological laggards tend to come from safer and more rural districts. They do very little outreach and have few communications demands. They are older, more established members who just do not need help with their communications. Every member elected for the first time in 1980 computerized his office.

The efficacy of computer applications for reaching electoral goals remains unclear. Computer users were only slightly more likely than nonusers to win or improve their electoral margins in 1976 and 1978. This may reflect the limited impact of computer applications, the complexity of factors associated with electoral success, and/or the probablity that members of Congress opting for computer services were the ones facing the most difficult challenges in 1976 and would not be expected to improve their margins much, if at all.

Table 6.2 shows that in 1976 Republican members were considerably more likely to use computers than Democrats. This uniqueness stood up when controlling for such factors as past marginality and other background factors.[5] It may have been that Republicans were playing it safe

TABLE 6.2   Computer Utilization and Party Identification of
             House Members, 1976 and 1979

| | 1976[a] | | 1979[b] | |
	Republicans	Democrats	Republicans	Democrats
Computer users	29 (62%)	31 (37%)	22 (58%)	52 (74%)
Non-computer users	18 (38%)	54 (63%)	16 (42%)	18 (26%)

a. Chi-square = 6.78; p < .01; Tau b = .2426.
b. Chi-square = 2.35; p < .10; Tau b = .1688.

after the disastrous 1974 election, in which most Republican members of
Congress suffered electoral reversals in the wake of Watergate. By 1979 the
partisan differential had reversed, with Democrats being somewhat more
likely to have their own computer applications.

Our profile of congressional innovators at this time characterizes them
as those whose electoral insecurity forces the search for alternative ways of
performing the representative task. The inconclusive consequences of
computer utilization and the lack of unanimity of computer use by
marginal members indicate that other forces are at work simultaneously.
Electoral insecurity provides the motivation for seeking alternative technologies, but natural tendencies to feel comfortable with the status quo
and fear of change crop up as barriers that not all are willing to overcome.

Technological Innovation and Risk Taking

The decision to step out from the crowd and use a technological
innovation introduces a number of potential risks. Socially, innovators put
themselves in line for criticism and possible ostracism (Chartrand, 1970:
185). The criticism of traditional ways of doing things stands out as an
implicit criticism of those holding on to the old ways. Whether out of
general fear of change or the specific challenge of being compared to
someone doing a task in a better or more efficient way, the challenged
traditionalist may take out his or her frustration on the proponent of
change. We would thus expect innovators to come disproportionately from
the group that is personally less traditional and that has few ties to others
with traditional outlooks.

The potential risks from computer usage are not minor. Politically,
those who supposedly benefit from the efficiency of a technological
innovation may rebel against the changes it implies. Constituents want
frequent, useful, and personal communications with their representatives.

The increase in constituency size and the growing awareness of citizens make the first two of these desires more important and the third more difficult. As long as congressional staffs used labor-intensive methods of hand-selected targeted mailings, robotyped stock letters, and signatures with an "autopen," the charade of personalized communications could be maintained. Computerizing the process raises the risk of discovery. Members of Congress have reduced the risk of being known for depersonalizing the communications process through the use of computers by keeping their constituents in the dark about their methods. One congressman with computer capability was willing to describe his system but not to reveal his identity since he "didn't want to be known as the first member who assigned a number to each of his constituents to keep track of their letters and his responses." Even Congressman Charlie Rose, one of the heaviest users of computers, felt it necessary to comment in a 1981 newsletter about a recent poll that "we are still in the process of reading and answering each one [response] personally." As computer use becomes the norm, constituents will have less basis for criticizing their representatives on these grounds. With the current flood of computerized mail, the American population is becoming more blasé about the use of computers (Chartrand, 1970: 186).

Risk taking has also been limited by introducing only those forms of computer usage in which the constituent would find it difficult to discover the computer's role. The process of reducing risk also carries over to the Congress as a whole. Money expended for computer applications, and records of those receiving it, is spread over a number of different accounts, many of which are impossible to identify. Few members are willing publicly to risk the criticism that this is "a government of machines, not men."

Potential congressional computer users must also recognize that they personally risk loss of flexibility, loss of control, and the possibility that new computer-associated human errors could embarrass them and/or damage their political future. Computer utilization requires the coding of information into limited categories according to fixed rules. Computers can accept only information organized into particular formats, which can severely limit flexibility in record keeping. Learning to communicate with the computer and preparing the initial data base involves significant "start-up" costs by members of Congress and/or their staffs. Ignorance about computer capabilities is legion and congressional attitudes toward them resemble the "love/hate" attitudes among the general population. The awe and wonder of flashing lights, whirring tapes, and instant responses is balanced against the horror stories of credit card foul-ups, misprinted checks, and other "computer" errors. It takes an act of risk taking and faith in the computer to place the efficiency of one's office and one's future political strength in the "hands" of a complex machine. A secretary can be chastised for sending a form letter to a big contributer, but the computer stands immune to such simple forms of reprimand and immediate correction.

Individual propensity to take risks varies with personality characteristics, but is mediated by social background and status factors that hinder or encourage innovation. Innovative individuals perceiving a non-supportive social setting or potential political disadvantages, or blinded by conventional wisdom will censor their own activities. We would thus expect innovative tendencies to flourish only among those members of Congress unfettered by such perception and outlooks.

The most frequent generalization from rural sociology and cultural anthropology is that socially marginal individuals are more likely to take the risks associated with innovation. Numerous studies show that "innovations are welcomed most readily by those who live, in some sense, at the outskirts of their societies" (Menzel, 1966: 705). Social marginality has been given at least two different meanings and subsequent operational definitions. The sociological tradition tends to define marginality as cosmopolitanism and/or contact with foreign ways of doing things (Menzel, 1966: 705). The theoretical assumption is that such people develop new frames of reference and observe the efficacy of alternative methods. Such individuals have their fears of risk reduced through familiarity with positive consequences in other settings.

Anthropologists tend to define social marginality as "poor integration into the home society" (Menzel, 1960: 705). While postulating different sources of such limited integration, the general operating assumption is that such individuals are not encumbered by traditional outlooks and have little to lose from taking risks, since their social acceptance and desire for integration into the traditional social structure is already low (Watson, 1973: 101).

Innovation and contact with outside influences

According to the sociological definition of marginality, representatives entering Congress with a richness of outside contacts and experiences will be more likely to take the risk of technological innovation, while those with more narrow political experiences will exhibit more retarded innovative tendencies. Although the figures are not statistically significant, it is clear from Table 6.3 that House members entering Congress without previous experience in political positions adopted computer application more readily than those schooled in the more traditional preelection career options. Again, the distinctiveness of the innovators is more dramatic early in the adoption era in 1976 than in 1979.

The content of outside experience also makes a difference in encouraging or discouraging technological innovation. Computers first gained acceptance in the business world, but business people in our sample are not more likely to use computers than members with other occupational backgrounds. The situation looks much different when we control for seniority. Recently elected members of Congress active in the business world after computerization became commonplace were more likely to accept the technology in their new jobs than were either other junior members or those with backgrounds in business entering Congress before computers were the rule in business, rather than the exception (see Table 6.4). By 1979, the uniqueness indicated by business background fades to a greater degree than uniqueness indicated by seniority.

Increasingly, members are coming into the House with legislative computer experience at the state level, and every member with such experience who entered Congress in 1978 and 1980 adopted computers. In 1969, Saloma (1969: 244) predicted that "the real change in congressional attitudes and skills will probably not be felt, however, until a new generation of political talent with practical experience with computers . . . begins to enter Congress."

The two above data sets indicate that the lack of familiarity with the traditional ways of doing things in Congress and proximate contact with outside technologies combined to open the horizon of members to new possibilities.

Innovation and social integration

In testing the anthropological assumption that risk taking accompanies the general lack of social integration, a number of different logical correlates of social marginality stand out as potentially associated with technological innovation. By viewing integration as a process of both feeling accepted by others with whom one must interact and taking on their values and operating assumptions, it becomes clear that integration will be a function of the time available for the process to run its course, the potential for social acceptance, and the perceived benefits of not risking one's concrete gains.

TABLE 6.3 Computer Utilization and Previous Political Experience of House Members, 1976 and 1979

	1976[a]		1979[b]	
	No Previous Electoral of Appointive Political Experience	Specific Political Experience in Elective or Appointive Positions*	No Previous Electoral or Appointive Political Experience	Specific Political Experience in Elective or Appointive Positions**
Computer users	19 (58%)	40 (41%)	25 (74%)	49 (66%)
Non-computer users	14 (42%)	57 (59%)	9 (26%)	25 (34%)

a. Chi-square = 2.65; $p < .10$; Tau b = .1428.
b. Chi-square = 2.88; $p < .30$; Tau b = .0631.

*62 percent served in state legislatures, 25 percent in other elective positions, and 13 percent in appointive government positions just prior to congressional service (former congressional staff members were deleted).

**47 percent served in state legislatures, 25 percent in other elective positions, and 28 percent in appointive government positions just prior to congressional service (former congressional staff members were deleted).

TABLE 6.4 Technological Innovation, Occupational Background, and Seniority Among House Members, 1976 and 1979

	1976[a]				1979[b]			
	Low Seniority*		High Seniority		Low Seniority*		High Seniority	
	Business	Nonbusiness	Business	Nonbusiness	Business	Nonbusiness	Business	Nonbusiness
Computer users	10 (71%)	25 (57%)	6 (27%)	19 (36%)	10 (83%)	30 (73%)	7 (47%)	27 (68%)
Non-computer users	4 (29%)	19 (43%)	16 (73%)	33 (64%)	2 (17%)	11 (27%)	8 (53%)	13 (32%)

a. Chi-square = 10.70; p < .05; Tau c = .2580.
b. Chi-square = .4972; p < .95; Tau c = .1107.
*Less than 4 terms.

Seniority. Since integration takes time to develop, more junior members of Congress should be less integrated and also more willing to take the risks associated with innovation. Research on the willingness to reform organizations in general (Zaltman et al., 1973: 73) and Congress in particular (Davidson et al., 1966: 81) indicates that new personnel enter with new expectations and methods, and think more highly of change. The data on computer utilization (see Table 6.5) indicate a rather clear trend in the same direction during the initial measurement point, with a confused picture by 1979.

Since low seniority is highly related to electoral marginality, which we have already pointed out as a precursor of innovation, it is necessary to determine the independent effect of each factor. By controlling for marginality it is clear that marginality is most important, but that seniority has an independent effect (see Table 6.6). Regardless of seniority, marginal members during both time periods were almost equally likely to stand out as innovators, and among the electorally secure members, only the most junior ones stood out as innovative. Even when electoral threat was not high, junior members in 1976 from secure districts sought out technological innovation more than their more senior colleagues. By 1979, the impact of the two variables had lessened dramatically, with the only unique noninnovators being secure senior members.

Age. Age serves as another surrogate measure of potential for integration. Younger members of any social organization have had less time to go through the integration process, and in Congress find themselves faced with an institution with a high average age (almost 50 for the years in question) and a power distribution heavily skewed toward older members through the seniority system. Although conventional wisdom speculates that youth are more venturesome, less tied to traditional ways of doing things, and more susceptible to fads, data collected in other realms by sociologists and anthropologists indicate inconsistent or nonexistent relationships between age and technological innovativeness (Robertson, 1971: 88-115; Hagerstrand, 1967: 150; Rogers and Shoemaker, 1971: 196, 352).

For congressional technological innovation, younger members in the initial sample do show a somewhat greater tendency to accept innovations than do older members. By 1979, age is much less important as a precursor to innovation (see Table 6.7). The independent effect of age carries through after controlling for such factors as party, margin, and political experience, but the data include a confounding twist for seniority. Members of Congress entering Congress after the age of 50 were somewhat more likely to accept computerization. While no solid explanation is

TABLE 6.5 Congressional Seniority and Technological Innovation Among House Members, 1976 and 1979

	1976[a] Number of Terms in Office			1979[b] Number of Terms in Office		
	1-2	3-6	7 or more	1-2	3-6	7 or more
Computer users	27 (60%)	21 (50%)	12 (27%)	23 (66%)	30 (77%)	21 (62%)
Non-computer users	18 (40%)	21 (50%)	33 (73%)	12 (34%)	9 (23%)	13 (38%)

a. Chi-square = 10.60; p < .01; Tau c = .2996.
b. Chi-square = 2.12; p < .30; Tau c = .0326.

TABLE 6.6 Technological Innovation, Electoral Marginality, and Seniority Among House Members, 1976 and 1979

| | 1976[a] | | | | 1979[b] | | | |
| | Junior Members* | | Senior Members | | Junior Members* | | Senior Members | |
	Marginal**	Secure	Marginal**	Secure	Marginal**	Secure	Marginal**	Secure
Computer users	18 (60%)	17 (61%)	9 (53%)	16 (28%)	19 (76%)	21 (75%)	6 (75%)	28 (60%)
Non-computer users	12 (40%)	11 (39%)	8 (47%)	41 (72%)	6 (24%)	7 (25%)	2 (25%)	19 (40%)

a. Chi-square = 12.522; p < .01; Tau c = .3157.
b. Chi-square = 3.093; p < .20; Tau c = .1588.
*Members with 4 terms or less.
**Less than 60 percent of the vote in the previous election.

TABLE 6.7 Age and Technological Innovation Among House Members, 1976 and 1979

| | 1976[a] Age | | | | | 1979[b] Age | | | | |
	25-39	40-49	50-59	60-69	70+	25-39	40-49	50-59	60-69	70+
Computer users	10 (59%)	21 (47%)	17 (47%)	11 (38%)	1 (20%)	20 (73%)	16 (59%)	27 (71%)	11 (85%)	0
Non-computer users	7 (41%)	24 (53%)	19 (53%)	18 (62%)	4 (80%)	7 (27%)	11 (41%)	11 (29%)	2 (15%)	3 (100%)

a. Chi-square = 3.27; $p < .50$; Tau c = .1462.
b. Chi-square = 9.66; $p < .05$; Tau c = .016

evident, such "late starters" seem to feel particularly politically and/or socially marginal. Computerization may be one way of providing them a better opportunity to compete with their age group cohorts who supersede them in seniority and other power sources.

CHANGING PATTERN OF INNOVATION

Innovation is generally a fairly slow process, especially when it involves changing fundamental ways in which people operate. Computerization in Congress has progressed with remarkable speed. Within ten years an intial oddity has become a common operating procedure. The rapidity of innovation can be accounted for partially by the physical proximity and ease of communication between initial innovators and potential innovation targets. Other research has shown the impact of colleagues on substantive decisions in the Congress. One would not expect less information transfer on procedural hints (Kingdon, 1981). Taking the innovative step often makes innovators outspoken converts; getting others to follow their lead justifies their initial decision.

The process has also been facilitated by active promotion by vested interests. Vendors with congressional applications rapidly sprung up to serve congressional needs and make a profit. The House Information System informed, cajoled, and help the hands of members as they moved into the computer age. More and more legislators and staffs moved to the position of not being able to conceive of going back to the old ways of doing things.

The rapidity of innovation may also be accounted for by the fact that computerization did not run into the kinds of opposition faced by other attempts to reform Congress. Members were given free rein to tailor computer use to their own needs. Unlike reforms such as those redrawing committee jurisdictions, where vested interests of chairpersons were clear, computerization gave something to everybody. Committee chairs, who may lose some of the power resources of information over junior members, often either did not perceive the shift or felt compensated in other ways from the new information resources they received.

In the process of expanding the base of computer users, the distinctiveness of the individual users began to erode. Members with less severe electoral needs saw applications for their offices. Increasing numbers of users reduced the risk of colleague ostracism, staff fear for their jobs, and constituent condemnation. The influx of newly elected representatives

TABLE 6.8 Degree of Overrepresentation of Categoric Groups of Members of Congress in Terms of Technological Innovation 1976 and 1979

	Percentage Difference in Technological Innovation Among Categoric Group Members and Overall Percentage of Technological Innovation	
	1976 (46% with computers overall)	1979 (69% with computers overall)
Marginal members	+11	+7
Junior members	+14	+7
Younger members[a]	+13	+5
Members with no previous political experience	+11	+5
Republicans	+16	−11
Nonretirees	+ 2	+4[b]
Low-seniority members with business background	+25	+14
Junior marginal members	+10	+2

a. Under 40 years old.
b. 1978 data.

brought in new members with different backgrounds, but who were almost universal in their acceptance of computers. Of the 80 new members elected in 1978, 78 accepted some form of computer application, and the millenium seemed at hand in 1980, when every new member took the computer plunge.

Table 6.8 compares the overrepresentation of particular types of members of Congress among the computer innovators at the two measurement points. While the key precursors to innovation still have utility in predicting likely innovators, the uniqueness of the innovators is greatly reduced.

Over the two time periods, the picture of the technological innovator in Congress emerges as that of a politician with greater need to bolster electoral strength and greater willingness to take risks. However, the distinctiveness of the innovative group has diminished greatly in a very short period of time. While the variables used to measure needs and marginality all have some degree of interrelatedness, each of them exerts an independent effect on the decision to use computer applications. The average innovator remains a young junior member, from a marginal district, who came to Congress with little previous political experience in elective office.

All indications are that computer use is well past the stage of being an innovation. It is now a well-established fact; and future generations of congressional legislators will have to justify to themselves and those around them the decision *not* to take advantage of modern information technology.

NOTES

1. The most exhaustive bibliography on the general topic of technological innovation can be found in Rogers and Shoemaker (1971: 388-466).

2. The Member Information Network (MIN) provides for the delivery of various information products directly to House member offices. The information products are constantly being expanded and currently include the Legislative Information and Status System (LEGIS), Summary of Proceedings and Debates (SOPAD), the Member Budget Information System (MBIS), the Library of Congress Bibliographic and Issue Briefs data bases, the Federal Assistance Programs Retrieval System (FAPRS), and a series of commercial data bases such as JURIS (Justice Retrieval Inquiry System) and the *New York Times* data base.

3. For each year, data on computer usage came from the *Report of the Clerk of the House,* for the following dates: 1976 sample (n = 108), January 1-July 30, 1976; 1979 sample (n = 132), July 1-September 30, 1979.

4. Estimated at 2-5 percent per election for members of the House. See Erickson (1971).

5. Controls for previous occupation, ideology, age, leadership, and seniority all indicated the independent effect of party.

7
THE ACCESS WARS

RHETORIC AND REALITY OF INFORMATION SHARING

Once Congress developed the capability for modern information processing through computerization, the battle turned from one of acquisition to one of access. Despite the fact that information reformers promoted change as a method of improving information access to all participants, the stark reality that controlling information creation and dissemination leads to power tempts many individuals to turn from information democrats to information dictators. It is one thing for a reformer to demand that information be shared down to his or her level, and quite a different thing to turn around and dissipate one of his or her power resources by sharing information even further. The story of providing access to information technology and information per se by Congress represents a tug-of-war between the pressure to share information freely in a democratic society and the organizational and personal desires to use information and information access to help reach one's more private goals. In Chartrand's (1971b: 170) words:

> From the beginning there has been a controversy as to the question of who should control this [computer] capability and the concurrent vestiges of power which accrue to those who control or monitor information resources.

From the organizational standpoint, limiting access to information by both insiders and outsiders has been publicly justified by raising fears of cost, overloading of the system, or legal constraints, while the real reasons were much more practical. As in all organizations, information serves as an organizational resource for Congress vis-à-vis its environment. In all government bureaucracies, controlling information helps the organization to maintain its reputation by inhibiting embarrassing information and facilitating the dissemination of positive information (Laudon, 1974: 59). Despite its position as a public entity, Congress has decided not to computerize, or to limit access to, information that might be interpreted as embarrassing. Controlling access also helps preserve the autonomy of an organization or its subunits by allowing them to use their exclusive information to provide a strategic advantage.

Individuals within Congress act on the basis of similar, but expanded motivations. They do not want to make it too easy for their political opponents to evaluate them and wish to have unique access to data they can use for their own purposes. To these arguments, members of Congress add that certain information represents their individual efforts and creativity, and the widespread dissemination of such material as voting lists, casework records, and staff analyses would not only violate canons of ethics, but would unfairly disadvantage them politically (Chartrand and Staenberg, 1978: 28).

The introduction of computer technology thrusts the questions of access to the forefront, since it makes it much easier to transport information across organizational boundaries. Congress is clearly part of the new information environment, which

> creates new forms of "property," i.e., organized information with transfer and transformative capacities far greater than before. It may tend to create a new powerful "property class," whose property is in their heads—those exclusively possessing the specific skills required for access to, and manipulation of, vital knowledge and information [McHale, 1976: 24-25].

Congress as an institution, as well as individual members of Congress, is increasingly becoming aware of this new power source, and has adopted rules for computer access that they hope will protect their competitive advantage in the production and analysis of, and access to, computerized information.

ACCESS TO THE TECHNOLOGY

In a collective decision-making body such as Congress, in which changes in resource allocations are subject to votes in which each participant's vote counts equally, there was never any consideration of limiting access to the terminals forever. The question of providing computer hardware was one of "when," not "if." The process of providing hardware access had to be perceived as fair and logical. Both the Senate plan of universal grants and the House approach of allowing members to use existing resources to purchase services met these criteria.

In experimenting with new hardware and expanded access by members to new data banks, both chambers used pilot projects. Individuals chosen for inclusion came from the ranks of those making the loudest demands for change and those whose presence on the overseeing subcommittees reflected their interest in computerization (not to mention their power over the decision). Attempts were made to allocate selective computer resources in a nonpartisan manner. Pilot projects always had representation from the minority party roughly equal to the party strength in the chamber.

When the leadership terminals were initially put on the floor to monitor ongoing votes, the capabilities of the minority and majority systems were identical. After the vote-monitoring terminals proved their utility, pressure from nonleaders led the House to install terminals in the back of the chamber that could access much of the same data. In providing terminals to committees, the right to access was equal for majority and minority staff members, although the initial terminals were placed in the majority staff offices. As district and state offices became an integral part of the member's operation, provisions were made to link these offices to the Washington office and to make available to them the same data bases. Following their traditional distribution approaches, the House required members to pay for such services, while the Senate offered terminals on request.

Congress paid little attention to providing hardware to potential outside information consumers. Terminals in the Congress can be used only by members of Congress or their staffs. The Library of Congress has a limited number of public terminals with access to some congressional data bases (see next section), but the potential for public terminals spread around the country has not gone beyond the talking stage.

Within Congress, early limited access to computer hardware was a short-term problem in the spread of modern information technology brought on by budget limitations, uncertainty as to the equipment to purchase, and the lack of an overall plan for distribution and access. Congress was clearly feeling its way. Today the battle is not over access to hardware, but over access to the data and analysis packages that make that hardware useful.

ACCESS TO THE DATA BANKS

The value of a data base often depends more on who may be excluded from using it than who may access it [Michael Duggan, quoted in Amara, 1974: 104].

The messy nature of congressional decision-making, with its lack of overall coordination and its multiple decision points, makes its failure to devise a master plan for computerization and information access understandable. Despite the lack of a sophisticated strategy for limiting access to computerized information, sporadic steps by Congress and its subunits reveal that members of Congress are not unaware of the advantage encompassed in the ability to control access to information.

The Individual Versus
the Organization and Its Members

Congress has clearly recognized the right of individual members to create and access their own data bases with little or no outside interference. Elaborate password procedures protect individual data bases from outside perusal. In the Senate, the Correspondence Management System limits the number of categories into which a letter writer can be placed; but no attempt is made to monitor an individual member's coding scheme, even to determine whether the senator is breaking Senate rules by storing blatantly partisan political information.

Individual members of Congress have also been granted the right to protect information relating to their own behavior and performance. In the House, the introduction of electronic voting allowed easy access to individual voting records and patterns, but members balked at providing the capability for such analysis until guaranteed that members could only access their own voting records. Although readily available, the CMS system in the Senate is not allowed to report publicly the amount of mail generated by individual offices. In their attempts to monitor computer usage in order to facilitate long-term planning, H.I.S., the Library of Congress, and the Senate Computer Center have all run into trouble from individual members who do not wish to be monitored. Neither chamber will readily publish even the fact that particular members are computer users, since many members wish to keep this information from their constituents. Up until a few years ago, the financial reports of congressional office expenditures were designed to obfuscate total expenditures by individual offices, and the *Digest of Public Bills* made it difficult, if not humanly impossible, to monitor the legislative record of members. The LEGIS system makes it possible to create "batting averages" for members, which measure their success at getting legislation passed, but the public access to creating such measures is much more laborious than would be possible if Congress really wanted to share it (Frantzich, 1979c).

Members Versus the Leadership

Compared to that of most organizations, the congressional leadership has not been able to centralize computerized congressional information under its control. By and large, the leadership has no more access to the general files than do regular members. Two exceptions stand out. Chairpersons of committees with their own data bases usually have first and sometimes exclusive access to those files. And on the floor of the House, the party leadership groups can do more sophisticated analysis of ongoing votes than can be done by regular members on their two terminals.

Committee Territorialism

Committees jealously guard their turf and the information that goes along with it. The power of individual committee chairpersons and the committees they control is often vested in the information they have. The jealousy of committees is exemplified by the experience of one staff member:

> Budget information had become a turf question. The Appropriations Committee had a corner on the market. The authorizing committees often did not know what budget items were in their jurisdiction. When I first arrived, I suggested to an authorizing committee that they just ask Appropriations for some data I knew they had, and the committee members just laughed at me.

While budget information is readily available, it has been relatively difficult to "ventilate" the budget system and get data down to the individual-member level. Initially the Congressional Budget Office limited usage to members of the committee. Slowly the access rights of individual members have emerged, but what this usually means is that the individual is placed on the priority list well below that position guaranteed to committee members; thus, the individual's analysis may never get done, or arrives well after the key decisions have already been made.

A classic case of limited access can be seen in the Individual Tax Estimation Simulation. After its creation by the Treasury Department, members of the Joint Committee on Taxation and Internal Revenue could approach Treasury, hat in hand, to do an analysis of a proposal (Dartmouth College, 1976: 25). The Joint Tax Committee was dependent on Treasury's priorities and its ability to affect the content of analysis done. Given a choice, the Department of the Treasury and its subunit, the Internal Revenue Service, prefer complex rather than simple tax laws, since the more complex the tax laws, the more need for bureaucrats to interpret the laws and catch violators. Proposals for simplified tax procedures were often turned away with explanations such as, "We don't have time for such an analysis," or, "The simulation model is not designed to answer such questions."

Acting as good bureaucrats, Treasury officials held on to access to the model and protected their power, which was based on access to information. Members of the Joint Committee wailed publicly that this was public information and the Congress deserved direct access. Congressman Charles Vanik (D-OH) complained that the IRS is "a sphinx protecting the privileged from Congress" (Cohen, 1973: 383). To counter such demands, Treasury argued that since the data came from individual tax returns, only the Department of the Treasury was legally able to protect individual privacy. After numerous skirmishes. the Joint Committee got the model and changed its tune. After arguing for the open right to information, members of the Joint Committee turned around and showed that they had learned their lesson well. They became the ones unwilling to open access to the model, arguing that open access would be impossible since the model was so complex and required a trained operator, the data was so confidential that only the Joint Committee could be trusted to protect individual privacy, and too much use would be costly and overburden the system. Currently the staff will do runs for other committees and individual members on request, but their right to use the system comes well after priority use by the Joint Committee. As long as the costs of limiting access in terms of criticism and ill feeling from colleagues are less than the benefits of controlling access to the simulation model, the Joint Committee on Internal Revenue and Taxation will thwart open access.

Congress Versus the Executive

Congress and the executive branch exist in a symbiotic relationship, in which each partner needs cooperation and information from the other. Traditionally, Congress has been the information stepchild, begging for scraps of data and information from the data-rich executive branch. While a massive imbalance still exists, there are areas in which modern information technology has increased the value of some of the information that Congress can provide to the executive branch. This availability of information on both ends of Pennsylvania Avenue has spawned a new dynamic tension over information access.

Congressional access to executive branch information

Most of the information exchange involves the transfer of executive branch information to the Congress. Increasingly, Congress has used its legislative power to require agencies to provide data in machine-readable form to the Hill, but open access is still a long way off. A number of problems stand in the way of open access.

Executive branch opposition and foot dragging. Realizing the advantage of controlling information, executive branch agencies find ways to discourage cooperation, whether by turning to legalism such as that shown by Treasury in sharing the tax simulation model, or by simple foot dragging. In the debate over the Congressional Budget Office, the late Senator Lee Metcalf (D-WY) exhorted Congress to demand more executive data, and observed that in the past the executive branch, and especially the Office of Management and Budget, had expressed "an attitude of passive resistance, with semantic sawdust as their weapon" (U.S. Congress, Joint Committee on Congressional Operations, 1974: 527).

Part of the lack of executive branch response to congressional information requests for information may stem from the timid way in which the Congress has approached the problem. Former H.I.S. Director Frank Ryan expressed the H.I.S. position when he stated that "we're exploring what information is available on their computers to see what they wouldn't have any objection to giving Congress" (Cohen, 1973: 380). The hesitancy of executives to provide legislatures with adequate information is not a new phenomenon. Speaking about Bismarkian Germany, Max Weber commented:

> Officials would give the legislature only the barest minimum of information, because they regarded it as an assembly of impotent grumblers, full of learned conceit and a drag on efficient operations [quoted in Heaphey, 1975: 479].

For many members of the executive branch these words summarize their current view of the Congress. With such an attitude, Congress may need to demand more information, and not simply ask for it politely.

Data transfer problems. Frustration over the transfer of information from the executive branch often stems from the overblown expectations members of Congress have concerning the availability and utility of such data. In summarizing Congress's move into the computer age, Chartrand observed that

> while there were millions of punched cards and thousands of reels of magnetic tapes, irregularly inventoried at best, there was very little that could be used in its present form. . . . But there continues to be, in certain quarters, this almost mystical quality of wanting to believe that if we just had all that Executive Branch information, especially on line, how many great things we could do [Chartrand and Morentz, 1979: 42).

There is a real danger of Congress being overwhelmed with a "feast of undigestable data" (U.S. Congress, Senate, Commission on the Operation of the Senate, 1977b: 127).

Even if the desired data exist, they may not be in the form Congress needs or can use. Executives and legislatures simply need different kinds of data. Executive branch data collection techniques were designed to serve their own unique needs. There is not even any coordination of data collection, coding, or analysis techniques within the executive branch, much less a capability to transfer data banks and analysis tools from one branch to another. In some cases it may be easier to start from ground zero and create a data base designed to fit Congress's needs, rather than attempting to understand and straighten out the lack of equivalencies between the data collected and the outputs needed. Washington is filled with "horror stories of those who tried to crack informational peanuts with a computer sledgehammer" (Thompson, 1976: 54).

Despite the problems, congressional access to executive branch information has improved both in terms of quantity and quality. Efficiency still suffers from duplicative data collection and lack of coordination, but more information is flowing between the two branches today then ever before.

Executive branch access to congressional information

Congress has had so little experience providing information to the executive branch that its initial efforts were marked by missteps and reflected the fact that the Congress as an organization had not thought out just how far it should go in terms of cooperation.

While the OMB has used budget analysis developed by the CBO, and White House researchers use the Library of Congress bibliographic data bases, the most important unique data bases Congress can share with the executive are those such as LEGIS and SOPAD, which monitor ongoing legislative activity. Access to these data bases would give the White House, particularly, a strategic advantage in knowing what decisions are about to be made, and in providing the raw material for strategy planning. The White House was rather slow in considering an integrated computerized information system. It was not until 1978 that the Carter administration moved the White House into the computer age (Bulletin of the American Society for Information Science, 1978: 15-21). Using Vice President Mondale's position as presiding officer in the Senate, the White House added the Library of Congress SCORPIO, LEGIS, and SOPAD files to its own administrative files. H.I.S. sent the White House tapes of chamber voting records, which served as the raw material for White House analysts to create their own voting profiles of members and the base for executive lobbying strategy. By the end of the Carter administration, the White House Information Center provided invaluable strategic information.

Reactions to the development of this cooperation varied. One senior congressional staff member praised the developments and had only minor quibbles:

It is in the best interest of the Hill to have the White House fully informed as to what we are doing up here. Full sharing of information is desirable. Attempts by the Carter White House to use the SCORPIO were not undesirable, but had two fatal flaws. First of all the information was provided to too many units in the White House and we got into some contractual problems with data base vendors who sold their services under the assumption that they would be used by Congress alone. Secondly, the White House tried to develop a lock-step monitoring program for the president's program. They just did not know how this place works. They assumed that every bill simply proceeded intact from one stage to the next instead of realizing that substantive ideas can be buried in omnibus legislation or added as amendments.

Other senior congressional staff members argued that "Congress is at enough of an information disadvantage compared to the White House, which has the full bureaucracy working for it. We shouldn't share all our information." The way in which the Carter administration went about getting access to congressional data left a bad taste in many members' mouths:

> Under the Carter administration, the White House became an unprincipled information thief. Vice President Mondale, who had a SCORPIO terminal in his official position as presiding officer in the Senate, used the terminal as a gateway to SCORPIO data files for the entire White House staff. Richard Hardin from the White House Staff was the worst of the lot. Not only did he steal our information, but the unprincipled swine bragged about it. He wrote "kiss and tell" articles about how clever they had been. There is now a memo of understanding with Vice President Bush that this will not happen in the Reagan administration.

With the bad experience during the Carter administration and the current divided party control between Congress and the White House, cooperation and access is much less likely. After a brief flirtation during which a naive Congress willingly succumbed to the ovations of an information-seeking White House, cooler heads are now discussing how Congress can cooperate without losing the limited information advantages it now has.

CONGRESS VERSUS THE PUBLIC

Congress clearly has not come to grips with how widely it wants to disseminate its data files to the public. While all the information was collected at public expense and should refer to the official functions of Congress, initial dissemination techniques indicate that Congress would like to make a distinction between public and private data. The public terminals in the Library of Congress currently allow anyone to access the bibliographic files and the Library of Congress version of LEGIS. However, the public cannot do some of the sophisticated analyses of the LEGIS files and does not have access to valuable research files such as voting records or the *Congressional Record Index*.

Open access to governmental data banks holds the potential for expanding citizen impact by allowing citizens to support or oppose legislative options with the same timely information used by legislatures, as well as by allowing continuous citizen monitoring of implementation (Michael, 1971: 299). Currently, citizens are largely the recipients of the outputs of congressional computers in an indirect manner, rather than being direct users. Legislation has been introduced to provide a toll-free telephone number for the LEGIS office, but wider dissemination of other congressional data bases is a long way off (Gregory, 1979b: 5).

CONTINUING ACCESS PROBLEMS

Conventional wisdom both inside and outside of Congress is committed to the doctrine that more information is better than less, and, at least in the abstract, open sharing of information is preferable to selfish hoarding. Despite these long-term goals, no general policy or specific set of applications serves as the guiding force for information policy either within Congress, between Congress and its environment, or even between environmental elements.

A number of pressing access problems continue to haunt Congress. The ethical questions brought up by the Common Cause suit, which stem from the blatant political payoffs incumbents receive from computer-facilitated franking procedures will have to be faced, whether or not the suit is won by Common Cause. In fact, the very existence of a legal action against the Congress has already led to some tightening of procedures.

The access to computerized information capabilities thrusts Congress into new areas for which few precedents exist. Computer proponents are constantly pushing Congress in an attempt to define the limits of what might be technologically possible but politically unacceptable. For example, in 1981 the Post Office and Civil Service Committee in the House requested funds to use the computer to provide demographic data to incumbents that would be helpful in reacting to redistricting plans. The committee unanimously accepted the proposal and dealt with it as just another logical extension of computer capability until the Republicans belatedly objected that this service to incumbents would help the Democrats, who had more seats to protect. Eventually, the argument that such an application would have partisan impact and would reflect unfavorably on the House won the day, but it was a close battle (Arieff, 1981a).

As the impact and utility of congressional computer applications emerge more clearly, congressional observers and members of Congress themselves will have to answer the questions of who should have access to these information resources, in what form, and how providing access can be accomplished. If the challenge of dragging Congress into the computer age was significant, the challenges of combining Congress's new information capabilities with the values of fairness and democracy promise to tax congressional ingenuity to the limit.

8
IMPLICATIONS OF A COMPUTERIZED CONGRESS

Never underestimate the power of a computer.... History's most profound revolutions have been underestimated by their contemporaries [Hubert Humphrey, in U.S. Congress, Senate, Congressional Record, 1964: 9075].

Technology is already tilting the fundamental relationships of government.... A new and heavy factor has entered the old system of checks and balances [Chartrand, in Krevitt Eres, 1980: 18].

Effects and advance in information technology on society have been viewed as more disruptive than any other technological impact.... It is possible that such impacts will change the very locus and function of power and society [McHale, 1976: 1].

Information technology is a tool which can easily be employed to promote personal and political interests as well as the public interest. It is simply naive to assume that the impact will be neutral [staff interview].

The emergence of Congress as a heavy computer user is more than a story of an institution and its members belatedly but wholeheartedly following other segments of society into the computer age. Installing new technologies involves more than a simple revision of procedures and capabilities. The availability of the fruits of the technology carries with it the potential for changing the structure, behavior patterns, and outputs of the institution and its members (Yin et al., 1977: 39).

Although Norton (1980) captures the magnitude of potential change when he describes computerization in Congress as the "quiet revolution," describing it as "quiet" emphasizes the fact that little attention is paid to the process or its consequences. Former Congressman Charles Mosher (R-OH), after serving in Congress and then reviewing the academic literature in preparation for teaching, expressed surprise that he found "missing any serious . . . any adequate analysis of Congress in terms of the influence of its information resources" (Chartrand and Morentz, 1979: 72). The lack of attention paid to the impact of information technology is not limited to the Congress. Worthley (1977a: 425), commenting on the whole spectrum of legislatures, concluded:

> Hardly a study [is] available which analyzes the consequences of modern legislative information systems for the legislative process, for democratic government, or for public policy making.

While everyone agrees that Congress is not the same since the introduction of computers, the specific contours of the resulting changes remain hazy. A number of factors contribute to beclouding the issue. Between 1970 and the present, when computer capabilities really took hold, the Congress went through an orgy of planned reforms, found itself subject to an influx of new members with different perspectives, and realized the dramatic changes in its environment. Improved information technology was just one of the factors that might account for changes in congressional behavior and performance.

A second difficulty in assessing the impact of computers arises from the lack of concrete measures for assessing relevant congressional behavior and performance. While it is relatively easy to quantify such factors as attendance, party support on votes, and number of hours in session, more important concepts such as power, efficiency, or quality of legislation avoid easy measurement. Even in those areas where we have intuitive and/or empirical benchmarks against which to compare the changes facilitated by computerization, the final results are not yet in. Some of the consequences of computerization will not be felt for many years. The impact in some areas will depend on a cumulative effect, while in others the impact will increase as more functions are computerized and more members take advantage of the available applications. The ultimate impact of computerization in Congress is not fixed. Numerous decisions still have to be made. Congressional decision makers will react to the current consequences as they perceive them and take corrective action to redirect the impact to better meet their goals.

Given the inherent limitations of predicting the consequences of computerization in a setting such as Congress, this chapter will offer some tentative conclusions. Where possible, hard empirical data will be employed, but to a large degree the conclusions will be based on softer speculations of observers and perceptions of participants. The process of analysis will be enhanced by the fact that it is not necessary to start from ground zero. Research in a wide variety of realms focuses on the impact of modern information technology on organizations and their members. Many of the same consequences discovered in business and state legislative settings should emerge in Congress.

While the analysis of consequences aims at objectivity, the biases of the author obviously emerge in the choice of consequences analyzed and the characterization of specific consequences as positive or negative. My yardsticks for evaluation stem both from personal proclivity and the stated objectives of those who promoted computerization. My evaluations will favor efficiency over inefficiency, improved representation over diminished representation, more widely shared information over information fiefdoms, more satisfying job components over less, and policy decisions based on explicit understanding of the consequences over "flying blind."

I will explicitly attempt to avoid both the assumption that actual consequences are the same as intended consequences and the assumption that change is inherently good. Computerization was hailed by its proponents as a reform, but

> "reform" denotes change for the better; but whether change is reform depends on one's point of view.... Nor is it possible to say with certainty whether a given innovation will resolve the problem for which it was designed ... change usually brings in its wake costs as well as benefits ... the passage of time may render obsolete even the most useful innovations. History is strewn with examples of one generation's reforms which exacerbated the next generation's problems [Davidson and Oleszak, 1976: 38].

We must remember that

> information technology is a malleable tool whose ultimate social meaning, content and consequences are highly subject to the influence of the specific political values and interests that inform its use [Laudon, 1974: 311].

IMPACT ON EFFICIENCY

Promoters of computerization argued that the introduction of modern information technology would increase efficiency in general by increasing output of higher-quality products using fewer resources. While the computer has reduced the per unit cost of producing letters, reduced the time required of a member to participate in a roll call vote, and reduced the costs associated with the publication of official records of Congress (U.S. Congress, House, Committee on House Administration, 1977: 3), the real savings have not emerged. With new computer capabilities, it is not only that some previous tasks are performed more efficiently, but also that tasks once out of the realm of possibility are grafted onto the previous demands.

In the realm of computer-facilitated mailings, the introduction of the computer, with the potential for reusing "canned" paragraphs and targeted mailing lists, reduced the cost of sending out a high-quality letter; but as Table 2.1 (in Chapter 2) dramatically points out, the result was more mail being generated by congressional offices. As congressional offices increasingly flood their districts with solicited and unsolicited communications, more and more constituents are encouraged to increase the demand on the congressional office with additional requests for information or expressions of opinion. During the 1981 budget debate, one staff member exclaimed:

> The irony of this is that we are spending more money to answer the horde of letters asking the government to spend less money. I would like to insert a line in President Reagan's speeches to say, "Write your congressman, but don't include your return address." If they write to us, we will write back, which will just encourage them to write again. Before we had computers, this vicious circle just did not exist.

While the use of the computer might free up some staff members and members of Congress themselves to focus on more substantive issues, there is little evidence that such a shift of effort has taken place generally.

The pattern of increased demands following computerization repeats itself in other realms. Prior to electronic voting in the House, the burden of a roll call vote discouraged many members from inflicting such a demand on their colleagues. With the availability of a less time-consuming voting process, the number of recorded votes jumped dramatically (see Table 2.1). Now, although the time per vote has been cut by two-thirds, the increased number of votes almost negates the time saved.

TABLE 8.1   Legislative Branch Appropriations, 1946-1979

Year	Appropriations	Year	Appropriations
1946	$54,065,614	1963	$150,426,185
1947	61,825,020	1964	168,467,869
1948	62,119,714	1965	221,904,318
1949	62,057,678	1966	197,965,307
1950	64,313,460	1967	221,715,643
1951	71,888,244	1968	282,003,322
1952	75,673,896	1969	311,542,399
1953	77,670,076	1970	361,024,327
1954	70,925,361	1971	443,104,319
1955	86,304,923	1972	564,107,992
1956	94,827,986	1973	645,127,365
1957	120,775,798	1974	662,180,668
1958	107,785,560	1975	785,618,833
1959	136,153,580	1976	947,185,778
1960	131,055,385	1977	977,280,715
1961	140,930,781	1978	957,386,500
1962	136,686,715	1979	1,137,991,500

SOURCE: U.S. Congress, House, Committee on House Administration (1978b); information for fiscal year 1979 is from the Senate Subcommittee on Legislative Branch Appropriations.

In terms of publishing and the creation of other computerized data files such as the Bill Status System, Congress has been encouraged to publish more and develop more sophisticated tracking and analysis techniques. The upshot is that, far from reducing the cost of congressional operations, the dollar figure has skyrocketed. There is no doubt that we are getting more in terms of high-quality information for our money, but we are also paying an increased price (see Table 8.1).

When computerization was first suggested in Congress, staff members feared for their jobs, and proponents of computerization intimated that while current staff members had no fear, the long-run consequences of computerization would be lower staff costs. Experience on the local government level reveals that personnel costs did not go down; lower-paid staff were replaced by higher-paid computer specialists, and offices retained duplicative "back-up" staffs (Kraemer and King, 1975: 6-1). This practice was repeated in Congress. Congressional staff grew unabated during the period of computerization in Congress (see Figure 8.1).

In some specific areas staff members were freed through automation, but tended to be absorbed into other expanded functions. In many

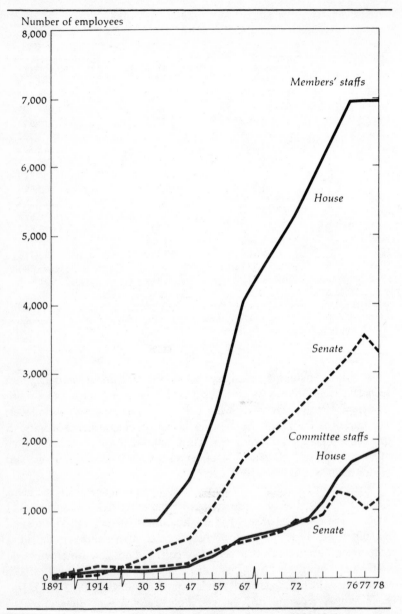

Number of employees

Figure 8.1 Staffs of Members and of Committees in Congress, 1891-1978
SOURCE: Bibby et al. (1980); reprinted by permission.

congressional offices, the arrival of the computer signaled the need for a new block of staff members to operate the terminals and program for special needs.

The fact that modern information technology has not reduced the absolute costs and number of staff members supporting Congress is not necessarily worrisome. Congress was not designed to be efficient nor cost-effective according to traditional criteria. Before passing judgment, it is more important to analyze the impact of computerization on what Congress does and how it does it.

POWER PAYOFFS

The computer is a well recognized source of power and a potential threat to existing power structure [Worthley, in Baaklini and Heaphey, 1977: 169].

In the realm of politics as elsewhere, the old forms of power, such as money or material rewards, have become relatively insignificant. The new "power currency" is information [McHale, in Thomas, 1978: 818].

Power in a social setting involves the ability of one actor to get another actor (the target) to behave in a way he or she had not intended. Compliance can be gained through a variety of potential resources running the spectrum from force, in which concrete rewards or sanctions serve as motivating forces, to leadership and authority, in which respect activates the power target, to persuasion, in which the individual is convinced that what the initial actor wants is really what he or she wants.

All power resources are to some degree dependent on information. In a persuasion situation information is especially important, for the person attempting to persuade must know enough about the target to determine which of the vast array of arguments will be most readily acceptable. The potential persuader with the widest knowledge of targets and the most complete knowledge of the possible arguments would be expected to be most effective. Leadership situations, in which the target gives up his or her own power to decide on a course of action and willingly follows the suggestion of the leader, often develop when the target perceives the leader to be more experienced and having more information. When authority serves as the basis for compliance, the target cooperates in deference to the legitimacy of the position held by the initial actor. Individuals attempting to use their authority need to know who sees them as legitimate and the limits on their ability to bring about compliance. When an actor must resort to forcing compliance through rewards and sanctions, it helps tremendously to know the kinds of rewards and sanctions of most utility in a particular case.

Information in all its various forms serves as a key power resource in politics. In a setting such as Congress, where there is relatively little interdependence among members, and no other political actor has access to the essential rewards and sanctions associated with a member's ability to stay in office, persuasion and leadership supersede authority or rewards and sanctions as important mechanisms for gaining compliance. Significantly, these two mechanisms are the most dependent on information.

Traditionally, information has been held quite tightly in Congress. Until recently, Congress was the bastion of "resident" information. The seniority system in Congress, which predetermined formal leadership positions with their guaranteed access to privileged information, is justified primarily on the basis of its contribution to expertise and continuity. Committee, party, and chamber leaders were revered for the body of information they carried around with them. They strengthened their positions by availing themselves of extra staff, leadership, meetings, and access to key members of the executive branch. The existence of information fiefdoms controlled by committee leaders, who gained power at the expense of party and chamber leaders, came about as legislative issues became more complex and the inability of the broader leaders to specialize and keep up with each substantive area put them at an information disadvantage.

When one analyzes the shift of power between institutions, it becomes clear that selective access to information and analysis also play a role. One of the main reasons the executive branch grew at the expense of Congress stemmed from the fact that governmental decisions became more complex, technical, and interrelated, and the executive branch had the staff and resources to gather the expanded information necessary to intimidate the Congress.

Thus information stands out as a key factor in determining who has power both within Congress and in government in general. The introduction of the computer threatened to upset the comfortable pattern of intrabranch and interbranch power holding.

Internal Power Shifts:
Congressional Battle Ground

The ultimate potential of democratizing congress

Just as Martin Luther stripped away the information advantages of the priests and redistributed the individual's power over his or her own spiritual life through the concept of a "priesthood of all believers," the computer holds the potential for turning political communicants into political priests. In settings such as Congress, where information serves as a key resource for power, power resides in those who establish the information-collecting procedures, those who know how to tap the information through their "access knowledge," and those who have the resources and the right to have access. The potential for modern information technology to democratize an organization hinges on the rules and procedures that govern access. To the degree that existing power holders can limit knowledge or access to modern information sources, the introduction of new technology will simply exacerbate existing information and power inequality.

If the right of access to information is relatively open, as it is in Congress, the potential for rather rapid power redistribution looms large. In a system dominated by traditional resident information, the individual's ability to accumulate enough information to compete requires a significant training period. When information technology presents such a massive amount of new and relevant information that no one's resident information is a match, power devolves to those who can gain the access information necessary to tap the new resource.

Access information, by its very nature, may be easier to acquire. It is likely to be a smaller body of knowledge. Second, and perhaps most importantly, it is reusable for a number of tasks, which increases the motivation to master it. The member of Congress with an in-depth, long-term body of resident information on particular aspects of the U.S. budget can use that information in a finite number of ways. The member mastering the technique of using the computer to get information on the budget can use that same technique for gaining access to myriad information packages. While members of Congress will always need some resident information to place new bodies of knowledge into context, reducing the amount of resident information necessary expands the time and capacity for using information stored in the computer in more sophisticated and creative ways.

The degree to which individual power rests on resident information, or on precomputer limitation on information access, defines those members of Congress who will be most threatened by the advent of computerized information systems with relatively open access.

The computer and the general trend
toward democratization in Congress

One of the more common assertions about the modern Congress revolves around the decline of leadership power and the rise of the individual member. Current members are less willing to follow party leaders, and more likely to oppose their own committees' proposals in public and on the floor, and reveal significantly less loyalty to Congress as an institution. Numerous possible causes of these phenomena have become part of the conventional wisdom. Currently, members of Congress are less dependent on their political parties for getting into office and reveal less willingness to repay their parties with loyalty. Chamber and party leaders have been stripped of many of the rewards and sanctions they originally held over the heads of members. The new breed of legislators come from a generation that is less willing to be led in general and that has become accustomed to "doing things their own way." To this list of possible causes, I would add increased access to relevant information.

Not all of the access to information can be traced to the computer. Just as party and chamber leaders lost out to the committee leader specialists, increased specialization in society and the incumbent needs for more specialized information for legislation led to the decline in power of committee chairs and the increased power of subcommittee chairs and individual members entering Congress with substantive specializations. The advent of the computer at once increased the potential and availability of specialized information, and gave individuals with some access knowledge choices of which substantive areas they wished to "bone up" on. Ambitious and able new members could get their information capabilities up to speed and compete successfully with members who had become fat and lazy resting on their resident-information laurels. Some examples of those who lost power will bring this point home.

Decline of the committee chair.

Power of certain functionaries or committee (and subcommittee) chairmen is vested, quite often, in the information they control [Chartrand, 1978: 183].

Committee chairpersons traditionally based their power on resident information. The classic example was Wilbur Mills (D-AR), former chairman of the House Committee on Ways and Means. Manley (1970: 124) concluded his study of this archtypical representative of a powerful committee chairman by asserting:

When asked to explain Mills's influence on the Committee, the reason most often given was the chairman's knowledge of the subject matter.

Members of the committee asserted that we "can always rely on his judgment and expertise," or, "There isn't anything in taxes he fails to understand or fails to relate to what has gone on before" (Manley, 1970: 124).

The Ways and Means Committee under the chairmanship of Wilbur Mills was decisive and cohesive. Mills never took a split committee recommendation to the floor and was generally able to get the committee to go along with him. His successor, Al Ulman (D-OR) suffered in comparison. Part of the diminished power of the Ways and Means Committee chairman may be due to the more limited resident information and skill of Ulman, but conditions have changed. As one member who spanned the two periods explained it:

When Mills was chairman new members would bring new proposals to committee only to be upstaged by Mills, who would sit back with his glasses perched on his nose and very patronizingly say, "Well, we considered that back in 1957 and this is why it both wouldn't work and would run counter to these parts of the tax code. . . ." The less knowledgeable new member would be awed by the performance, slink down in his seat and only be heard from when he voted in support of Mills' proposals. Toward the end of Mills' reign, and especially when Ulman took over, the scene was quite different. The ambitious new member would have his proposal run through the Tax Simulation Model. It soon became a battle of the member's projection, computer projection versus the chairman's. Experience and expertise did not count for much.

Academic observers and congressional participants alike agree that increased access to information by the average member reduces the power of committee chairs. Loomis (1980: 15) concluded that

increased ability of all members to draw upon massive amounts of available information may represent more of a democratizing influ-

ence in the Congress (and especially the House) than committee
reform, or the modifications of the seniority system.

The late Representative William Steiger (R-WI) observed that "information
systems and computers will strengthen members in contrast to the committee" (U.S. Congress, House, Committee on Congressional Organization
and Operation, 1973a: 314).

It is not only that members now have more information relative to
committee chairs, but also the fact that members need the chairperson
less. In the past the member who needed information had to go to the
chair to request it. The "gift" of information made by the chairperson
would obligate the member. Since the member could not repay the chair
with equally valuable information, the debt would be paid with loyalty to
the chair and the chair's proposals.

The ultimate consequence of increased power in the hands of individual
members and reduced power of committee chairs is likely to be increased
conflict on committee decisions and less cohesion when proposals hit the
floor. With independent sources of information and the lack of power
resources in the hands of the chair to enforce decisions, individual members feel free to go their own way and follow their own policy proclivities,
leading to increased conflict and reduced pressures for compromise.

Decline of party and chamber leaders. While the growth of available
information and the need for specialization doomed the generalist party
and chamber leaders in their attempts to dominate substantive policy
decisions, specific computer applications served to reduce their power even
more. Traditionally party and chamber leaders played an intermediary role
between the chamber and the White House. Presidents would hold leadership breakfasts and the leaders would bolster their positions by selectively
retailing the inside information from the president to cooperative party
members. While this process still goes on, the emphasis is reduced. There is
simply less "inside" information. In many cases the White House researchers depend on the same sources individual members of Congress or their
staffs can utilize. With the potential for monitoring voting patterns of
individual members of Congress, it is also easier for the president to bypass
the leadership and focus his efforts on the most likely supporters of his
proposals.

Electronic voting in the House has also reduced the power of the
leadership. In the past, many crucial votes were not recorded and individual members had some leeway. On these less public votes, it was easier

to swing votes. Now, with more recorded votes, members of Congress are on display and can ill afford to be known as people who forsake constituent concerns in the pursuit of party loyalty.

Electronic voting shortens the time available for bargaining. The New York State Assembly adopted electronic voting in 1965 and later dropped it, because the leaders felt they could influence the vote more effectively with the slower voice-vote method (Nations's Business, 1973: 70).

Decline of the generalist, the intermediary, and the captive of routine. Aside from democratizing Congress, the computer holds the potential for shifting power between classes of individuals within the Congress. While the committee system forces members to specialize and rewards them for it, all members of Congress must also be generalists who vote on a wide array of problems. In the past the generalist with some basic knowledge, a good political sensitivity, and intuitive skill often influenced fellow members of Congress and affected the outcome. When information was costly in terms of resources and time, the intuitive generalist who was available and could give quick and timely direction carried more weight. With the advent of information technology that can deliver timely and relevant information instantaneously, the imprecise generalist is more likely to be superseded (Foreign Policy Association, 1968: 96). Modern information technology allows the specialist to specialize even more and provides an opportunity for the motivated nonexpert to marshal useful information for specific decisions.

Computerization changes the roles of information intermediaries. While power once went to intermediaries who translated raw information into workable generalizations, direct and easy access to original data removes the need for such translators. The new Brahman caste of intermediaries is made up of those individuals who provide access information. Computer programmers, trainers, and analysts become important above and beyond their knowledge of substantive policy-related knowledge. As keys to needed information, they can become irreplaceable.

As information sources change, power goes to those who are able and motivated to remain current. In Kingdon's (1981: 233) words:

Like the rest of us, Congressmen are creatures of habit. They rarely seek out new information sources. . . . The congressmen who develop new information, furthermore, have disproportionate influence on Congressional outcomes.

Or, from the perspective of a staff member:

> The primary advantage in decision-making is in saving time. Staff
> members with computer skills can service their members' needs
> much more quickly. Those who have information in the legislative
> process gain effectiveness over those who don't.

Two scenarios for the future stand out as possibilities. Within Congress
as well as society, we could see a group of "haves" and a group of "have
nots." The haves would be composed of "datacrats" who have mastered
the access information and find the acquisition of new and better knowledge easier and easier. They would increasingly solidify their power position by limiting access to information. They would quickly move to the
top of the organization and become the new elite. The "have nots" would
not know how to use the new technology for their own benefit. They
would be captives of their old, outmoded information and information-
collection techniques. They would have little opportunity for improving
their lot and would become alienated (McHale, 1976: 33; U.S. Congress,
Office of Technology Assessment, 1981: 119).

The opposing scenario sees Congress and society moving more toward
an informational priesthood of all believers, in which power would be
evened out through open access to information and access skills. Although
some dislocation is likely as we change from traditional to modern information processes, those who wish to retool will be encouraged. Shifts of
power based on information will be open to those with ambition and
motivation. No one will be intentionally left behind.

Of the two scenarios, the second seems to apply most correctly to
Congress. Despite some evidence of limiting access and tradition-bound
members and their staffs, information-based power is going to those who
want it, not to those somehow preordained to receive it. Perhaps the most
positive indication of democratization is revealed by the generational
pattern of computer usage in Congress. While it is difficult to teach old
congressional dogs new tricks, newer members and their staffs enter with
open minds concerning computerization and seek out applications with
little hesitancy. In actuality, those with dark fears that current power
holders will somehow realize their stake in limiting access and reverse the
relatively open policy toward computerization harbor an image of Congress that imbues the leaders with too much foresight, rationality, and
power.

Countervailing power trends

While the general trend of power shifts due to computerization indicate a more even distribution of power within Congress in which factors of skill, motivation, and creativity count more than expertise or formal position, some divergent tendencies also appear. Current power holders have successfully limited access to data bases by making them the perquisites of particular committees or persons in specified positions. In other areas, potentially useful information is simply not collected in machine-readable form. In the words of one staff member:

> There are some limits to the degree that computers have democratized Congress. Much of the really critical decision-making information does not go on the terminals. If the leadership feels threatened they will block access or the collection of the data.

Perhaps the most useful power resource for the congressional leadership is the ability to perform sophisticated analyses of ongoing House votes through the leadership terminals connected to the electronic voting system. Although the traditional calling of the roll gave the leadership more time to influence votes, it was difficult to keep up with the tally to target potential vote switchers and to give them a rationale for changing (Haber, 1972: 1964). One of the staff members experienced in using the terminals on the floor explained the process:

> We begin with a pretty good idea of who is with us and who is against us. During the vote, we identify subgroups such as party, state or committee who should be solidly backing us. If a party member shows up as the only one from that state delegation voting against us, we can dispatch someone to corner them and it is often possible to convince them that they have overlooked something.

The utility of the vote monitoring system for giving the leadership more control over its followers emerges from recognizing the lengths to which members will go to lessen leadership targeting and pressure. On tough votes, in which members feel they must oppose the leadership, more and more members wait until the last possible moment to vote, pick a voting station close to the door, and dash out of the chamber as soon as the vote is recorded (Whalen, 1980: 20).

Not only can the leadership monitor ongoing votes, but the Speaker has some control over the length of the vote. While the voting terminals must remain open for fifteen minutes, the speaker has the discretion to keep them open a few minutes longer. Such a delaying technique has been used to round up nonvoters and to provide more time to change some votes.

As in many realms of society, the introduction of the computer threatens to reduce some individual freedom. The ability to easily monitor a legislator's current and past votes, legislative activity, campaign contributions, and the like reduces the traditional "backstage" areas in which to hide (Thompson, 1969: 101). While this is clearly desirable from the perspective of "keeping public servants in line," the availability of such information does reduce the power of individuals to control their own destiny.

Increasing the Power of Congress as an Institution

> The efforts of legislatures to regain their lost status focus on the improvement of their data gathering ability, by either improved staffing, or the use of computers and other informational hardware [Rourke, 1975: 2].

One of the primary motivations of computer promoters in Congress stemmed from the desire to regain some of the power lost to the executive branch and outside interest groups due to an imbalance of relevant information. The experience on the state level clearly indicated that when legislatures improved their information-handling capabilities, they were able to venture successfully into new policy areas (Baaklini and Heaphey, 1977: 168) and generally improved their competitive advantage over the executive branch (Worthley, 1977b: 22).

Although some have argued that reforms such as computerization may be little more than methods of helping legislatures to deal psychologically with their decline in relative power (Patterson, in Welch and Peters, 1977: 219), there seems to be a bit more substantive impact on Congress. While it is difficult, if not impossible, to devise measures of relative power between Congress and the executive branch that are not tainted by the idiosyncracies of particular time periods, issues, and personalities, some evidence exists as to the computer's contribution to Congress's ability to maintain, if not enhance, its current power position. The very fact that sharing of data and analysis is no longer a one-way street from the executive to Congress should be encouraging to Congress. The almost lustful desire of the Carter administration to gain access to congressional data bases and the interchange of budget analysis is only one example. From a more intuitive perspective, the modern Congress, with its independent information sources, seems to be giving executive branch and interest group proposals more careful scrutiny, using its own data and analysis. Congress has just scratched the surface in pursuing the potential for using computers to facilitate oversight of the executive. While some may bemoan a shift of emphasis from legislative creativity to oversight, it is more important for the balance of power system to maintain Congress as an independent branch than as a purely legislative branch, and modern information technology has an important role to play toward reaching that end. Information alone will never lead to a system of congressional hegemony, but lack of independent and relevant information will surely lead to congressional demise.

CHANGING THE NATURE
OF CONGRESSIONAL DECISION-MAKING

Improving the Quality of Policy Decisions

At least in the public rhetoric, improving the quality of policy decisions supersedes all other arguments for improving the information-handling capabilities of Congress. In the past, one congressional participant commented, "lack of information [was] a perfect excuse for some of the bad bills that became law" (Gregory, 1979a).

Providing better information

The computer holds the potential for providing the timely, relevant, and unimpeachable information Congress needs to make decisions. The process of data collection, storage, and retrieval via the computer requires forethought and careful planning:

> The effective use of computers requires disciplined human thought. In order to program computers, policy makers must undertake a more exacting analysis of issues than they might otherwise do [Brademas, in Perloff, 1971: 322].

Congress's development of independent computerized information sources has done a great deal to reduce the honest mistakes that led to misinformation in the past. As two staff members explained:

> Sharing of computerized information files leads to an upgrading of the quality of the output. We see each other's mistakes and can correct them.

The presence of CBO estimates and projections has done a great deal to keep OMB honest. We have taken some of the "crystal ball" out of the process. We are all professionals who attempt to understand how and why our projections differ.

In those situations where the spreading of misinformation could be a potential strategy, the expansion of information sources reduces its likelihood. One staff member observed that the major impact of computers in Congress was that "everyone is better informed. Much less is done by stealth on the Hill today than in the past. You just can't get away with it."

Participants and observers alike comment that committee and chamber deliberations are more sophisticated. The questions are tougher and the analysis sharper. Commenting on budget deliberations, Gatty (1978: 41) concluded that the upgrading of Congress's information sources and technology swept away "the old boy network of Defense decision-making."

A CRS staff member described how computerized data bases helped in briefing a member and created a new awareness of information equality in these words:

> The data bases have improved hearing preparation. I was recently asked to help a congressman opposed to a piece of legislation. Facing a hearing stacked in favor of the bill by the chairman, he knew that little opposition information would come from the hearings. We looked up the witnesses in the NEW YORK TIMES and other indexes. During the hearing, one witness tried to prove his qualifications by referring to an article he had written. The opposing congressman kept him honest by say "Oh, you mean this one" as he showed it to him. It was one of the articles our search had looked up. The committee chairman was taken by surprise and looked at his staff aid, saying, "Hey, why haven't I seen that article?"

One area of improved information involves the ability to identify the interaction effects of policy in areas previously thought to be unrelated (Mesthene, 1971: 156). In order to allow broad and integrated public policies, it is necessary to "structure salient information so that relationships become apparent and meaningful" (Chartrand, 1967b: 2). The most obvious examples of such usage are the tax simulation models used by the Joint Committee on Taxation, which allow manipulating a number of parameters of tax policy simultaneously.

Computerized data banks also make possible calculations and information retrieval procedures previously thought to be beyond human will, time, or energy (Laudon, 1974: 48). For example:

> If . . . the U.S. Congress had two reliable pieces of information—(1) How much it was costing not to grow cotton, and (2) How much it was costing to promote the use of cotton—The very juxtaposition might give rise to some better decisions [Bemer, 1975: 17].

The utility of the computer for "quick and dirty" information retrieval was dramatically revealed during the Reagan administration's budget-cutting search:

> Someone asked the computer to list all the National Institute of Drug Abuse research that used the word "social" and that became the list for cutting $9 million in studies, or 20% of the agency's budget [Washington Post, 1981: A8].

While all observers of Congress value more information over less, and the computer has an "unlocking effect" (Laudon, 1974: 6) on information sources, some dangers lurk. The availability of information does not necessarily predetermine its wise use. With increased information, poor decisions can now be bolstered with awesome facts and statistics (Wilensky, 1971: 281). The decisions associated with collecting, coding, and retrieving computerized information have consequences in and of themselves:

> A computer system that permits the asking of only certain kinds of questions, that accepts only certain kinds of "data," and that cannot, even in principle, be understood by those who rely on it, such a computing system has effectively closed many doors that were open before it was installed [Weizenbaum, 1976: 38].

While it may be that moving to computerized data bases in Congress has discouraged and perhaps permanently closed the door to some sources and data, it has certainly opened more doors than it has closed.

It is probably not possible to prove that computers in Congress have improved the quality of decisions or lead to specific policy biases. We do know that members of Congress are able to update themselves more quickly and have access to a wider array of information on societal problems, possible solutions, and projections of consequences. Congress's increased role in the budget-making process is almost unthinkable without the computer. While all the evidence leads to the conclusion that modern information technology has improved decisions, the justification for computers does not rely solely on such a judgment. Even if the quality of decisions did not change, the computer played an important role. Computerization came to Congress at a time when the demands on legislators were increasing from constituents, problems were becoming more complex, and the information explosion threatened to overwhelm even the most diligent members of Congress and their staffs. At a minimum, computers served as a facilitating mechanism, which allowed members to keep abreast of the burgeoning issues and demands. It helped members of Congress to run faster so that they could stay in place.

Changing the Level of Policy Conflict

Perhaps the greatest impact of a computerized information system for Congress as a whole will be a change in the basis for policy decisions and ultimately an increase in policy conflict. Traditionally, "not all congressmen who support a bill do so for the same reasons, and not always for the reasons that would satisfy analytic standards" (Schick, 1976: 215). Such "coalitions of mixed expectations" thrive in low-information settings. As the ability to predict the consequences of proposed legislation increases, and the possibility of measuring the implications of past decisions becomes more commonplace, fewer members of Congress will have the luxury of disagreeing on the consequences of their actions. While the ideal of a fully informed rational choice between alternatives stands out as a goal of information specialists (Laudon, 1977: 15), the hope for electronic "philosopher kings" fails to take into account the practical need of putting together more mundane political coalitions to pass legislation. In a political setting such as Congress, members arrive with different sets of values, different parochial interests to protect, and varying patterns of past decisions with which they need to maintain consistency. Only intermittently will the implications of new information be so overwhelming that values, parochial interests, and consistency wither in its light. Far from making political decisions easier, new information often exacerbates the problem by laying bare the conflicts over values or parochial interests that were muted when such information was not readily available (see Simon, 1975: 226; Mesthene, 1971: 159; Loomis, 1980: 16).

While new information challenges the creation of coalitions of mixed expectations in all settings, the explicit constituency base of members of Congress increases the problem. With better information, members of Congress will more often be able to determine not only the aggregate impact of legislation, but also the specific impact on their districts. Congress attempts to play a distributive policy role in which government services are parceled out in such a way that there are no complete winners or losers. Centralizing information and allowing it to be accumulated on the basis of electoral districts increases the awareness of the redistributive aspects of policy making (Schneier, 1970: 22). With the winners and losers each knowing the other's identity, conflict will increase. If such information on winning and losing becomes available to the general public, members of Congress will be judged more severely on their ability to look out for the interests of their districts, which will heighten the "zero-sum game" view of politics, which is inherently more competitive. There is dramatic pressure in Congress to use the computer to provide data that would allow comparing districts according to social characteristics and government expenditures. As the House Information System (1979b: 4) analysts concluded:

> Providing House offices information on topics at any level of detail may be doing a disservice to the country if it becomes commonplace to look only at data from a district or regional point of view and the national picture is ignored.

Inside observers are not only aware of the parochialism-based conflict that is likely to increase, but also conflict based on values and ideology. Few congressional participants put much stock in the seemingly naive assumption that the introduction of modern information technology will usher in a new age of rationality in which conflict over values will be superseded by nonideological decisions based on enhanced information and analytic models (see Laudon, 1974: 310; Mesthene, 1971). On the contrary, values will loom much larger. Far from the once-predicted end of ideology (Bell, 1969), Congress seems to be becoming more ideological and value oriented. Commenting on the various econometric models, some of the most sophisticated policy-related uses of computers in Congress, in the 1981 budget debate, Representative Ratchford (D-CT) pointed out that "the debate over forecasts is more than a squabble over numbers. The dispute involves basic disagreement over how the economy works" (U.S. Congress, House, Congressional Record, 1981: H1073).

The potential increase in conflict caused by information advances stems from another source as well. Members of Congress perceive consistency as a worthy and electorally advantageous goal. In an era of limited information, decisions could be made relatively early in the process without fear of embarrassment. With the computer facilitating instantaneous analysis of fresh data and information, members are less sure of when they can make public commitments. One budget committee staff member explained the dilemma:

> Our frequent updates of information get us into trouble with some congressmen. Just as they have established a political strategy, it is threatened by new information. We are technocrats and don't time our releases of information to embarrass members.

Far from being a benign influence or a force that guarantees more placid and simpler decision-making, the potential for predicting policy consequences is likely to increase conflict dramatically. Not only does the wide dispersion of information give more people the resources to play the game (Johannes, 1977: 56), but each player knows whether he or she is winning or losing and who the prime competition is.

Emergence of Minimum Winning Coalitions

Despite the rules of logic and the specific theory of minimum winning coalitions expressed by Riker (1962), most votes in Congress are considerably more one-sided than the majority-plus-one predictions one might expect in a managed coalition. A number of reasons help explain the lack of correlation between theory and reality. First of all, many coalitions that form around legislative proposals in Congress are not fully managed. Only some of the participants are "bought into" the coalition through compromise, persuasion, threats, or promises, and thus the coalition manager is in no position to expend only as many bargaining resources as needed to barely win. Second, and even more important, even when coalitions are fully managed, the managers have lacked the perfect information as to the size of the coalition at any one point in time. With the monitoring capability of floor voting in the House, we may well see an increase in minimum winning coalitions, where the managers seek out just enough votes to win. There was some evidence of this during the 1981 budget fight. As one Democratic strategist explained it:

> We went into the vote knowing that the Republicans were united and some of our people were committed to go over to the other side.

As the vote progressed, we realized that we needed four votes to win the day. This meant either switching two members or getting four no voters to the floor. We found four members who had not yet voted and went out to find them. Even though the Speaker held the vote open after the fifteen-minute time limit, we were only able to produce one of the four. I am sure that the Republicans were monitoring the vote just as we were and paying attention to those last few crucial votes.

The increased ability of the leadership to monitor ongoing votes via computer has been joined by quicker and more accurate vote recording and publishing via computer to make the job of members of Congress a more public one. With more recorded votes and better monitoring of them, members of Congress simply have fewer "free" votes, in which they can hide behind anonymity. Coalitions will be hard to create and, when created, they will tend to be closer approximations of the minimum winning model.

Changed Nature of Decision Demands

The introduction of computers into Congress has at once made the decision-making demands on members easier and heavier. The easing of pressures comes from the fact that the monitoring programs for floor activity and bill status allow members to structure their time better and predict upcoming votes. As a staff member phrased it, "Any member with a half-way decent staff has no excuse for getting caught with his pants down. He should know what is on tap." Once the upcoming decisions have been mapped out, members have easy access to background information to bring themselves up to speed (Rieselbach, 1977: 82).

For the individual member, the computer increases realistic responsibility for a broader spread of government concerns. The results constitute a mixed blessing, as one Senate staffer explained:

> LEGIS helps the Senator to keep track of legislation in committees of which he is not a member. In the past you needed a friend on the committee to keep you informed. Now there is less chance of something going by unnoticed. On the other hand, it stretches the senator's out. They can't just throw up their hands and say, "Oh! I just did not know about that." Now they have a broader responsibility.

Part of the increased pressure comes from the fact that there are simply more decisions to be made, and most of them are public. With modern information capabilities, the time cushion between the occurrence of problems and their entrance into the public policy dialogue is decreased. Policy makers are increasingly placed in the posture of day-to-day crisis management (McHale, 1976: 77). As information bases move from providing background information to becoming "real-time" systems that continually monitor ongoing events, provide warnings of emerging problems, and provide guidelines on possible corrective action, the decision life of specific policies becomes shorter (Mesthene, 1971: 156; Sackman, 1971: 222-223). Decision-making will be more continuous and it will be less possible to put problems behind us. The good news is that although it might be easier to make mistakes with such a system, Congress will have available quicker feedback and the likelihood of compounding errors will decrease. The leisurely life of the member of Congress who only had to face up to a few key public issues each session is likely to go the way of the buggy whip. The temperature in the congressional pressure cooker will increase rather than diminish due to expanded information capabilities.

IMPACT ON ORGANIZATIONAL STRUCTURE

Initial studies of computer adoption in industry almost universally indicated that the automation of information leads to centralization (Mueller, 1969: 27). Jack W. Carlson flatly stated that

> modern information technology is a cause of, and contributes to, centralization of authority and decision-making and this is a movement towards increased government role for government [Chartrand and Morentz, 1979: 114].

Other analysts disagree, and assert that there is nothing inherently centralizing about computers (De Sola Pool et al., 1971: 248). They argue that if computer power is dispersed, the result, if anything, is decentralization (Toffler, 1980: 96). The long-term picture for Congress is unclear. In general, Congress has avoided centralized control of policy, data bank creation, and access and has not even been able to completely coordinate duplicative functions. Only when absolutely necessary have members of Congress deigned to cooperate on data entry formats and choices of collective data banks. Suggestions for creating a computer network are floated periodically by H.I.S. and the Senate Computer Center, but they fall on deaf ears. Even though the proposals are rather timid, allowing individual members a great deal of freedom to contract for specialized services, Congress has steadfastly adopted a "free market" approach and developed a piecemeal system with a great deal of control by individual members and other users (U.S. Congress, House, House Information System, 1979b: 166; Flato, 1977: 254). Given the initial history of computerization in Congress and the general acceptance of the status quo, it is hard to foresee a dramatic turn toward centralization of information resources.

IMPACT ON WORK STYLE AND SATISFACTION

Much of this book has focused on members of Congress per se. While the introduction of computers to Congress is clearly evident to members when they are forced to dash over to the floor and are limited in the time they have to insert their plastic voting cards to register their preferences, much of the computer power on the Hill is transparent to the members themselves. They see the products of bibliographic searches, bill status tracking, or simulation models, but do not necessarily know how they were produced. Their mail goes out quicker, relieving some staff effort for other activities, but from the member's perspective the result could just as easily have been produced by a more efficient staff as by a computer. Members of Congress are result oriented, and they applaud or condemn the results much more than the process that produced them.

To more clearly delineate the personal impact of computers on day-to-day activities and lifestyles, one must focus on the staff. The introduction of computers into congressional offices has changed the staff in terms of recruitment, job description, training, power, location, and job satisfaction. Traditionally, congressional staff positions have been the extreme in patronage appointments. Congress has carefully avoided including itself in equal opportunity legislation and other rules that might limit its members in hiring staff who are completely loyal and attuned to the members. Computerization has forced members to seek out staff members with more specific skills. While staffs were once filled with generalists who could muddle through any problem that arose, the modern staff requires technocrats to run the word processor and program the computer and office managers to manage the flow of information and job assignments (Worthley, 1976: 105). As in other realms where computerization became commonplace, the middle-level generalists, who filtered and analyzed information for people on the top, using their generalist skills and resident information, have been bypassed due to the direct access to information the computer provides (Kraemer and King, 1975: 6-5). The middle-level information manager in the congressional office is slowly being replaced by individuals who create and manage information systems, or who can deal with the unexpected problems that baffle the computer (Hellriegel and Slocum, 1979: 543). These crisis managers, who are still very important in Congress, are being backed up by a whole new breed of less skilled workers who handle the routine jobs such as data entry (Laudon, 1974: 26). The middle-range staff generalist who can contribute neither to crisis management or to sophisticated information management, or who is unwilling or unable to deal with the routine, is going to be less and less common on the Hill.

The decade of the 1970s in Congress saw a mad dash of old staff "dogs" attempting to learn new tricks. CRS and H.I.S. initiated massive training programs. While initial staff attitudes bordered on hostility, and many found it demeaning to be retrained to do what they often saw as "clerical skills," most saw the handwriting on the wall, and hostility frequently evolved into indifference and finally acceptance. With the rapid turnover in Congress and the natural desire for job security, there were often waiting lines for training seminars. As one staff member involved in training put it:

> We really knew we had made it when members were personally contacting the director of CRS trying to pull some strings and get their staff to the head of the line for training.

Staff members who gained some access information and learned how to use the computer often reaped some power and status benefits. One office told of a college intern who arrived at the office after spending a few hours on the public terminals at the Library of Congress. When the congressman needed a quick update on a bill, the intern quietly went over to the dust-covered terminal and retrieved the information, while the rest of the office was running around trying to get through to the Bill Status Office and to call their contacts. The intern proved his utility and was soon "in charge" of the computer. After a few months he was asked to stay on as a legislative assistant, with a big increase in status, pay, and power; all because he was at least semiliterate on the computer. Other success stories abound. Another staff member moved from a position in a congressman's mailroom to one of chief leadership strategist on the floor because he knew how to use the computer.

For some offices, the availability of the computer has led to work being done in different locations. While the introduction of computers did not cause the growth of district and state offices, the ability of staff members out in the districts to access data on bill status and federal programs has enchanced the kind of work that can be done away from Washington. The Capitol Hill office is increasingly becoming the core office for legislative tasks, while the district office deals directly with constituent services and requests. Some Senate offices are having their computer-generated letters printed out directly in the district, which speeds response time. The computer more directly splits the office staff in the Senate, where most senators run satellite offices away from their main offices to handle computerized mailings. Inhabitants of these letter-generating "boiler rooms" have little contact with the glory, excitement, and status of the main office.

While the staff initially feared that computers would take over their jobs, the actual result has been redefinition, rather than elimination. For the higher-level staff members who manage offices or only use the computers periodically, the computer did require some retraining, but the results were positive on the whole. They could wow their congressional bosses with instantaneous information or rest on their laurels for efficiently sending out massive piles of high-quality, computer-generated targeted mailings. The computer clearly helped them look better while freeing them of some of the drudgery associated with more traditional office and research procedures (Sanfield, 1979: 16).

For the lower-level staff, the impact of the computer was less positive. As was the case in other realms, computers required a vast army of clerical workers whose data entry and checking responsibilities involved routine, impersonal tasks with limited intrinsic rewards and more intensified performance monitoring (Kraemer and King, 1975: 6-3). The ultimate result is unlikely to be anything but lower job satisfaction as the computer reduced necessary job skills and autonomy (Laudon, 1974: 26). The data entry specialists interviewed indicated that the glory of being on the staff of a member of Congress was severely diminished by the nature of the job. Rather than freeing them, the computer controlled their work schedule. With too much mail to process and limited lines to connect them to the Correspondence Management System (CMS) over in the Senate, staff members complained of having to work weekends and holidays in order to get on the computer, or having to come in at 6 a.m. in order to beat everyone to the line. One staff member told the plaintive tale of being virtually locked to the terminal. Once getting a line, she did not want to lose it. This meant that she had to take some action every ten minutes or the computer would automatically cut her off. She barely had time to run to the restroom, and had spent a number of months eating her lunch at her desk so as not to lose the line. While this case may be extreme, it is sometimes unclear as to who is the master and who the servant.

On a personal note, some truths do not sink in without personal experience. While both the literature and interview subjects commented on the subtle ways in which computers control the operator, the reality of these changes did not really impress me until I experimented with using a portable terminal at home to write and edit this book. The fact that I could only have the terminal at home for short periods drove me to use it every spare moment. At the office I stare at the terminals, which are always available, without effect; but walking by the "wasted" empty terminal at home gave me pangs of guilt. I found myself rushing to the terminal as soon as the system was up in the morning and grasping at straws for ways to use it. The rational sequence of a need leading to seeking out the machine became reversed. I truly felt relieved when I had to take the terminal back, because I was relieved of the necessity of using it.

The impact of the terminal went well beyond challenging my sense of mastery over my environment. Since the terminal tied up our only phone line and the only convenient outlet was in the family room, the presence of the terminal isolated us from the outside world for hours on end (not a complete detriment), and my children were denied their daily fix of modern culture through the family room television. I am not convinced that my family will ever be the same. The next time someone tells me that access to the computer changed his or her life, I will conjure up more than images of increased efficiency and productivity, for the more subtle changes in work habits and job satisfaction engendered by my portable terminal are still fresh in my mind.

IMPACT ON POLITICAL SECURITY

The general pattern prevails: more help for incumbents through the wonders of modern, in-House media [Robinson, 1981: 62].

One has only to look at the types of computer applications most ardently sought out by members of Congress to conclude that the computer is a very powerful contribution to the long list of resources we provide to incumbent legislators from the public treasury. While it might be impossible to sort out the independent impact of computers on reelection, it is safe to say that computers will further help lock incumbents into secure positions.

The efficacy of computer applications for reaching electoral goals is hard to prove conclusively. House members using computers in 1976 and 1978 were somewhat more likely than nonusers to improve their electoral margins, but that may not be a fair test. As we saw in Chapter 6, members of Congress in the deepest electoral trouble were the most likely to turn to the computer for help, and they are the very ones we would not expect to improve their margins much, if at all.

Perhaps the clearest evidence of the electoral benefits accruing from the computer emerges from the ways in which congressional offices use the computer. The heavy evidence of utilization of the computer for constituent services and communications stands as a strong indicator of how the participants themselves view the contribution of computerization.

IMPACT ON THE PROCESS OF REPRESENTATION

> Technological advances promise greater accessibility of Senators and Congressmen to their constituents, individually and collectively, and greater access of citizens to the Senators and Congressmen as well [Brademas, 1972: 154].

> The new technology will make it easier to bridge the gulf between the citizen and his government. "Vote for the computer-competent Congressman!" may well be one of the common campaign slogans of the year 2000 [Brademas, 1971: 320].

The primary rationale for the existence of Congress lies in its potential contribution to representative government. In order for representative government to work in any credible way, citizens need to know enough about their elected officials to give them direction and hold them accountable on election day, and elected officials need to know enough about the citizenry to determine with clarity the signals they are giving. Traditionally citizens have found out about Congress in a haphazard and fragmented way, and elected officials have only received intermittent and selected signals. The more active proponents of computerization argue that computers can help inform elected officials and the public in such a way that the average citizen can "become more integrally involved in the managing of our country" (Chartrand, in Krevitt Eres, 1980: 20).

Making Elected Officials More Accessible

The increased number of recorded votes spawned by the electronic voting system increased the opportunities for having members of Congress go on record and should facilitate the opportunities for informed judgments by the electorate. The increased ease and efficiency of communicating with constituents through targeted mailings and high-quality computerized letters holds the promise of communicating with constituents on issues that are of particular interest to them. While the potential for such things is there, some potential dangers also lurk. The opportunity to communicate useful information facilitated by the computer exists side by side with the capability to communicate selective information or misinformation in a sophisticated manner. As one staff member put it:

> We now have the capability to inform only those groups who favor the legislation—rather than using the news media and possibly offending some group [Burnham, 1980: 97].

Modern mailing list technology could potentially exacerbate citizen inequality. If you are on your representative's mailing list and your friend is not, you have a special channel of communication (Frank Ryan, in Dartmouth College, 1976: 24). In a potentially more limiting situation, citizens could be rebuffed by members of Congress familiar with sophisticated analysis techniques with a brush-off such as, "We can't let you participate because planning is so complex. You don't even know the language" (Westin, 1971: 218).

Although the average citizen is not generally aware of it, the computer has given the public access to a great deal of potentially useful data for evaluating incumbent members of Congress. Using the bill status system, it is relatively easy to trace the legislative efforts and effectiveness of individual members of Congress. Increasingly, congressional challengers are using such information in their opposition research. While not all of the useful information is available to citizens or potential challengers, the computer data bases open to the public take a significant step toward equalizing the information gap between congressional incumbents and their challengers.

Making the Public's Views More Accessible

Congressional offices realize that they only hear from a random subset of their constituencies, but even among the people they hear from, it has not been possible to get an accurate measurement of opinions. Commenting on the spillover effects of a mail recording and tracking system, one staff member pointed out, "In the past we used to weigh the mail. Now we have accurate mail counts from the computer." Members clearly have a better sense of what their constituents in general think, and are able to analyze identifiable subgroups of the letter writers.

The computer is just beginning to be used to help members of Congress poll their constituencies more scientifically. While the traditional poll was more of a public relations gimmick, random samples generated by the computer, with tracking of responses and follow up letters to boost response rate, show some promise for giving members direct knowledge of constituent opinions. H.I.S. has even proposed a massive polling effort funded by Congress to provide similar information (U.S. Congress, House, House Information System, 1979b): For those who are not fearful of too much citizen impact, the computer may herald a new day of more direct democracy.

The catalog of potential implications of computerization could go on and on. It will take a great deal more time to separate the wishful thinking and undue alarm from the real consequences. In the short term, computerization in Congress suggests some problems that eventually will have to be faced.

PROBLEMS ON THE HORIZON

Now that modern information technology is well entrenched on Capitol Hill, proponents and observers feel more free to temper their enthusiasm and suggest an agenda for dealing with the mixed "blessings" of computerization. The shift in orientation shows up dramatically in the comments of participants in two seminars put together by CRS information specialist Robert Chartrand. The thrust of comments during the 1969 seminar focused on the potential contributions of computers and the possibility of developing a comprehensive information system (Chartrand, 1972). In a seminar involving many of the same participants in 1977, the thrust was quite different. After some experience with computers in Congress, speakers emphasized the limits of computerization for solving all problems and admitted a growing concern with the human dimension of information technology (Chartrand and Morentz, 1979).

Aside from the general awareness that computers are not a panacea for the ills of Congress or of society in general, it is now becoming more clear that the introduction of computer technology has brought with it some unique problems with which Congress will have to deal.

Cost Factor

The cost of computerization in Congress is astronomical. Without taking into account the $15,000 House members are each allowed to spend out of their office accounts for outside services, computer expenditures in Congress increased from $48 million in 1970 to $613 million in 1980 (Chartrand and Borrell, 1981: 14). The growth in computer expenditures has far outstripped inflation and patterns in other areas of congressional support and services. Some concern is beginning to be expressed regarding the efficiency of expenditures. The pattern of allowing individual members to contract independently for services predominent in the House, and the duplication evident in providing many services, mitigates against gaining the benefits of economy of scale. Computer services have until recently been purchased with little attention to cost. Even the budget cuts exacted in 1981 evidenced less concern with a careful cost-benefit analysis of particular services and instead focused on a "meat ax" overall cut. There is little incentive in Congress for pursuing cost effectiveness in the provision of modern information technology. As one staff member expressed it:

> There is probably too much computer power on the Hill. Everyone wants his own machine from the top on down so he can control its capabilities and use. Everyone touts the possibility of a less costly information network which would reduce duplication and lower costs, but no one is willing to give up what he has. Congressmen avoid coordinated information systems, or contracting for outside services to serve many members simultaneously even if they are cheaper out of an inordinate fear for security and control. Programmers within Congress discourage mini-computers because the big bucks are in programming big computers. Congressmen have become accustomed to getting everything they want, how they want it, and when they want it. Like a spoiled child at Christmas, cost has never been a consideration.

In the current era of budget cutting and closer scrutiny of what Congress spends on itself, Congress will have to pay more attention to the value it gets for its expenditures, and will have to plan for acquiring services on the basis of well-thought-out priorities, not isolated whims. In the long run, it may be necessary to balance competing desires, such as control over applications, security of data, and speed of availability, against cost factors. This may well mean more services provided by a centralized information network.

Ethics

New technologies often stretch traditional ethical codes to the breaking point. The introduction of computers into Congress opens a number of ethical problems. In the realm of constituent communications, the potential for unsolicited targeted mailings makes it difficult to divine which applications are part of the member's official responsibilities and which are simply effective reelection tactics. The guiding premise that members of Congress retain a total right of scrutiny over their mailing lists makes it impossible to enforce even the simplest limitations, such as the prohibition against maintaining partisan political information in data files financed through tax dollars. We simply do not know the degree to which data files are being misused.

The ability of the computer to consolidate data files and track the attitudes and behavior of individuals reduces privacy. While the problem of privacy in a computerized society goes well beyond Congress, current congressional applications contribute to reducing the individual's protection from surveillance and interference. For example, should a congressional office be able to combine a list of farmers getting prices supports with a list of those constituents writing to them on reducing government expenditures in order to develop a targeted mailing list for sending out unsolicited letters touting the member's exemplary performance in helping to accomplish both goals? To take the example a step further, should the incumbent be allowed to provide such a list to his or her campaign committee to target potential contributors? In modern society each individual leaves a "paper trail," and no one has fully determined who has the right of access to its content. In the past, Congress has not been particularly sensitive to its potential contribution to this problem. Perhaps the increased ability to consolidate data files relating to members of Congress themselves and to track their official and less public attitudes and behavior will eventually serve to sensitize them to the broader question of citizen rights to privacy.

Discerning Quantity of Information from Quality

Modern information technology excels in collecting more data, faster, and presenting it in a seemingly more sophisticated manner. The quantity of data presented does not necessarily correspond to an increase in quality. As one information specialist in Congress put it:

> We can now collect, store and retrieve garbage at fantastic rates. And it is often packaged in some attractive ways—We've got to keep searching for ways to get around the "fringe benefits" of our technology—wherein we tend to lose whatever grasp we may have originally had over the nature and quality of the subjects we're dealing with [Price, in Chartrand and Morentz, 1979: 47].

Congress needs to develop ways in which to separate useful information from useless information, and information from misinformation. Traditionally this is done through trial and error, but the importance of the problems with which Congress deals cries out for a more sophisticated evaluation system. Data must be constantly checked for its accuracy by comparing alternative sources. Decision makers must develop a deeper understanding of the sources and biases of the data they are using. Information producers must be more honest about the limitations and problems of their data. One budget analyst admitted privately:

> We have had some data and software glitches. In one case two of our data bases did not agree for a number of weeks. Luckily no one was aware of the multi-billion dollar error nor made a major policy decision based on the faulty data.

The capacity to generate massive amounts of computerized information threatens to exacerbate the "white plague" of paper that the computer revolution was supposed to solve. Piles of computer printouts may be no less burdensome than similar piles of traditional printed material. Information specialists James Price challenged his fellow experts to "consider information as an anti-commodity rather than a commodity.... Something from which we have to protect our clients" (Chartrand and Morentz,

1979: 47). In this computer age as well as in the past, the challenge of reducing information load will be one of establishing the correct selection rules that will allow the necessary and useful computerized information to reach the decision makers, while sorting out the extraneous.

Access

Information, whether based on computer technology or not, serves as one of the most important power resources in our political system. Modern information, with its capacity for information technology, requires access information that can usually be gained more easily than the resident information more important in prior periods. This fact, combined with the information explosion that inundates the information-processing capabilities of existing experts, opens the door to a more democratic society, in which ability and motivation to access and utilize the new information means more than one's current formal power position or expertise. The degree to which computers democratize Congress will depend on the rules for access. Inside Congress, computerized information is widely shared and the presumption is for open access. In only a few specific cases will Congress have to determine whether particular data bases deserve special rules of limited access. The sharing of computerized information with outside observers presents a more mixed picture. Pleading financial constraints and rights of privacy, movement to computer storage of congressional data has not increased access to that data by constituents, interest groups, or members of the executive branch. While it would be feasible for Congress to provide direct access to its data files through terminals in libraries around the country, or through contracts with commercial interests to market the data, action on these possibilities have not gone beyond the talking stage. The fear in Congress of letting the public know too much and its natural conservatism have meant that Congress has already missed the boat in recovering some of its costs through selling its information. A commercial firm is already marketing a form of the bill status system to interest groups and other private parties. Putting aside the question of commercial payoffs from congressional computerization, the broader question remains unanswered. In the near future Congress will have to decide which data files the public deserves access to and the best means of granting it. The answer to this question may well decide whether computerization enhances or diminishes citizen power.

CONCLUSION

As this evaluation of the overall impact of computers on Congress shows, the balance clearly falls on the positive side. Above and beyond being almost inevitable, access to computerized data bases and manipulation capabilities have left Congress better informed and better able to select and use relevant information. Both sides of the representation equation have been improved, as members of Congress know more about what their constituents want and are more efficiently able to communicate with them. Relatively open access to information has democratized the decision-making process and set the stage for better public policy made by individuals more fully aware of the complete range of consequences.

While extensive, the impact of computerization has not been uniform across all categories of needed information. To date the deepest impact has been on *word-processing* applications for solving communications challenges. The introduction of computers for dealing with *secondary data* allowed Congress to at least hold its own in selectively assimilating the vast and growing amount of data standing on its threshold. The vast capabilities of computers have only been used sporadically for creatively analyzing *primary data*, although significant advantages have been found for monitoring budgets and legislative activity.

Not all of the consequences of computerization are as positive. The potential for efficient and creative communications with constituents invites overuse and further denegrates the chances of electoral challengers by giving incumbents the potential for reelection without real responsiveness. Computerization has also increased the financial costs of congressional operations and may exact more costs in the forms of changed power relationships, enhanced parochialism, and increased decision-making conflict.

The relatively smooth incremental process of adopting modern information technology by Congress meant that little long-term planning and projection of potential consequences took place. The fact that few major negative consequences emerged was more a matter of luck than of preparation.

Although computerization in Congress has come a long way in the last decade, the millenium has not arrived. As late as 1977, congressional scholars Roger Davidson and Walter Oleszak (1977: 5) listed shortcomings in the utilization of information technology as one of their major criticisms of the system:

> Congress lacks sufficient modern information technology to assist it in making informed policy judgements. Compared to the executive branch, Congress seems far behind in developing an independent automatic data-processing capability.

While some improvement has been made since then, existing computer applications only scratch the surface of what is possible. In the long run, the important decision for Congress may not have been whether to adopt computers or not, but rather the past, current, and upcoming decisions as to how to use the capabilities. Congress is clearly still feeling its way.

The ability to assess the ultimate impact of computers in Congress is a long time away. With only ten years' experience, we are still at the early stages of development. As Congressman Charlie Rose stated it:

> The Congress has come a long way since the initial computerization, but it is still in early adolescence. The shape of adulthood will depend on the type of congressmen elected and the efforts of information specialists both in and outside of Congress. We need to elect more young and imaginative Congressmen who are computer literate and can see the potential applications. Information specialists must open the doors to new possibilities and devise new approaches to pricing and utilization. Currently, technology is ahead of the people. People don't have their own perspectives straight enough to know computer potential. Electronic computers are prisoners of human "computers" that have severe software malfunctions. There is a tremendous future in electronic computers for running the world, if we can develop aware and credible human computers to direct the electronic ones [personal interview].

Our initial analysis of the path toward computerization in Congress teaches some lessons. Despite its unique responsibilities, composition, and traditional working patterns, Congress is quite similar to other organizations in terms of the process of technological innovation and the impact of computers. The threat or promise of computers looms a bit larger in Congress due to the important role information plays in decision-making and the distribution of power. The cry in the halls of Congress, that "the

Computers Are Coming," has been replaced with the recognition that "the Computers Are Here." Congress and the society of which it is a part are unlikely to ever be the same.

REFERENCES

ADAMS, J. M. and D.H. HADEN (1973) Computers: Appreciation, Applications, Implications. New York: John Wiley.

ALBRECHT, G. L. (1979) "Defusing technological change in juvenile courts: the probation officer's struggle for professional autonomy." Sociology of Work and Occupations 6 (August): 259-282.

AMARA, R. [ed.] (1974) Toward Understanding the Social Impact of Computers. Menlo Park, CA: Institute for the Future.

ARIEFF, I. B. (1981a) "House OK's committees' 1981 investigative funds." Congressional Quarterly Weekly Report (March 28): 546.

——— (1981b) "Group of House Republicans oppose funding increases for chamber's committees." Congressional Quarterly Weekly Report (March 7): 429-430.

——— (1979) "Computers and direct mail are being married on the Hill to keep incumbents in office." Congressional Quarterly Weekly Report (July 21): 1445-1448.

BAAKLINI, A. I. and J. J. HEAPHEY [eds.] (1977) Comparative Legislative Reform and Innovations. Albany, NY: Comparative Development Studies Center.

BARNETT, G. (1953) Innovation: The Basis of Cultural Change. New York: McGraw-Hill.

BECKER, S. W. and T. L. WHISLER (1967) "The innovative organization: a selective view of current theory and research." Journal of Business 40 (October): 462-469.

BECKMAN, N. (1971) "Congressional information processes for national policy." Annals of the American Academy of Political and Social Science 394: 85-99.

BELL, D. (1973) The Coming of Post-Industrial Society. New York: Basic Books.

——— (1960) The End of Ideology. New York: Macmillan.

BEMER, R. W. (1975) "The frictional interface between computers and society." Computers and People 24 (January): 14-19.

BEREANO, P. [ed.] (1976) Technology as Social and Political Phenomenon. New York: John Wiley.

BEZOLD, C. (1975) "Congress and the future." Futurist 9 (June): 132-142.

BIBBY, J., T. MANN, and N. ORNSTEIN (1980) Vital Statistics of the U.S. Congress, 1980. Washington, DC: American Enterprise Institute.

BIGONESS, W. J. and W. D. PERREAULT (1981) "A conceptual paradigm and approach for the study of innovators." Academy of Management Journal 24 (March): 68-82.

BOLLING, R. (1975) "The management of Congress." Public Administration Review 35 (September/October): 490-494.

BORTNICK, J. (1979) "Legislative and legal information systems." Bulletin of the American Society for Information Science 5 (August): 26-27.

BRADEMAS, J. (1972) "Prognostications regarding the growth and diversification of computers in the service of society: the congressional role," in R. L. Chartrand (ed.) Computers in the Service of Society. New York: Pergamon.

——— (1971) "Congress in the year 2000," in H. Perloff (ed.) The future of the U.S. Congress. New York: George Braziller.

BRIGHT, J. R. (1964) Research, Development and Technological Innovation. Homewood, IL: Irwin.

BRYDGES, E. W. (1965) "The electronic Solon." National Civic Review 35 (July): 350-353.

BRZEZINSKI, Z. (1971) "Moving into a technetronic society," in A. F. Westin (ed.) Information Technology in a Democracy. Cambridge, MA: Harvard University Press.

BUHL, L. C. (1974) "Mariners and machines: resistance to technology change in the American navy, 1865-1869." Journal of American History 61 (December): 703-727.

Bulletin of the American Society for Information Science (1978) "The presidency in the information age." Vol. 4 (December).

——— (1975) "Congress in the information age." Vol. 1 (April).

BURNHAM, D. (1980) "Congress's computer subsidy." New York Times Magazine 130 (November): 96-102.

CALIFANO, J., Jr. (1971) "Congress has been bypassed in analysis technology." Washington Post (July 19): A18.

CAPLAN, N., A. MORRISON, and R. J. STAMBAUCH (1963) The Use of Social Science Knowledge in Policy Decisions at the National Level: A Report to Respondents. Ann Arbor, MI: Institute for Social Research.

CARTER, C. F. and B. R. WILLIAMS (1957) Industry and Technical Progress. Oxford: Oxford University Press.

CHARTRAND, R. L. (1980) Information Services for Legislative Policy Making. Brussels: NATO, Advisory Group for Aerospace Research and Development.

——— (1978) "Congressional management and use of information technology." Journal of Systems Management 28 (August): 10-15.

——— (1976a) The Legislator as User of Information Technology. Washington, DC: Congressional Research Service.

——— (1976b) "Legislative information services for Congress," in J. Worthley (ed.) Comparative Legislative Information Systems: The Use of Computer Technology in the Public Policy Process. Albany, NY: Comparative Development Studies Center.

——— (1976c) "Information in the legislative process." Annual Review of Information Science and Technology 11: 299-344.

——— [ed.] (1972) Computers in the Service of Society. New York: Pergamon.

——— (1971a) "Redimensioning congressional information support." Jurimetrics Journal 11 (June): 165-178.

——— (1971b) "Congress needs the systems approach," in A. F. Westin (ed.) Information Technology in a Democracy. Cambridge, MA: Harvard University Press.

——— (1970) "Congress, computers and the cognitive process," in T. Beyle and G. T. Lathrop (eds.) Planning and Politics: Uneasy Partnership. New York: Odyssey.

——— (1967a) "Automatic data processing for the Congress." Legislative Reference Service Report TK6565.

——(1967b) "The systems approach: a tool for the Congress." Legislative Reference Service Report TK6565.

—— and J. BORRELL (1981) "The legislator as user of information technology." Congressional Research Service Report 81-187 SPR.

CHARTRAND, R. L. and J. W. MORENTZ [eds.] (1979) Information Technology Serving Society. New York: Pergamon.

CHARTRAND, R. L. and J. B. STAENBERG (1978) Information Support for the State Legislatures: The Role of Advanced Technology. Washington, DC: Congressional Research Service.

CHARTRAND, R. L., K. JANDA, and H. MICHAEL (1968) Information Support, Program Budgeting and Congress. New York: Spartan.

CLAYTON, A. (1979) "The information revolution comes to Parliament." Optimum (March): 5-15.

COHEN, R. E. (1973) "Information gap plagues attempt to grapple with growing executive strength." National Journal 5 (March): 379-388.

COLEMAN, J. (1977) "Policy research in the social sciences," in U.S. Congress, Senate, Commission on the Operation of the Senate, Policy Analysis on Major Issues. Washington, DC: Government Printing Office.

—— E. KATZ, and H. MENZEL (1966) Medical Innovation: A Diffusion Study. Indianapolis: Bobbs-Merrill.

Common Cause (1981) Plantiffs' motion for summary judgment. Common Cause v. William F. Bolger and the House Commission on Congressional Mailing Standards, U.S. District Court for the District of Columbia. Civil Action 1887-73.

Congressional Quarterly (1979) Inside Congress. Washington, DC: Author.

Congressional Quarterly Weekly Report (1971) "House computer finding." November 20: 2382.

Congressional Record (1981) Debate on legislative funding. March 25 (daily): H1073-H1120.

—— (1972) Remarks of Congressman Wayne L. Hays, speaking on electronic voting in the House of Representatives. Vol. 118, October 13: 36005-36012.

—— (1971) Remarks of Congressman Frank Thompson, Jr., speaking on providing funds for computer services for the House of Representatives. Vol. 117, November 9: 40015-40016.

—— (1970) Robert Chartrand, "Congress: the three dimensional chessboard—the role of information technology." Vol. 116, August 13: 28893.

—— (1969) Remarks of Congressman Jack Brooks, speaking on data processing techniques to aid Congress. Vol. 115, January 3: 129-131.

—— (1968) Remarks of Congressman Robert McClory, speaking on computers for Congress. Vol. 114, January 29: 1322.

—— (1967a) Robert Chartrand, "Automatic data processing for the Congress." Vol. 113, January 30: 1801.

—— (1967b) Remarks by Senator Hugh Scott. Vol. 113, February 16: 3732.

—— (1966) Remarks of Congressman Robert McClory, "An automatic data processing facility to support the Congress." Vol. 112, October 19: 27824.

—— (1964) Remarks of Senator Hubert H. Humphrey, speaking before the Eastern Spring Computer Conference on "The Computer Revolution." Vol. 110, April 25: 9075.

COOPER, J. (1977) "Congress in organizational perspective," in L. Dodd and B. Oppenheimer (eds.) Congress Reconsidered. New York: Praeger.

——— (1975) "Strengthening Congress: an organizational analysis." Harvard Journal on Legislation 12 (April): 328-356.

CROLEY, J. C. (1977) The Congressional Guide to Computers. Washington, DC: Congressional Management Foundation.

CYERT, R. M. and J. G. MARCH (1963) A Behavioral Theory of the Firm. Englewood Cliffs, NJ: Prentice-Hall.

DANZIGER, J. N. (1977) "Computers, local governments, and the litany to EDP." Public Administration Review 37 (January/February): 28-37.

——— and W. H. DUTTON (1970) Technological Innovation in Local Government: The Case of Computers in U.S. Cities and Counties. Washington, DC: National Science Foundation.

Dartmouth College (1976) Computers and Public Policy. Hanover, NH: Author.

Datamation (1981) Congress and Its Members. Washington, DC: Congressional Quarterly Press.

——— (1973) "Senate upstaged on Dial-a-Bill system." April: 124.

DAVIDSON, R. H. (1979) "Paradigms of innovation: House and Senate Committee reorganization." Presented at the American Political Science Association Convention.

——— and W. OLESAK (1977) Congress Against Itself. Bloomington: Indiana University Press.

——— (1976) "Adaptation and consolidation: structural innovation in the U.S. House of Representatives." Legislative Studies Quarterly 1 (February): 37-65.

DAVIDSON, R. H., D. M. KOVENOCK, and M. O'LEARY (1966) Congress in Crisis: Politics and Congressional Reform. Belmont, CA: Wadsworth.

DECHERT, C. R. (1966) "Availability of information for congressional operations," in A. de Grazia (ed.) Congress: The First Branch of Government. Washington, DC: American Enterprise Institute.

DE GRAZIA, A. [ed.] (1966) Congress: The First Branch of Government. Washington, DC: American Enterprise Institute.

DERTOUZOS, M. L. and J. MOSES [eds.] (1975) The Computer Age: A Twenty Year View. Cambridge: MIT Press.

DERY, D. (1981) Computers in Welfare: The MIS-Match. Beverly Hills, CA: Sage.

DE SOLA POOL, I., S. McINTOSH, and D. GRIFFEN (1971) "Information systems and social knowledge," in A. F. Westin (ed.) Information Technology in a Democracy. Cambridge, MA: Harvard University Press.

DEXTER, L. A. (1969) The Sociology and Politics of Congress. Skokie, IL: Rand McNally.

DODD, L. C. and R. SCHOTT (1979) Congress and the Administrative State. New York: John Wiley

DONHAM, P. and R. FAHEY (1966) Congress Needs Help. New York: Random House.

DOWNS, A. (1967) "A realistic look at the final payoffs from urban data systems." Public Administration Review 27 (September): 204-210.

DREYFUS, D. (1977) "The limitations of policy research in congressional decision-making," in C. H. Weiss (ed.) Using Social Science Research in Public Policy Making. Lexington, MA: D. C. Heath.

DUTTON, W. H. and K. L. KRAEMER (1976) Determinants of Support for Computerized Information Systems. Irvine, CA: Public Policy Research Organization.

Electronics (1971) "Digitalizing Congress." Vol. 43 (August 31): 41-46.

EMARD, J. P. and J. B. STAENBERG (1977) "An overview of computerized legal information systems—an update." Law and Computer Technology 10 (First Quarter): 2-16.

ERICKSON, R. S. (1971) "The advantage of incumbency in congressional elections." Polity 3 (Spring): 395-405.

ETZIONI, A. (1978) The Active Society. New York: Macmillan.

EVELAND, J., E. M. ROGERS, and C. KLEPPER (1977) The Innovation Process in Public Organizations: Executive Summary. Washington, DC: National Science Foundation.

FELLER, I. and D. C. MENZEL (1978) "The adoption of technological innovations by municipal governments." Urban Affairs Quarterly 13 (June): 469-490.

FENNO, R. (1973) Congressmen in Committees. Boston: Little, Brown.

FLATO, L. (1977) "Computers and legislators." Datamation 23 (September): 253-256.

Foreign Policy Association [ed.] (1968) Toward the Year 2018. New York: Cowles Education Corporation.

FRANKLIN, M. (1976) "The use of computers in the British parliamentary process," in J. Worthley (ed.) Comparative Legislative Information Systems: The Use of Computer Technology in the Public Policy Process. Albany, NY: Comparative Development Studies Center.

FRANTZICH, S. (1979a) "Technological innovation among members of the U.S. House of Representatives." Polity 22 (Winter): 333-348.

——— (1979b) "Technological innovation among congressmen." Social Forces 53 (March): 968-974.

——— (1979c) "Who makes our laws?: the legislative effectiveness of members of the U.S. Congress." Legislative Studies Quarterly 4 (August): 409-428.

——— (1979d) "Computerized information technology in the U.S. House of Representatives." Legislative Studies Quarterly 4 (May): 255-280.

——— (1978) "Congress by computer." Social Policy 8 (January/February): 42-45.

Futurist (1978) "Information: The Ultimate Resource." 12 (February): 55-56.

GATTY, B. (1978) "Shoot-out on Capitol Hill." Army 28 (June): 41-43.

General Accounting Office (1980) Annual Report, 1980. Washington, DC: Author.

GLASS, A. J. (1970) "Congress moves into the computer age but divides control of new systems." National Journal (May 30): 1150-1157.

Government Executive (1977a) "Congress automates its information." Vol. 9 (November): 46-48.

——— (1977b) "How computers are making congressmen more effective." Vol. 9 (June): 46-48.

GREGORY, N. (1980) "Changing information needs of Congress," in B. Krevitt Eres (ed.) Legal and Legislative Information Processing. Westport, CT: Greenwood.

——— (1979a) "Congress and the politics of information." Presented at the meeting of the Data Processing Management Association.

——— (1979b) "The U.S. Congress—on-line users as policy makers." Presented at the Online Information Meeting, Commonwealth Institute, London, December 5-8.

――― (1978) "Congress—the politics of information." Data Management 16 (January): 96-100.

GREIDER, W. (1981) "The education of David Stockman." Atlantic Monthly (December): 27-54.

GRIFFITH, E. (1951) Congress: Its Contemporary Role. New York: New York University Press.

GRIFFITH, J. (1981) "Studies of SCORPIO training and use." U.S. Library of Congress. (unpublished)

GROBAN, G. (1981) "Progress too fast, H.I.S. is C.U.T. by House." Roll Call (May 14): 5, 8.

GROSS, B. (1969) Social Intelligence for America's Future. Boston: Allyn & Bacon.

GRUMM, J. G. (1979) "A theory of legislative reform." Presented at the International Political Science Association Congress, Moscow, August 12-18.

HABER, JUEGEN (1972) "Updating of census data caused delay, revisions in first revenue-sharing payments." National Journal 4 (December 23): 1964-1967.

HAGERSTRAND, T. (1967) Innovation Diffusion as a Spatial Process (A. Pred, trans.). Chicago: University of Chicago Press.

HAYDON, W. (1980) "Confessions of a high-techo politico: Mr. Wang goes to Washington." Washington Monthly 12 (May): 43-48.

HEAPHEY, J. J. (1975) "Legislatures: political organizations." Public Administration Review 35 (September/October): 479-482.

HEDLUND, R. D. (1980) "Measuring activity or performance and developing a theory of legislative change." Presented at the American Political Science Association Convention, Washington, D.C., September.

HELLRIEGEL, D. and J. W. SLOCUM (1979) Organizational Behavior. St. Paul, MN: West.

――― (1978) Management: Contingency Approaches. Reading, MA: Addison Wesley.

HOLMES, E. (1977) "Congressional DP service seen enmeshed in politics." Computerworld 11 (July 18): 7.

HOLOIEN, M. O. (1977) Computers and Their Societal Impact. New York: John Wiley.

HOPKINS, B. R. (1972) "Congressional reform: toward a modern Congress." Notre Dame Lawyer 47 (February): 442-513.

HORNBLOWER, M. (1981) "AT&T debate." Washington Post (July 7): A1.

INGRAM, H. M. and S. J. ULLERY (1980) "Policy innovation and institutional fragmentation." Policy Studies Journal 8 (Spring): 664-682.

IVANCEVICH, J. M., M. J. WALLACE, and A. SZILAGVI (1971) Organizational Behavior and Performance. Santa Monica, CA: Goodyear.

JANDA, K. (1968) Information Retrieval Applications to Political Science. Indianapolis: Bobbs-Merrill.

JOHANNES, J. R. (1977) "Statutory reporting requirements: information and influence for Congress," in A. I. Baaklini and J. J. Heaphey (eds.) Comparative Legislative Reform and Innovations. Albany, NY: Comparative Development Studies Center.

JOHNSON, D. (1976) "Legislative information processing in the State of Florida," in J. Worthley (ed.) Comparative Legislative Information Systems: The Use of Computer Technology in the Public Policy Process. Albany, NY: Comparative Development Studies Center.

JONES, C. O. (1976) "Why Congress can't do policy analysis (or words to that effect)." Policy Analysis 64 (Spring): 251-264.

JOST, S. (1979) "The automated congressional office." Data Management 17 (May: 46-50.

KANTER, J. (1967) Computers and the Executive. Englewood Cliffs, NJ: Prentice-Hall.

KAPLAN, A. (1964) The Conduct of Inquiry. San Francisco: Chandler.

KINGDON, J. (1981) Congressional Voting Decisions. New York: Harper & Row.

KNIGHT, K. (1967) "A descriptive model of the intra-firm innovation process." Journal of Business 40 (October): 478-496.

KORNBLUH, M. (1977) "Legislative implications of socio-economic models." Congressional Research Service Report 77-128.

KOVENOCK, D. (1967) "Influence in the U.S. House of Representatives." Presented at the American Political Science Association Convention.

KRAEMER, K. L. and J. L. KING (1975) Municipal Information Systems: Evaluation of Policy Related Research, Volume 1: Summary of Research Findings. Washington, DC: National Technical Information Service.

KREVITT ERES, B. [ed.] (1980) Legal and Legislative Information Processing. Westport, CT: Greenwood.

LAUDON, K. (1977) Communications Technology and Democratic Participation. New York: Praeger.

——— (1974) Computers and Bureaucratic Reform: The Political Functions of Urban Information Systems. New York: John Wiley.

LIGHTMAN, D. (1979) "Our million dollar congressmen." Baltimore Sun (September 28): A1, A4.

LOOMIS, B. A. (1980) "Policy speculation and the Congress: an issue based approach." Presented at the meeting of the American Political Science Association, Washington, D.C., September.

——— (1979) "The congressional office as a small business." Publius 9, 3: 35-55.

LOY, J. W. (1969) "Social psychological characteristics of innovators." American Sociological Review 34, 2: 73-82.

McHALE, J. (1976) The Changing Information Environment. Denver, CO: Westview.

MAIDIQUE, M. A. (1980) 'Entrepreneurs, champions, and technological innovation." Sloan Management Review 2 (Winter): 59-76.

MAISEL, L. S. (1979) "Information and decision-making in House offices." Presented at the American Political Science Association Convention.

MALVEY, M. (1981) Simple Systems, Complex Environments. Beverly Hills, CA: Sage.

MANLEY, J. F. (1970) The Politics of Finance. Boston: Little, Brown.

MANSFIELD, E. (1968) Industrial Research and Technological Innovation. New York: Norton.

MARCH, J. G. and H. A. SIMON (1958) Organizations. New York: John Wiley.

MAYHEW, D. (1974) Congress: The Electoral Connection. New Haven, CT: Yale University Press.

MENZEL, H. (1960) "Innovation, integration and marginality: survey of physicians." American Journal of Sociology 25 (October): 704-713.

MESTHENE, E. G. (1971) "How technology will shape the future," in A. F. Westin (ed.) Information Technology in a Democracy Cambridge, MA: Harvard University Press.

MEYER, D. N. and T. M. LODAHL (1980) "Pilot projects: a way to get started in office automation." Administrative Management 4 (February): 36-37, 62-64.

MICHAEL, D. N. (1971) "Democratic participation and technological planning," in A. F. Westin (ed.) Information Technology in a Democracy. Cambridge, MA: Harvard University Press.

––– (1966) "Some long-range implications of computer technology for human behavior in organizations." American Behavioral Scientist 9 (April): 29-35.

MILLER, P. J. and A. ROLNICK (1981) "The CBO's policy analysis: an unquestionable misuse of a questionable theory," in R. G. Penner (ed.) The Congressional Budget After Five Years. Washington, DC: American Enterprise Institute.

Modern Data (1969) "Congress and the computer." Vol. 2 (September): 68-71.

MOHR, L. B. (1969) "Determinants of innovation in organizations." American Political Science Review 63 (March): 111-126.

MORISON, E. (1966) Men, Machines and Modern Times. Cambridge, MA: Harvard University Press.

MOYNIHAN, D. P. (1969) Maximum Feasible Misunderstanding. New York: Macmillan.

MUELLER, E. (1969) Automation in an Expanding Economy. Ann Arbor, MI: Institute for Social Research.

MUELLER, R. K. (1971) The Innovation Ethic. New York: American Management Association.

MULHOLLAND, D. P., S. W. HAMMOND, and A. G. STEVENS (1981) "Informal groups and agenda setting in Congress." Presented at the Midwest Political Science Association Convention, Chicago, April.

MYERS, C. [ed.] (1967) The Impact of Computers on Management. Cambridge: MIT Press.

Nation's Business (1973) "Congress puts the computer to work." Vol. 61 (May): 69-73.

NICHOLS, J. H. (1976) "Foreword," in J. Worthley (ed.) Comparative Legislative Information Systems: The Use of Computer Technology in the Public Policy Process. Albany, NY: Comparative Development Studies Center.

NORTON, B. (1980) "The quiet revolution of information technology in Congress," in B. Krevitt Eres (ed.) Legal and Legislative Information Processing. Westport, CT: Greenwood.

O'DONNELL, T. O. (1980) A Study of the General Information Requirements of Member Offices. Washington, DC: House Information Systems. (unpublished)

OLSON, M., Jr. (1965) The Logic of Collective Action. Cambridge, MA: Harvard University Press.

ORNSTEIN, N. [ed.] (1975) Congress in Change. New York: Praeger.

––– (1974) "The strategy of reform: recorded teller voting in the U.S. House of Representatives." Presented at the Midwest Political Science Association, Chicago, April.

PERLOFF, H. S. (1971) The Future of the U.S. Government. New York: George Braziller.

PERRY, J. (1978) "Campaign act: congressmen discover computer and use it to keep voters in tow." Wall Street Journal (March 15): 1, 33.

PORAT, M. V. (1976) The Information Economy. Stanford, CA: Stanford University Institute for Communications Research.

PORTER, H. O. (1974) "Legislative experts and outsiders: the two step flow of communication." Journal of Politics 36 (August): 703-730.

PORTER, R. (1972) "Congress and computers." American University, Washington, D.C. (unpublished)

REILLY, A. M (1979) "How Congress educates itself." Dun's Review 114 (September): 72-78.

RIESELBACH, L. M. [ed.] (1978) Legislative Reform: The Policy Impact. Lexington, MA: D. C. Heath.

――― (1977) Congressional Reform in the Seventies. Morrison, NJ: General Learning Press.

RIKER, W. (1962) The Theory of Political Coalitions. New Haven, CT: Yale University Press.

RIVLIN, A. M. (1978) "Sharing fiscal information: a legislative branch view." Bulletin of the American Society for Information Science 5 (December): 25-26.

ROBERTSON, T. (1971) Innovative Behavior and Communication. New York: Holt, Rinehart & Winston.

ROBINSON, J. A. (1966) "Decision-making in Congress," in A. de Grazia (ed.) Congress: The First Branch of Government. Washington DC: American Enterprise Institute.

ROESSNER, J. D. (1975) "Incentives to innovate in public and private organizations." Administration and Society 9 (November): 341-365.

ROGERS, E. M. (1962a) "Characteristics of agricultural innovators and other adopter categories," in W. Schramm (ed.) Studies of Innovation and of Communication to the Public. Stanford, CA: Stanford University Press.

――― (1962b) Diffusion of Innovations. New York: Macmillan.

――― and F. F. SHOEMAKER (1971) Communication of Innovation. New York: Macmillan.

ROSE, C. (1978) "Information sharing: a view from the Hill." Bulletin of the American Society for Information Science 5 (December): 14-15.

ROSENTHAL, A. (1981) Legislative Life. New York: Harper & Row.

ROURKE, F. (1975) "Administrative secrecy: a contemporary perspective." Public Administration Review 35 (January/February): 2-25.

ROWE, L. A. and W. B. BOISE (1974) "Organizational innovation: current research and evolving concepts." Public Administration Review 34 (May/June): 284-295.

RYAN, F. (1976) "Computing as an aid to political effectiveness," in Dartmouth College, Computers and Public Policy. Hanover, NH: Dartmouth College.

SACKMAN, H. (1971) "A public philosophy for real time information systems," in A. F. Westin (ed.) Information Technology in a Democracy. Cambridge, MA: Harvard University Press.

SOLOMA, J. S. (1969) Congress and the New Politics. Boston: Little, Brown.

SANFIELD, P. (1979) "Congress has moved fully into computer age." Roll Call (July 12): 1.

SAPOLSKY, H. M. (1967) "Organizational structure and innovation." Journal of Business 40 (October): 497-510.

SCHICK, A. (1976) "The supply and demand for analysis on Capitol Hill." Policy Analysis 2 (Spring): 215-234.

SCHLAPPE, R. D. (1974) "The computer information system of the U.S. House of Representatives: how Congress uses the computer." Computers and People 23 (February): 11-13.

SCHLOSS, L. (1970) "Congress needs computers—but they are many years away." Government Executive 42: 42-43.

SCHNEIER, E. (1970) "The intelligence of Congress: information and public policy patterns." Annals of the American Academy of Political and Social Science 388 (March): 14-24.

SCICCITANO, M. J. (1981) "Legislative goals and information use." American Politics Quarterly 9 (January): 103-110.

SHEPARD, H. A. (1967) "Innovation-resisting and innovation-producing organizations." Journal of Business 40 (October): 470-477.

SIDLOW, E. I. and D. H. SHUMAVON (1981) "Congressional budget committee staffs and the use of information." Presented at the Midwest Political Science Association Convention, Chicago, April.

SIMON, H. (1975) "The consequences of computers for centralization and decentralization," in M. Dertouzos and J. Moses (eds.) The Computer Age: A Twenty Year View. Cambridge: MIT Press.

SOUTHWICK, T. P. (1977) "Computers aid Congress in work, politics." Congressional Quarterly Weekly Report 35 (May 28): 1045-1051.

SPECTOR, B., R. E. HAYES, and M. J. CRAIN (1976) The Impact of Computer-Based Decision Aids on Organization Structure in the Task Force Staff. Arlington, VA: CACI, Inc.

STAATS, E. B. (1978) "Social indicators and congressional needs for information." Annals of the American Academy of Political and Social Science 435 (January): 277-285.

STAENBERG, J. B. (1978) "Use of computers in supporting members offices." Bulletin of the American Society for Information Science 4 (April): 33-34.

——— (1977) The Use of Computers by House Members and the Staff for Official and Campaign Purposes: Legal and Ethical Issues. Washington, DC: Congressional Research Service.

Staff Journal (1981) "Information flow: types, trends and tips." March/April.

——— (1980) House information system tailors aid to individual members." May/June.

——— (1979) "Hill tries new information aids." September/October.

——— (1978) "House provides computer graphic capability with IMAGE system." May/June.

STEVENS, A. G. and S. P. RICHARDSON (1981) "Indicators of congressional workload and activity." Congressional Research Service Report 81-96 Gov.

TAPPER, C. (1970) "Computers and legislation." Alabama Law Review 23 (Fall): 1-42.

THOMAS, W. V. (1978) "America's information boom," pp. 803-820 in Editorial Research Reports Staff, Editorial Research Reports November 3. Washington, DC: Congressional Quarterly.

THOMPSON, R. C. (1976) "Information for legislatures: the New York experience," in J. Worthley (ed.) Comparative Legislative Information Systems: The Use of Computer Technology in the Public Process. Albany, NY: Comparative Development Studies Center.

THOMPSON, V. A. (1969) Bureaucracy and Innovation. Tuscaloosa: University of Alabama Press.

——— (1968) "How scientific management thwarts innovation." Trans-Action 5 (June): 51-56.

Time (1978) "Living: pushbutton society." Time 11, 8 (February 20): 47.

TOFFLER, A. (1980) "A look at the next civilization." Industry Week 20 (March 31): 90, 95-96, 101.

TOWELL, P. (1981) "Inflation, spending projections." Congressional Quarterly Weekly Report (April 18): 681.

U.S. Congress, Congressional Budget Office (1981) "Congressional budget office computer requirements." (unpublished)

U.S. Congress, House, Clerk of the House Reports (quarterly) Washington, DC: Government Printing Office.

U.S. Congress, House, Commission on Administrative Review (1978) Administrative Reorganization and Legislative Management. Washington, DC: Government Printing Office.

——— (1977a) State Legislative Use of Information Policy. House Document 95-271. Washington, DC: Government Printing Office.

——— (1977b) Final Report of the Commission on Administrative Review: Communication from the Chairman. House Document 95-272. Washington, DC: Government Printing Office.

U.S. Congress, House, Commission on Information and Facilities (1976a) Information Resources and Services Available from the Library of Congress and Congressional Research Service. House Document 94-527. Washington, DC: Government Printing Office.

——— (1976b) Automated Information Resources for the U.S. House of Representatives. Committee print. Washington, DC: Government Printing Office.

——— (1976c) Inventory of Information Resources. House Document 94-537. Washington, DC: Government Printing Office.

U.S. Congress, House, Commission on Organization and Procedure (1973) Information Systems for Congress Revisited. Washington, DC: Government Printing Office.

U.S. Congress, House, Committee on House Administration (1981) Providing for the Expenses of Investigations and Studies to Be Conducted by the Standing and Select Committees of the House. House Report 97-11. Washington, DC: Government Printing Office.

——— (1980a) Congressional Handbook. Committee print. Washington, DC: Government Printing Office.

——— (1980b) Providing Funds for the Expenses of the Committee on House Administration. House Report 96-813. Washington, DC: Government Printing Office.

———(1979a) The Legislative Information and Status System for the U.S. House of Representatives. Committee print. Washington, DC: Government Printing Office.

——— (1979b) The Electronic Voting System for the U.S. House of Representatives. Committee print. Washington, DC: Government Printing Office.

——— (1979c) Providing Funds for the Expenses of the Committee on House Administration. House Report 96-23. Washington, DC: Government Printing Office.

——— (1978a) Providing Funds for the Expenses of the Committee on House

Administration. House Report 95-878. Washington, DC: Government Printing Office.

——— (1978b) Studies Dealing with Budgetary, Staffing, and Administrative Activities of the U.S. House of Representatives 1946-1978. Committee print. Washington, DC: Government Printing Office.

——— (1977) Providing Funds for the Expenses of the House Information Systems of the Committee on House Administration. House Report 95-137. Washington, DC: Government Printing Office.

——— (1976) Providing Funds for the Expenses of the House Information Systems of the Committee on House Administration. House Report 94-961. Washington, DC: Government Printing Office.

——— (1975a) The Bill Status System for the U.S. House of Representatives. Committee print. Washington, DC: Government Printing Office.

——— (1975b) Computer Based Information Resources for the U.S. House of Representatives. Committee print. Washington, DC: Government Printing Office.

——— (1975c) The Electronic Voting System for the U.S. House of Representatives. Committee print. Washington, DC: Government Printing Office.

——— (1971) Effectiveness Audit of the Data Processing Office, Office of the Clerk. Committee print. Washington, DC: Government Printing Office.

——— (1970) Second Progress Report of the Special Subcommittee on Electrical and Mechanical Office Equipment. Committee print. Washington, DC: Government Printing Office.

——— (1969) First Progress Report of the Special Subcommittee on Electrical and Mechanical Office Equipment. Committee print. Washington, DC: Government Printing Office.

U.S. Congress, House, Committee on Standards of Official Conduct (1980) Study and Analysis of the Voting Anomalies in the House of Representatives on May 14 and July 30, 1979. House Report 96-991. Washington, DC: Government Printing Office.

U.S. Congress, House, House Information System (1981a) "Remote data communications project." (unpublished)

——— (1981b) "Budget book." (unpublished)

——— (1979a) "Besides answering the mail, what else is there?: supporting advanced computer applications." (photocopied seminar summary)

——— (1979b) "Strategic plan for information technology services at the U.S. House of Representatives, 1980-1981." (unpublished)

U.S. Congress, House, Select Committee on Committees (1974) Congress and Information Technology. Committee print. Washington, DC: Government Printing Office.

——— (1973a) Information System Support to the U.S. House of Representatives: Working Papers on House Committee Organization and Operation. Committee print. Washington, DC: Government Printing Office.

——— (1973b) Committee Organization in the House. Hearings. Washington, DC: Government Printing Office.

U.S. Congress, Joint Committee on Congressional Operations (1974) Congressional Research Support and Information Services. Committee print. Washington, DC: Government Printing Office.

U.S. Congress, Office of Technology Assessment (1981) Computer-Based National Information Systems. Washington, DC: Government Printing Office.

——— (1980) "Appropriations supplemental report." (unpublished)

U.S. Congress, Senate, Commission on the Operation of the Senate (1977a) Senators: Offices, Ethics and Pressures. Committee print. Washington, DC: Government Printing Office.

——— (1977b) Policy Analysis on Major Issues. Washington, DC: Government Printing Office.

——— (1977c) Committees and Senate Procedures. Committee print. Washington, DC: Government Printing Office.

——— (1977d) Techniques and Procedures for Analysis and Evaluation. Washington, DC: Government Printing Office.

——— (1976a) Interim Report of the Commission on the Operation of the Senate. Senate Document 94-165. Washington, DC: Government Printing Office.

——— (1976b) Policy-Making Role of Leadership in the Senate. Washington, DC: Government Printing Office.

——— (1976c) Toward a Modern Senate. Senate Document 94-278. Washington, DC: Government Printing Office.

U.S. Congress, Senate, Committee on Appropriations (1979) Oversight on Computer Services in the Legislative Branch. Hearings. Washington, DC: Government Printing Office.

U.S. Congress, Senate, Committee on Rules and Administration (1980) Annual Report of the Technical Services Staff to the Chairman. Committee print. Washington, DC: Government Printing Office.

——— (1977a) Information Support for the U.S. Senate: A Survey of Computerized CRS Resources and Services. Committee print. Washington, DC: Government Printing Office.

——— (1977b) Report on the Subcommittee on Computer Services. Committee print. Washington, DC: Government Printing Office.

U.S. Congress, Senate, Policy Coordinating Group for Technology Development (1978) First Annual Report. Committee print. Washington, DC: Government Printing Office.

VAGIANOS, L. (1976) "Today is tomorrow." Library Journal 101 (January): 147-156.

VERBA, S. and N. NIE (1972) Participation in America. New York: Harper & Row.

WARNER, K. E. (1974) "The need for some innovative concepts of innovation." Policy Sciences 5 (December): 433-451.

Washington Post (1981) "White House uses social sciences, but cuts funding for research." June 29: A1, A8-A9.

WATSON, G. (1973) "Resistance to change," in G. Zaltman (ed.) Processes and Phenomena of Social Change. New York: John Wiley.

WEAVER, W. (1972) Both Your Houses. New York: Praeger.

WEBBER, D. J. (1981) "Necessary political conditions for a legislator's use of policy information." Presented at the meeting of the Midwest Political Science Association, Chicago, April.

WEINBERG, H. (1979) "Using policy analysis in congressional budgeting," in F. M. Zweig (ed.) Evaluation in Legislation. Beverly Hills, CA: Sage.

WEISS, C. H. (1977) Using Social Science Research in Public Policy Making. Lexington, MA: D. C. Heath.

WIEZENBAUM, J. (1976) Computer Power and Human Reason. San Francisco: Freeman.

WELCH, S. and J. C. PETERS [eds.] (1977) Legislative Reform and Public Policy. New York: Praeger.

WESTIN, A. F. [ed.] (1971) Information Technology in a Democracy. Cambridge, MA: Harvard University Press.

WHALEN, C. W. (1980) "A decade of reform in the U.S. House of Representatives: 1969-1979." Woodrow Wilson Center, Washington, D.C. (unpublished)

WILDAVSKY, A. and E. TENENBAUM (1981) The Politics of Mistrust. Beverly Hills, CA: Sage.

WILENSKY, H. (1971) "The road from information to knowledge," in A. F. Westin (ed.) Information Technology in a Democracy. Cambridge, MA: Harvard University Press.

WILSON, B. J. (1980) "The human factor in change." Journal of Micrographics 13 (May/June): 27-29.

WILSON, J. Q. (1966) "Innovation in organization: notes toward a theory," in J. D. Thompson (ed.) Approaches to Organizational Design. Pittsburgh: University of Pittsburgh Press.

WOOD, F. B., V. T. COATES, R. L. CHARTRAND, and R. F. ERICSON (1979) Video Conferencing via Satellite: Opening Congress to the People. Washington, DC: George Washington University Program of Policy Studies in Science and Technology.

WORTHLEY, J. A. (1979) "Legislatures and information systems: challenges and responses in the states," in A. Baaklini and J. J. Heaphey (eds.) Comparative Legislative Reform and Innovation. Albany, NY: Comparative Development Studies Center.

――― (1977a) Legislatures and Information Systems: An Overview and Analysis of Recent Experience. Albany, NY: Comparative Development Studies Center.

――― (1977b) Legislatures and Information Systems: Challenges and Responses in the States. Albany, NY: Comparative Development Studies Center.

――― [ed.] (1976) Comparative Legislative Information Systems: The Use of Computer Technology in the Public Policy Process. Albany, NY: Comparative Development Studies Center.

YIN, R. (1981) "Life histories of innovations: how new practices become routinized." Public Administration Review 4 (January/February): 21-28.

――― K. A. HEALD, and M. E. VOGEL, (1977) Tinkering with the System: Innovations in State and Local Services. Lexington, MA: D. C. Heath.

ZALTMAN, G., R. DUNCAN, and J. HOLBECK (1973) Innovations and Organizations. New York: John Wiley.

ZWEIG, F. (1979) Evaluation in Legislation. Beverly Hills, CA: Sage.

ZWEIR, R. (1979) "The search for information specialists and nonspecialists in the U.S. House of Representatives." Legislative Studies Quarterly 4 (February): 31-42.

INDEX

ABOUT THE AUTHOR

STEPHEN E. FRANTZICH is Associate Professor of Political Science at the U.S. Naval Academy. After receiving his Ph.D. from the University of Minnesota, he did research in the Philippines with the Ford and Rotary Foundations, and taught at Denison University and Hamilton College. Aside from teaching, he currently serves as a consultant on internship programs and political campaigns, and offers seminars on using the unique resources of Washington, D.C. He is the author of *Storming Washington: An Intern's Guide to National Government* and *Presidential Popularity in America,* as well as numerous articles on congressional careers, power distribution, and adaptation. In the classroom he is an active advocate of innovative teaching techniques employing interactive videotape and computers and videotape in tandem. He is currently working on a project to utilize C-SPAN (the coverage of Congress on cable television) for educational purposes.

DATE DUE

NOV 1 6 1994			
MAR 0 6 1995			